The Great Scot

The Great Scot

A Biography of
DONALD GORDON

Joseph Schull

McGill-Queen's University Press
Montreal

©McGill-Queen's University Press 1979

ISBN 0–7735–0349–8

Legal deposit third quarter 1979
Bibliothèque nationale du Québec

Design by Naoto Kondo AIGA
Printed in Canada

Contents

Illustrations

Preface

Of many acknowledgments I should like to make, the first goes to the late W. R. Wright, who was for several years an associate of Gordon in the railway and whose enthusiasm for the man and his story was a great factor in enlisting support for the book. It is a matter of regret to all concerned that Dick Wright's untimely death, just as the work was getting under way, prevented him from carrying out much of the research and interviewing he proposed to do in support of the writing. What he had done, in the form of several taped interviews, was made available through the kindness of Brian Philcox of Ottawa, Wright's literary executor.

To Donald Sutherland, director of McGill-Queen's University Press, and to Dr. Dale Thomson of McGill, R. M. Fowler, director of the C. D. Howe Research Institute, and Professor F. W. Gibson of Queen's who composed the editorial committee, I offer my thanks not only for cooperation but for an occasional suspension of critical judgment where they disagreed with my treatment of subjects or choice of incident. That lenity I may perhaps come to regret; but the faults of the book are my own.

I am grateful to Queen's University and the University Archivist for access to the Gordon Papers, which were a principal source of reference. The Bank of Nova Scotia, the Bank of Canada and the Canadian National Railways have all been most cooperative in assisting research in their archives. The Public Archives of Canada has been, as always, a source of unstinting help. In acquiring a general understanding of the work of the Wartime Prices and Trade Board I have been much indebted to Dr. Pauline Jewett's thesis, 'The Wartime Prices and Trade Board: A Case Study in Canadian Public Administration'. For the chapter on Gordon's time with Brinco I found a rich and clear background in Philip Smith's *Brinco: The Story of Churchill Falls*.

These and other published sources and official papers will be found referred to in the notes. Beyond that it will be evident to any reader how much I have depended on the sixty or more relatives and friends of Gordon who were kind enough to grant me interviews and answer innumerable questions. I have to thank Mrs. Gordon herself for several interviews, for access to private papers and photographs and for courtesy and cooperation in every respect. Other members of the family have not only been equally accommodating; they have also been equally frank in revealing the man as he was, 'warts and all'. Among the friends and associates who contributed their reminiscences I have particularly warm memories of J. Ross Tolmie, Q.C., of Ottawa, who went to the trouble of assembling half a dozen distinguished members of the Five Lakes Fishing Club at the club itself for a long joint interview which occupied much of a weekend and provided a mine of valuable information.

There were, of course, among those interviewed some who had fought with Gordon on various lively occasions and some who saw his faults in larger perspective than others. What has emerged for me, out of all the interviews and the whole range of the research, is a very large figure rich in interest as a fallible human being and deserving of being remembered as a significant force in the country. I hope some of that image is conveyed.

Publication of this book was assisted by Canadian National; content was left to the unfettered judgment of the author and the publisher.

Joseph Schull

CHAPTER 1

New Canadian

Donald Gordon was born on December 11, 1901, in Old Meldrum, Aberdeenshire, Scotland, between the fringe of the Grampian highlands and the coast of the North Sea. Fifty miles to the west was Moray Firth and nineteen miles southeast, an overshadowing presence, was the city of Aberdeen.

Old Meldrum, with a population of about fifteen hundred, had a core of ancient buildings expanded but not improved on by a few modern additions, a bowling green, a sports field and a cluster of weathered houses lined along narrow streets. It was a grey inland town, enjoying the climate though not the location of a port. Somewhat mystifyingly, even to local inhabitants, it boasted the statue of a sailor who could not see salt water and who looked out for the most part on peat, granite and moor country and some very hard-won farmland. In 1960 a correspondent of the *Weekly Scotsman* who visited Donald Gordon's birthplace and described it as 'Scotland's Shangri-La' tended to weaken his case with photographs of a grisly, rain-washed square and of a town hall in the worst tradition of late-Victorian Glasgow.

At the same time he uncovered substantial evidence of a hardy and long-lived race. Ninety-eight-year-old Jonathan Henderson, who would have been just on the edge of his forties when Donald Gordon was born, was found shovelling draff at a local distillery and rejecting thoughts of retirement. 'I can still shovel twice as hard as my laddie —I'll never retire—not till the man with the scythe comes for me.' Ninety-three-year-old Alexander Pirie, the schoolmaster of Donald's day and long after, had fallen head first into the river shortly before the visit and had come out unscathed with his fishing tackle and salmon. He was discovered by the correspondent reading Cicero's *De Senectute* after a long tramp on the hills, and put down the book to count off on his fingers half a dozen neighbours who were well into their nineties.[1] Willie Gordon, a far-flung cousin of Donald, sent him the clipping from the *Scotsman* with the remark that Old Meldrum reminded him of a town he had known in South Africa 'where they had to shoot somebody to get the cemetery started'.[2]

As the eighth in a family of nine children, Donald Gordon grew up in respectable poverty to hard work, hard learning and a general lack of prospects. John Gordon, his father, was a man of many talents, almost all of them frustrated. 'Watchie' Gordon, in his shop at Old Meldrum, came from a family of watchmakers and had always detested the trade. He had won a graphology contest far back in his youth and still cherished the prize. He had letters of recommendation as to probity, ability and energy from several distinguished citizens, but they were in support of applications for posts he did not get. He read much, wrote verse and prose and supplemented the income from his shop by acting as correspondent for an Aberdeen newspaper and by serving in Old Meldrum as town clerk and postman. None of it brought him much, either in money or satisfaction. Donald was to know his father only as a man with stubbly, whitening hair, a mouth hardening in defeat under a ragged grey moustache and a sardonic way with words.

He remembered himself long afterward in the course of a St. Andrew's day address as 'a barefoot boy who ran through the hills and the meadows, "paidl'd in the burn and pou'd the gowans fine"' and explored the secret passage of Barra Castle 'to the very cave where I myself got lost one Saturday afternoon of fearsome memory'. In the same nostalgic vein he recalled as a man of sixty the 'big square' of Old Meldrum where 'as a wee laddie I earned an honest penny in tending the cattle and the sheep and the horses of the surrounding farmers who brought them in for a hard-fought sale on market day'.

As the time came for school there were six years of thoroughgoing Scotch teaching. He read the books at home and borrowed others where he could. The man in later life seemed to draw easily from a compendious knowledge of the scriptures and to produce quotations or at least know where to go for them in many of the major classics. His always weak eyes, he said, had been damaged through studying by firelight, and he had sat on a high stool so that if he drowsed over a book he would fall off and wake up. Big and bursting with energy, then as always, he played as hard as he worked. In a lively household of five brothers and four sisters debate and discussion went with the thumb-marked books. Very soon for Donald there were also part-time jobs. The newsboy went to the railway station to meet 'Meldrum Meg', the way-train from Inverurie bringing the daily papers.[3] He was there in 1912 on the bleak April day that followed the sinking of the *Titanic* and could recall white-faced people gasping at the black headlines and grabbing at the dank sheets. Lingering quite as vividly among the Scotsman's recollections were the faces of the half-dozen who had turned away without paying.[4]

One memory, pervading the country round him, may have sunk deep. In the autumn of 1906, when the boy was not quite five, the University of Aberdeen celebrated the four hundredth anniversary of its foundation. The Lord Chancellor presiding over the ceremonies was Donald Alexander Smith, born at Forres within sight of Moray Firth and now Lord Strathcona, returned after sixty-eight years in Canada as a prince of the Hudson's Bay Company and a builder of the CPR.

Aberdeen had seldom, if ever, seen quite such a celebration. Largely through the help of Smith's money, the dour old city was aglow with banners and bunting and flooded with the robes of academic dignitaries from Europe, Asia, Africa and North America. Edward VII was present, saluting his 'Uncle Donald'. A vast hall, specially built for the occasion by and at the expense of Strathcona, accommodated not only the notables but the twenty-five hundred undergraduates of the university at a climactic banquet. All were served with a profusion of splendid wines and foods by seven hundred imported waiters. The toastmaster of the Lord Mayor of London, 'brought down at a higher fee than would have fetched a great physician, and cheap at the price', orchestrated a giant revel which soon shed its solemnity. Even the weather seemed to have been commanded if not paid for by this son of an obscure tradesman who had gone out from Forres in hob-nailed boots and homespun. Through the whole three days of the festival sunlight warmed the green and usually wet lawns, and they were smiled over at night by a great round harvest moon.[5]

For the other Donald, nineteen miles away and eighty-one years younger, it would have been a hard act to follow. Nothing suggests that he ever intended to do so. There are vague, oblique references indicating that the example of Smith might have been in the minds of the Gordon family when it emigrated to Canada. It could hardly have failed to be, since it was in the minds of most Scots. When it came to a return, however, sixty-odd years later, Donald's effort, though memorable, was much in his own style.

Arriving in Aberdeen as the internationally known banker, the equal and intimate of cabinet ministers and the head of the CNR, he hired a Rolls Royce, equipped himself with a chauffeur, and loaded in a crate containing twelve bottles of champagne. Proceeding in state to Old Meldrum, he passed down remembered Cowgate Street, already collecting a train of interested followers, and ordered a stop at the Meldrum House, the town's best hotel.

Climbing the mossgrown stone steps, he pushed through the doorway and loomed before the guests inside, six feet four inches tall, two hundred and forty pounds of well-groomed, beaming benignity. 'I'm Donald Gordon,' he announced to all and sundry, 'and I've done well. Will you come and join me in a drink?'[6]

It was about the middle of 1913, when the older children of the family were well into their twenties, that the migration of the Gordons began to get under way. Charles, the eldest, and George, the third of the sons, were the first to take off for Canada. James followed with his wife and his three-month-old son, John Alexander; and Annie, the eldest sister, went with her husband, James Smith. By the beginning of 1914 all were established in or around Toronto and were writing home with favourable reports on their prospects.

John Gordon in Old Meldrum, with his household steadily diminishing and trade slow in his shop, was settling into the mood that he would express a few years later: 'Looking back on myself I have made but a pitiful job of my opportunities, although mind you I sometimes flatter myself that I made the most of it. . . . I am convinced that people who should have known better were narrow, ignorant and prejudiced and that . . . I did not often get a fair deal.'[7]

For Old Meldrum, during that period and in that mood, he summoned his poetic talents in a hauntingly allusive tribute:

Land of the Cowgate Street where Webster's horse
Will block the passage while the vanmen curse
. . .
Where Upper meets and Lower pause a while,
The cobblestones are starting from the soil
. . .
And rude pedestrians seldom make a stir,
The bulk of them are old, and young Jok Burr
As pusher's wagon on a rainy day
Starts with its hideous canvas canopy;
O highway to the poorhouse where for life
Lives lazy Jamie Duguid, aul' Bell Fyfe
And Robbie Tweetie lookin' for a wife

The local religious, the better-housed and the official classes are all saluted in the piece, with more than a touch of bile:

Wee, modest, crimson tippit' Crashie Doo
With staff in hand and spectacles on broo
Blinks in the sun and with his firewood's pay
To Adam's Hotel hies his gentle way
To get a dose of early piety

. . .

Brave Ellenbank blooms in the wilderness,
It has the only bathroom in the place

. . .

And near the poorhouse lane within thy bounds
We see the gateway green and house and grounds,
A man of many surnames there resides,
A town and parish councillor besides
And he his steed to Fochel daily guides,
His further name and title we might mention—
But what's the use, he soon will get a pension.[8]

The young Donald, by then just coming to the end of his thirteenth year, was to have the masterpiece recalled to him fifty years later and be stirred by a touch of nostalgia as he remembered his father labouring over it in the kitchen. There was not much warmth in the memory, however, for John Gordon, resenting lifelong poverty and still unable to escape it, was an abstracted and remote figure as head of the family. He read, wrote, tinkered with the hated watches and involved himself as little as possible in the concerns of his sons and daughters. He was not stirred to enthusiasm by the letters coming from Canada. He thought perhaps he might move, but only to Aberdeen, where he still hoped for newspaper work or a post suited to his talents.

It was at this point that his wife intervened decisively.[9] Margaret Watt had been small, slender and chic at the side of her towering bridegroom, a girl with wide, direct eyes and a smiling mouth. She was no longer slender, she had borne nine children and a quarter-century of hopes and dreams deferred, but the eyes were still direct and the mouth as gentle as ever. The bairns had been all-in-all to her and she as much to them, but it had never led her to oppose her husband's will. This time it did. There would be a move, she said, but not to Aberdeen, not to another round of apprenticeships and small trades and the genteel poverty of Scotland. The Gordons who had left were reporting well of Canada; it was time for the rest to follow.

By the spring of 1914 she had made her point. John Gordon, for lack of a better proposal, had assented to the great uprooting. In early April he, his wife and the five remaining children landed at Halifax and took the train for Toronto. Old Meldrum with its stone houses and narrow streets, Scotland with its moors and glens and lovely, rolling farmlands was all put behind them. It might have been that with all the tearing of heartstrings and all the excitement of departure Margaret Gordon had failed to realize the enormity of what she had done in imposing this decision on her husband. It seemed to dawn on her now; she seemed for once to be depressed as the backyards of dreary, wood-built towns went straggling by and raw fields and stone and barbed-wire fencing dwindled into forest patches where the last of the winter snow lingered under the fir trees. Donald remembered that, and remembered her discovering comfort as they passed a stretch of pasture. 'Ah weel,' she murmured to herself out of a long, reflective silence, 'the coos are a' the same.'[10]

By May 1914, three months before the beginning of the First World War, the Gordon family was together again in Toronto. Of several early addresses the best remembered was a two-storey house on Markham Street, which accommodated the parents and the three youngest children on the first floor with the rest of the brood on the second. It was a crowded, temporary arrangement made necessary by the lack of money, and dispersion soon came.

James, who had become a baker, was the first to set up on his own with his wife and son. Charles and George enlisted in the army as soon as war began, and were not to see Canada again. George was killed on the Somme and Charles made his home in Scotland after demobilization. John, the fourth and most footloose of all the Gordon brothers, drifted to the United States. He was to return later, often as a boon companion and occasionally an affliction to Donald, but he was an absent wanderer through most of the early years.

For those remaining there was a hard period of adjustment during the first stresses of war. The strange new city was strange even to itself. During 1913 a decade of boom years had begun to falter to its close, filling the streets with queues of the unemployed. They were dissolving now and becoming waves of khaki, but peacetime trades and industries were in the midst of a panicky slump. The conversion to war production was not yet under way, and for newcome Scottish immigrants it was hard to find a job. During one grim interval James with his wife and son and his baker's salary of twelve dollars a week was the sole support of the family.

John Gordon, senior, with small means and less apparent enthusiasm, was slow to resume his trade. The other Gordons, however, scratched about for work, and Donald as the second youngest seems to have led the way. The soles of his shoes gave out and he patched the holes with cardboard, but he found a job in a box factory at six dollars a week. He supplemented that income as a delivery boy for shopkeepers and by any other errands that could be made to command a price. It taught him the names of streets and some of the ways of the people, and when he had accumulated ten dollars which bought him a second-hand bicycle he was a knowledgeable Torontonian in a modest way of business.

He was not yet fourteen, however, and his first career was short. A Toronto truant officer, heartily supported by his mother, soon saw to it that he would continue his education. Enrolled perforce in the Manning Avenue High School, he plunged into books and lessons and continued the search for work. A newspaper route replaced his lost jobs, solved the problem of after-four leisure and brought an experiment with transport that foreshadowed one of his careers. The pick-up point for his daily stock of papers was halfway across Toronto from the starting-point for his route, and streetcar fare to get to it would eat up most of the profits. It was possible, however—or possible for Donald Gordon—to persuade a friendly conductor to carry the papers free. The future president of the CNR would load his bundle on the car, see it safely off, and race through the streets on his bicycle to make connections at the stop.

Meanwhile James did well, jobs cropped up for the girls and conditions eased a little. Margaret, the Presbyterian, saw to it that there was always kirk, though religious duties never became oppressive. Donald studied in the evenings and John Gordon read, islanded away in his books. Yet he could break out of them for horseplay, which he tolerated without joining, and he was often submerged in talk. Ideas, opinions, arguments were free and uninhibited, and a little money came in. Always hard up and always individualists, lively, literate, affectionate and disputatious, the Gordon family managed to make ends meet.

Through 1915 there were other separations as married sisters moved away with their husbands. By April, John and Margaret Gordon with their younger children had moved to a house on Queen Street across from Osgoode Hall. Once more, as it had been in Old Meldrum, it was a home combined with a shop; for John Gordon in the new world was repeating the pattern of the old. After weary days with watches he read and brooded in the evenings, and occasionally attempted writing. He was much heartened when, on April 24, 1915, the Toronto *Evening Telegram* published one of his efforts—free of charge, he noted, when he had been told he might have to pay as much as fifteen dollars for the favour. 'I was struggling at the time,' he wrote later, 'to get a living fighting against great odds. It was said that if I could write something good to the *Telegram*, that the Editor, a millionaire Scot, might notice and help me.'[11]

That, judging by the piece, would seem to be problematical. 'Watchie' Gordon repeated an oft-told story to the *Telegram*'s readers: 'I found it necessary to cross the Atlantic and carve out a living for myself and my household under new conditions in the city of Toronto.' He had found conditions dull, but 'after a period of enforced idleness I opened a small shop on a busy street for the repair or "fixing" (as they call it) of watches and clocks, and by practising Scottish thrift and industry I have contrived to make a living'.

On the cluttered Queen Street of the time, with its shops, movies and restaurants and small establishments of more or less repute, he had made the acquaintance of the 'Soakers', the con men of his day. One respectable-looking old gentleman who claimed to have been locked out of his house by accident had requested a loan of thirty-five cents to send a telegram to his wife. A younger and more modest operator claimed to be a stranded trades-man needing five cents for carfare, and a tall man in a hurry had been prepared to accept five dollars for a watch and other jewellery obviously worth fourteen. He, Watchie reflected, 'may now be serving His Majesty in some capacity over the Don'. The thirty-five cents had been refused the elderly gentleman, but the five cents had been granted since 'it will neither break me nor make me'. It was amazing, concluded the philosopher from Old Meldrum, how many in the new world got along without work.[12]

There is no evidence that John Ross Robertson, the 'millionaire Scot', was impressed by the piece in his newspaper. John Gordon was to continue much as before, a tradesman by force of circumstance and wryly contemptuous of his work. He was in no position to contribute to Donald's schooling, and the boy was a hard-headed realist becoming a man in a hurry. He was getting all that was to be had at Manning School; he was losing the edge of his burr and absorbing Canadian ways. But he was serving out a term, restrained only by a law that prescribed fifteen as the school-leaving age. Education was good but it was reserved for those who could afford it; his own job was to get on. He could not then enlist as his older brothers had done, and the weak eyes behind the thick lenses of his spectacles ruled out future hopes. By the late spring of 1916, however, as the school year came to an end, he was approaching fifteen. He would be within three months of it by September when the new term began. The authorities might shut their eyes to a little judicious haste, particularly now with the demand for workers growing. There were more jobs to be had and, perennially fascinating to a Scot, there was the prospect of a job in a bank.

Mr. Richardson, his principal, had had an approving eye on the bustling young Gordon, and was inclined to provide assistance. The Bank of Nova Scotia, short-handed like all banks, was inclined to be a receptive employer. Donald Gordon was interviewed and some time after the occasion had his picture taken.[13] He stands up in the photograph against the usual photographer's background with his hand on the usual chair, spectacled and smiling primly, with the mischief hidden in his eyes like a teller behind a wicket. Five feet ten inches tall and weighing only 118 pounds, he could almost be imagined as frail under the wrinkled, ready-made suit. Only the hands dispel any such illusion. They stand out, as they always would, protruding from the overlong sleeves, huge, restless and formidable, eager to be put to work.

He left a note of the great day of the beginning. 'Record with the Bank of Nova Scotia—at Ossington and Dundas branch Entered Service Junior Clerk at salary of $300. per annum on June 5, 1916.'[14] As he walked in by the sombre counters and cages, the glass-panelled door with the sign, 'Manager', gleamed at the end of the office. He remembered the sight of it later, and also his own reaction. 'That,' he said to himself, 'is where I'm going to be.'

CHAPTER 2

'Possibly a bit impetuous'

'T his young man's work has been first class; considerably above the average junior,' read the first of the staff reports on Donald Gordon.[1] At Ossington and Dundas, as a checker-off of clearings, a stoker of the cranky furnace and a runner of innumerable errands he had been more than satisfactory. His Christmas reward on December 24, 1916, was a bonus of $25.

By June 1917 he had earned a spell on a ledger. In August he relieved a teller on summer holidays and by late October, though he was back on a ledger again, he had considerably advanced his status. There had been an annual increase of $50 in April, another of $100 in July and still another in October. The Christmas bonus for 1917 was $50, and by the end of 1918, as he rose to teller-accountant, two more increases had brought his annual income to a total of $750.

'Unfortunately,' said the staff report of February 1919, 'he recently cashed a bogus cheque for $200. without referring it to the manager. He is worrying considerably over this blunder, and more so by reason of the fact that he has been asked to make good the amount.'[2]

Worry, however, with Gordon, was not a passive condition. Even while the report was being written the seventeen-year-old teller-accountant was spending his evening hours prowling the streets. He remembered the looks of his man, could make a guess at his habits, and he favoured direct collection. Late one snowy night, as the writer of the bad cheque emerged from a Queen Street movie house, a great paw descended on his shoulder, he was swung round with adequate accompanying comment and marched off in the direction of the nearest police station. There, or on the way there, he was moved not only to repentance but at least partial disgorgement. Gordon arrived at the bank next morning with $180 to apply on his shortage and the name and address of a thoroughly scared culprit as fair security for the rest.

In November 1919 came the first of a series of moves. He was sent as trouble-shooter to an apparently untidy branch at Dundas and Brock where his work was 'to locate differences in Bills Discounted, Remitted Balances and Savings Ledger Balance'. Then as always, he regarded an unbalanced ledger as a personal challenge, to be met if it took all night. He occasionally worked all night, and emerged fresh in the morning. Within three months he was not only acting accountant at Dundas and Brock, but had had a spell as relieving manager at a small country branch. Returned to Dundas and Brock, he was growing restless; and a restless Gordon was a trial. 'He complains,' complained his manager, 'that he has not enough to do.'[3] That dilemma was resolved for him, at least temporarily, when he was transferred to head office in the summer of 1920 with a breath-taking increase of $300.

On the top floor of the old Bank of Nova Scotia building on the south side of King Street, he was removed by several levels not only from the main city branch which was on the ground floor below, but from the drudgery of branch routine. He moved among executives here, first as relieving clerk to the chief accountant, then as relieving clerk to the general manager. By 1921, as secretary to the general manager, he was in the main stream of promotion that led toward the highest posts.

There was a long way to go, but he was a highly visible figure in a highly strategic place. In the seasoning and moving around which were an essential part of the business he would be watched with interest, not only by H. A. Richardson, the general manager, but also by J. A. McLeod, the shrewd, goateed, soft-spoken little president, who was one of the prominent bankers of the day.

Burly, thrusting, ebullient and wholly in love with his work, the Gordon of the early Twenties was already a man worth watching. Legend speaks of him as being 'afraid of nothing and nobody'.[4] He had the faculty, said another colleague, of regarding whatever he was doing at the moment as the most important work in the world. Big as he was and careless as he was in most of the formalities of life, he had the banker's care for his appearance. Forty years later, as president of the CNR, he rode up in an elevator with one of his senior officials and with an office boy whose shoes needed a shine. When the car stopped and the boy got off at his floor Gordon looked after him for a moment and gave a grunt of distaste. 'How does a fellow ever expect to get anywhere,' he asked, 'with shoes like that?'[5]

His own problem, as he felt through much of his life, was a lack of education. Queen's helped him in that, and earned a grateful admirer. By 1919, while he was complaining of not having enough to do at Dundas and Brock, he was taking the correspondence courses in banking and commerce sponsored by the university. 'Passed with *Honours* in the Canadian Bankers Examinations,' he noted proudly in August 1920;[6] and by June of 1922 he had graduated as a Fellow of the Canadian Bankers' Association and earned a diploma which would hang framed and prominent in many of his later offices. Night school courses in Toronto supplemented the work at Queen's, while at the same time he was widening his range of interests. In 1919 he was one of a youthful group who got the help of their elders and formed the Bankers' Educational Association. It proved to be an important body which brought distinguished lecturers and evenings of lively discussion on banking, commercial law and allied subjects. Later on, extending to other fields and developing into a forum for public speaking, it became the famous Thirty Club which is still in active existence.

All of it stimulated Gordon, brought him back to his desk with new ideas, and fuelled his enormous zest. By 1923 his impressed seniors were reporting on him in almost lyrical terms. 'He has made a complete cleanup of the work in arrears in the past . . . has revised and modernized many records and now asks for more advanced work. He towers above those of the same age and length of service . . . a great student . . . apt in commercial law . . . possessed of a good brain, temperament, judgment and forcefulness . . . he is possibly a bit impetuous.'[7]

The family had moved by then to another house at 352 Quebec Avenue, where Donald, Jessie and Elizabeth were still living with the parents. Jack, returning from the United States to a job with the Goodyear Tire and Rubber Company, had also joined the establishment and spent much time with Donald. James, with his own bakery business, was now doing well, and as the richest member of the family was driving a second-hand car. It often brought him to Quebec Avenue with his wife, Mary, and the children, and the other sisters came with their husbands for lively Sunday dinners.

Uncle James and Aunt Mary were the great favourites of Donald, and he himself was 'a fine uncle' to their children. Margaret, the youngest, remembers some of those Sundays as varied and seldom tranquil. The Gordons, who came in all heights and sizes, were 'a funny mixture of warmth, aggression and competition'. For all their mutual affection, they could be sharp, witty and devastatingly critical of each other, and each in his own way was a citadel of independence. John Gordon, senior, was not prospering in his shop, and was more and more withdrawn in quirky resentment. He could still be gay and funny when the mood took him, there was no doubt that he enjoyed the family gatherings, but he was often not quite part of them. He had his old habit of burying himself in a book while argument flared around him, and he had transmitted that gift to the children. All Gordons read whenever they felt inclined to, and on other occasions filled the room with noise or with their beloved Scottish songs. To little Margaret Uncle Donald was equally familiar sitting impregnably remote, absorbed in a banking treatise, or romping in the backyard with Jack as aide and abettor. She was terrified but not surprised, one afternoon, to discover him hanging by his feet from the third-floor window, yelling for Jack to come and take his picture.[8]

To his mother, 'a lovely, gentle, quiet woman', Donald remained devoted. He had an almost equal affection for his Aunt Mary. A stronger woman than Margaret Watt Gordon, she was the 'iron butterfly' who stimulated the boy's ambition and to whom he often came for advice. From his mother there was unfailing support for anything he wanted to do, and from his father there was a queer stimulus that was half-rooted in jealousy. The son was crude and ignorant by many of the old-world standards that were dear to John Gordon, but he was making his way in a world that still defeated the father. Or he seemed to be; to John Gordon that remained to be proved. The boy came home with salary increases and promotions as a self-important banker, and his father began to refer to him as 'the great man'. It was familiar Gordon irony in a family that refused to be impressed, but there was always an edge of scepticism. It provided a challenge for the son, but it strained relations with the father which had never been very close.

The gap widened as other promotions came. In October 1924 Donald Gordon was appointed to the bank's inspection staff and began to travel the country. He was the very green and junior member of a team of two, but 'in six months,' according to one of his colleagues, 'he started to take it over'.[9] He had new ideas and methods, he was not satisfied with old, traditional routine, and he had a way of asking questions that were hard to answer. He was a terrible figure as an inspector to a branch with sloppy ways, but no way was sacred. If it could be improved by change, why not? If it had always been done, why?—did it still have to be done? He was brash, blunt, thrusting, devouringly anxious to get on, and after hours he was over-given to play. Yet the senior men he worked with were driven to extend them-selves; Gordon could somehow push without bringing resentment and he usually knew what he was about. Possibly, in one area, he was stimulated by an important friend of later years. In October 1925 a young Royal Bank executive by the name of Graham Towers delivered an address to the Toronto Bankers' Educational Association on 'International Banking and Foreign Exchange'.[10] Within a few months Gordon developed an interest in the foreign business of the Bank of Nova Scotia and transmitted the interest to his seniors. The result was closer control, requiring inspection trips to the bank's branches in Jamaica, Cuba, Puerto Rico and the Dominican Republic. The green young inspector, eager to see the world, had a first glimpse of the Caribbean countries.

There was more than that ahead of him. In the spring of 1926, a bachelor banker twenty-four years old, he was travelling down to the Maritimes on the Ocean Limited. With him, and officially in charge of him, was R. A. S. Elliott, a senior inspector and a sedate English gentleman who was reputed to have connections in the peerage. To Elliott the fact that a strikingly handsome young woman was sitting ahead of them in the car was hardly a reason to look up from his book. To Gordon, however, growing more fidgety and restless mile by mile, it was obviously a challenge to adventure.

At length, under Elliott's disapproving glare, he made his way down the aisle, bent over the lady and eventually settled in with her, not rebuffed. It was a long talk and, as it proved, a fateful one. Maisie Barter was twenty-three years old, a year younger than Donald. She was slender, not very tall, with lively Irish eyes and jet-black hair. Born in St. John's, Newfoundland, of a moderately prosperous family which had been one of the first supporters of the Salvation Army on the island, she had had a year of teaching school in one of the outports. She had not much cared for that, she had been restless in the strict atmosphere of her home and she was clearly not destined to be a Salvationist. When sent out to distribute some religious pamphlets she had simply thrown them away. Maisie's eyes were directed to mainland Canada, and she had finally been given her head. When Gordon met her she had had two years at a finishing school in Toronto, followed by an illness which had brought the threat of tuberculosis and required a period of rest at the sanatorium in Gravenhurst. She was going home, according to family legend, to marry a one-time suitor; but it was a marriage not to come off. The hopes of the other man crumbled during the rest of the journey on the train.

By late May Gordon was back in Toronto, an engaged man, and Maisie was returning from St. John's. The marriage was arranged for June, but it was preceded by complications. All went well with the career; the nomad bachelor inspector was to have a new post more suitable to a married man as assistant chief accountant in the main branch at Toronto. He was to have an imposing starting assignment, which could have delighted only the devoted: to assist with a complete revision of the bank's *Manual of Rules of Procedure*. Before that, however, came a last tour of inspection, the most trying and longest-remembered of all the trips he had taken.

In Ontario, at a small, obscure sub-branch, trouble was obviously brewing.

The manager was known to be unsteady, he was said to have threatened suicide, and he had apparently been consigning all the head office communications of the past year to his waste-basket without troubling to read them. When the inspector arrived the mess was worse than expected and his own comments sharp. 'Enjoy your job today,' was one which legend attributes to him, 'because you won't have it tomorrow.' That night, putting the office pistol to his head, the manager passed beyond the need of all jobs; and a badly shaken Gordon, four days before he was scheduled to become a bridegroom, was left to act as manager till the place was filled. Relief arrived in time, but the event was not to be forgotten by the man born in Old Meldrum, carrying the fears and mysteries and strange foreknowings of the Highlands under his self-assurance. 'He was always afraid of the dark,' said one of his sons, 'and not of robbers or holdups but of ghosts and demons.'[11] On the morning after the suicide when he came into the bank it was to tell a white-faced clerk, with a white face himself, that he had dreamed of it all exactly as it took place.

Dreams changed no plans, however, and on June 12, 1926, Donald Gordon was married to Maisie Barter. The home he left was in process of breaking up. He was to lose his father before the end of the year and his mother a year later. On July 11 came a letter from John Gordon, senior, who had not been present at the wedding nor seen his son since. It was wry and chatty and filled with family gossip. The Orangemen would be passing his 'wee shop' next day 'with many great men in the procession. Had I been one of them on a white charger beplumed and behatted I would have shown myself a greater ass than any of them, but I can only look on and wonder at the vast idiocy that permeates all through the lot of them.' The plaster had fallen in the kitchen and 'we are getting a mannie to fix it this week'. Lizzie was 'out a-walking with her boy friend, now with her a confirmed habit' and 'everything moving along here much as usual. Jamie and Mary kindly come across nearly every Sunday and take your mother and I an outing.' The handwriting of the man who had won a graphology contest many years before was still clear and firm, and there were few complaints in the letter. Yet it was a little remote and tentative; the old Scot was writing to a young stranger: 'I have not, as you know, written to you since you embarked on the sea of matrimony. It was not that I had forgotten about you but just because I thought it was needless to overload you with any commonplace letter of mine, seeing that I could wait a little. And of course I offer you congratulations and heartfelt wishes for your happiness in the present and the future. I hope to meet your wife sometime soon.'[12]

CHAPTER 3

A Push from Maisie

Marriage brought to the banker a new perspective on life and a new thrust to his career. Maisie Barter, providing a vivid companionship, was also a complement and stimulant widening the range of his ambition. 'I'm a lazy bugger,' he was to say long afterward. 'It was Maisie that pushed me on.'[1]

If he was lazy, it was not by any ordinarily recognizable standard. For the better part of a year his long days as assistant chief accountant went on into night sessions over his beloved revision of the *Manual of Rules of Procedure*. He found time for night school, was religiously regular in his attendance at the meetings of the Bankers' Educational Association and was an enthusiastic participant in its courses in public speaking. He was up in the mornings well before breakfast for what must have been a trying routine. Standing in front of a mirror, pronouncing 'thirty-three' over and over again, he was gradually eliminating the Scottish roll from his 'r's. He acquired a dictaphone from the office and formed the habit of leaving each Friday afternoon with a huge file of papers and a box of dictaphone records. To the girls in the stenographic pool, as he returned with the papers disposed of and all the records filled, he was a Monday morning nightmare.

On September 12, 1929, his first son, Donald Ramsay, was born. On March 26, 1931, installed in a new house on Indian Road Crescent, he became the senior of two assistant managers in the main Toronto branch. His salary was reaching up toward $5,000 a year, he was as well regarded as ever on the higher levels, and in the way of promise and prospects little seemed to be lacking.

If there was a lack, or if there was laziness, it was in the development of a settled purpose. The road up in the bank seemed too clear to be a challenge, and at the end there was only money. Gordon wanted money—he was always in need of money—but he wanted more than that. Or he would when he knew himself, as Maisie did already. Sharp-tongued, vigorous and more ambitious than he was, she sensed the qualities of the man and his need of scope to develop them. But money came first—you had need of money to look to wider fields—and in the meantime life was fun.

It was almost too much fun in the early years. The partners had joined forces in the midst of the roaring Twenties, when the always-climbing stock markets were creating daily fortunes and brokers' clerks, bootblacks and even tellers and ledger-keepers were counting paper profits. The times were infectious for the banker and the student of business conditions who believed too much of what he read. When the crash came, carrying the mighty down, Gordon was one of the lesser thousands riding the same toboggan.

'He lost his shirt,' said one of his early colleagues, and though it was not much of a shirt the loss would be long felt. Gordon would be a central banker and a nationally known figure before the last of his debts were paid. They hung over him through the Thirties, but they hardly changed his ways. 'He was always a gambler, you know . . . always hoping that he would be lucky and make a lot of money.'[2] Somewhere in the back of his mind and haunting his conversation there was usually a large scheme, mercifully held in abeyance for lack of capital. After the crash, with monthly deductions for his loans eating away at his salary, financial plunges were limited to occasional days at the races. Maisie went too, always enjoying excitement, and on the worst days trudged home beside him with even their carfare lost.

Hard up as they were, the Gordons maintained a house that was worthy of the banker's position. It was lively and well-filled, for there was a growing cluster of friends. 'Fats' Bell and George Poole, both later to be senior officials of the bank, were boarders in the Gordon home, helped with the paying of the rent and hugely enjoyed their stay. Joe Barter, Maisie's favourite brother and equally a favourite of Donald, was another frequent visitor. Future presidents and high executive officers, then as junior and impecunious as Gordon, came for Saturday afternoon bridge games that often went on to disturb the peace of the Sabbath. No one could afford much liquor and Gordon drank little, but he was responsive to what he took. 'Two drinks,' says one friend, 'were enough to set him off. . . . I remember one night he got bored with the bridge game and went out and started jumping fences. I'll never forget that night—we had to catch him and bring him in.' There was always plenty of song around the piano, Gordon played an accordion to which he was much addicted, and occasional evenings were memorable for displays of Maisie's temper. 'I've seen Maisie slap Donald's face,' another friend recalled, 'just to say, "Here—you're doing something I don't like and this is the only way I know how to stop you".'[3]

Fondly remembered as 'Peck' is E. L. Pequenagh, a diminutive Swiss on the inspection staff whose spectacles were as thick as Gordon's and whose wit was quite as sharp. A sparring partner and needler, he weighed some 110 pounds, reached about to Gordon's shoulders standing on tiptoe, and was quite undaunted by the size of his towering rival. The owl-eyed pair were frequent disrupters of bridge games and still worse when they were brought together on a golf course. Neither could see the ball nor be taught respect for the game and one foursome which included them is said to have begun on the first tee at eight o'clock in the morning and ended approximately on the fifth green at four in the afternoon.

Never much given to any physical exercise, Gordon did a little canoeing because he could do it sitting down. His golf, however, was much like his home carpentry; he bought the tools and equipment but nothing could be made to work. At the Royal York Hotel Golf Club, now become St. George's, he played what was probably his concluding round in Toronto. Well out on the course and well along in frustration, he addressed his ball, swung mightily and missed, and proceeded to hack up turf till the club in his hand broke. Then, throwing the others away, he stalked back to the clubhouse and betook himself to the showers. Under the soothing water, with his temper partially restored, he began to fill the clubhouse with waves of Scottish song. It was too much for one of the neighbouring showerers, who reached over with a back-brush, whacked him hard on the bottom and ducked out of the room. Gordon emerged from the stall, rubbing his sore backside, and scooped up the tray from the shower floor with its antiseptic solution and its gallons of soapy water. As the shower room door reopened he let go with the tray's contents, expecting the returning culprit. The man entering, however, proved to be the club manager, correctly and fully dressed and looking for the cause of the uproar. As enlightenment and the water hit him simultaneously Gordon's welcome on the premises came to an official end.[4]

He was into his thirties now, six feet, four inches tall and still rangy, but showing the effects of desk work. He already walked like a bear who preferred to be sitting down. He could be a noisy nuisance, a disastrous guest and an unpredictable host. Maisie, volatile enough herself, had often to cope with the raw practical jokes which he played on anyone present, frequently with brother Jack. Still a wanderer and still a favourite with Donald, Jack stayed at the house when the mood seized him and made himself much at home. Nothing was changed, where Jack was concerned, by the birth of Donald Ramsay, and his occasional habit of making gin in the bathtub meant fewer baths for the child. As the background of an industrious and rising banker, the Gordon ménage foretold a colourful career. So too did some of the banker's methods.

The story of 'The Story-Tellers of the Air' seems oddly enough to have enhanced the banker's standing. It permeates the Gordon legend, and it began with a bad loan. Early in March 1931, just installed as senior assistant manager, Gordon was approached at the counter by an attractive potential customer. The interview, soon transferred to the private office of the manager who happened to be away ill, went on for a long time. The Bank of Nova Scotia, it developed, was being given its first opportunity to invest in a new art form. Facing the banker at the desk was a young actor, formerly of the New York theatre, who had a contract from station CKGW of Toronto to produce thirteen half-hour radio dramas on a budget of $3,000. All that stood in the way was an initial lack of money; he required $1,500 to provide for writing and casting and to get the series going.

Here was a first ripple of the advancing wave of the future. Radio drama, and the possibilities of advertising interspersing the drama, had hardly been touched as yet. They could be seen, however, by a banker envisioning the future and facing the bright young man. The manager could not be reached, might well not have been impressed, and Gordon had no authority to advance the money. Nevertheless he did so, and the axe fell in the morning. The contract was not collateral, or at least acceptable collateral, and Gordon would be held responsible for the full amount of the advance. More than that, there were rumours from CKGW, all too soon confirmed. The young man with the money was not creating drama; he had skipped for the United States. The senior assistant manager, with $1,500 added to his debts, had acquired a contract for thirteen radio programs not presently in existence.

Not for the first or last time the Gordons were facing a crisis. In its very dimensions, however, and still more in its novelty, there were the seeds of inspiration. Donald was given to song on the slightest provocation; his accordion and his rich, booming baritone were a byword in all his circles. Maisie not only sang; she was a trained elocutionist and she had played in dramas at finishing school with a good deal of success. Neither doubted for a moment that they could find ideas and write; and if not plays it would be stories and if not stories they would sing. The two persuaded themselves, and later persuaded the station, that they could fill the thirteen periods as 'The Story-Tellers of the Air'.

As a result that fall the audience of CKGW enjoyed one of the first radio dramatic series ever to be heard in Canada. The scripts, written by Donald and Maisie, shifted from the dramatic to the narrative form and frequently invoked music. Where a play or story was short it was eked out by song; and 'Little Old Lady', 'If I Forget You' and 'Danny Boy' became admired Gordon duets. They were particularly admired, perhaps, by intrigued listeners from the bank who saw the hard commercial fact of a bad loan being eaten away by art. As cultural contributions the level was not high, and Gordon in later years was understandably reluctant to show the scripts to his sons. Yet he kept one or two; he was artist enough for that.

One play, oddly foreshadowing his role as a central banker, somehow involved the hero in a discussion of foreign exchange. Gold and the gold standard were both dismissed in the tag-line with a final flash of wit. 'What's the good of a gold standard, anyway? Why not have a cement standard—that'd be more concrete!' At about the same level in another story is 'Jimmy, the Lucky Guy', an enterprising young salesman who comes to his moment of truth. Is he to win a big contract or beat up the potential customer who is mauling his pretty wife? Honour wins over greed and a bruised Jimmy, confronting his president next morning, is told that he is being fired for losing the contract. 'In a blind heat of rage the injustice of it finally mastered him and he finished chokingly, "You damned old hypocrite, you can't fire me. I quit".' As he started for the door, however, the president stood confronting him in the best manner of sterling old industrialists. 'Thank God, Jimmy, you had it in you. I've been waiting for years to find out if you were anything but a good-natured fool before I fired you as salesman and hired you as my Sales Manager!'[5]

Playing all the major parts, supplying the musical interludes and drafting friends to build up their small casts, the Gordons for thirteen weeks were consumed and irrepressible. They acted at home, they were given to rehearse in public, and any potential audience could be a stimulant for a new scene. Robert L. Dales, later to be one of the senior executives of the bank, was at that time a frequent and nervous companion. 'When you got on a streetcar with them—streetcars were always crowded in those days—I'd go sit at the back. Not Donald and Maisie. They'd get on at different ends and come at each other yelling in pig Latin, or they'd hang on the straps, fighting—Donald with his great big voice and Maisie with her sharp tongue—and the people around gaping at them, thinking it was the real thing. Then they'd come to their stop and walk away together, both laughing their heads off.'[6]

At the same time, in the midst of the creative excitement, the commercial purpose remained. While the program paid off the loan it could also be made to sell, and Maisie evolved a product. It was 'IT' cold cream, suitably titled for the days of Clara Bow. Made in the Gordon kitchen and promoted on the Gordon program, it was sold under Maisie's direction door-to-door. By the end of the thirteenth week, though the program was not renewed and the older debts remained, the Gordons had fought their way through one disaster.

Senior executives of the bank, whatever they thought of his antics in recovering bad loans, were impressed and tolerant with Gordon. He was a handful but he was an asset, and the credits outweighed the debits by a large margin. J. A. McLeod, the strait-laced little president, and A. Y. Merrick, the Toronto branch manager, watched and scolded Gordon but drove him with a light rein. The debts and horseplay were one thing, but the real ability was another.

'Donald was intense, you know,' says Thomas A. Boyles, a later head of the bank, 'always a man at his best when he had to work hard.'[7] A stickler for branch routine, he was a ruthless weeder-out of the inefficient, and the drones of the staff were quickly put on transfer. He had a good mind, ripening steadily with experience, and he was as decisive as he was impulsive. 'He could gather things together so quickly,' says Robert Dales. 'Where figures and balance sheets were concerned he really had a photographic memory; he could read a page, quote it and hardly miss a word—sometimes I couldn't believe it.'[8]

His work on rules and procedures and his studies of banking methods were also bearing fruit. By 1930 his earliest contributions were appearing in the *Journal of the Canadian Bankers' Association*. Dealing with 'Machinery in Banks', he welcomed the 'maze of mechanical devices seemingly possessed of human ingenuity . . . in the busier offices of the day the pen-and-ink ledger is gone. Gone too is the bleary-eyed ledger keeper who worked far into the night hunting for an elusive difference. His place has been taken by the error-proof machine operated by a vision in bobbed hair and bright raiment whose knowledge of Debit, Credit and Balance is confined to the pressing of keys.' With a philosophical sigh for the passing of 'the good old days', he went on to consider the future. 'The writer ventures to say that the time is not far distant when photography will play a large part in bookkeeping and the ledger of the future may quite conceivably consist of a photographic record of all transactions.' There would be no more of 'the romance seen in the careers of present-day General Managers and Senior Executives who started their banking careers by lighting the office fire in the bank office of some humble hamlet'. He saw the banker of the future as the product of colleges and universities, and ended on a note of crashing male chauvinism. Drudgery would be left to the sex in bobbed hair and bright raiment, 'the machine-operator type of help whose duties will be purely of a mechanical nature and whose salaries will not increase beyond a fixed maximum of from $1,200. to $1,500. per annum'.[9]

With theorizing in journals went hard-fisted daily work in the promotion of the bank's business. Around the main office in the heart of the financial district were the brokerage houses issuing the stocks and debentures that floated on call loans. Through the late Twenties and on into the Thirties, in spite of hard times, there was a large and active brokerage business, most of which was handled by the Royal Bank. A good deal of that business began to pass through the ledgers of the Bank of Nova Scotia as the new assistant manager got into his stride. It was a matter of going out and meeting clients, and Gordon thrived on that. Constantly supported by Merrick, 'he made the Bank of Nova Scotia one of the top brokerage banks in Toronto—he really took business away from the Royal'.[10] Thomas Boyles, watching him, saw the developing qualities of a public relations man. 'He had no hesitation in putting on his hat and walking round to the various brokers and making himself known. They liked him, they liked his energy, they liked his looks and attitude, and he saw that they got service.'[11]

By 1934, with his radio program behind him and the bank's business showing the effects of his work, the staff reports reflected his rising status. He was now 'a young executive . . . having the courage, tact, mental equipment and poise to take him far'.[12]

He was already farther on his way than anyone realized, and the direction pointed to Ottawa. In 1933, Fraser Elliott, the federal commissioner of income tax, had been concerned with a nagging problem. Much income earned by foreign-based individuals and corporations was being used quite legitimately for the purchase of bearer bonds. When the bonds were cashed, however, they were as anonymous as a dollar bill and the money could flow from the country free of tax. It was a costly, irritating loophole, particularly in hard times, and somehow had to be closed.

W. A. Mackintosh, the head of the Department of Economics and Political Science at Queen's University, and a perennial government adviser, offered a useful suggestion. Since the question involved banking, the banks should be called in. Early in February the invitations went out, and in most cases the response came from presidents and general managers. At the Bank of Nova Scotia, however, the high executives were involved in other affairs. The nod went to the assistant manager, Toronto, and when the meeting came to be convened it included Donald Gordon.

It was a first and memorable glimpse of him at the centres close to power. Big, young and crude, he was quite unawed by the imposing elders round him. Yet he was as good a listener as a talker, and he was concerned with a practical problem that was well within his sphere. By the second day he had produced a practical solution. It lay simply in the destruction of anonymity. The foreign holder, when he cashed his bearer bonds or transferred funds in any form that resulted from Canadian earnings, should be required to acknowledge ownership and the fact of foreign residence. On that base taxation could be established; and Gordon produced the form of ownership certificate upon which the Canadian withholding tax came to operate. Out of his long interest in banking methods and machinery he had brought off a notable coup. From the commissioner of income tax to the president of the Bank of Nova Scotia went one of those letters that help to decide destinies. In the solution of the problem of the withholding tax, Fraser Elliott wrote, 'the efforts of your Mr. D. Gordon played a major part'.[13]

In the same year, with a notable lack of enthusiasm on the part of the chartered banks, came the proposal for a central bank. The idea was not new, and it had been mooted in many forms as the country struggled with depression. Most of the Commonwealth countries already had central banks. The Bank of Canada, as it came to be established in 1934, was to control the currency of the country, issue all bank notes, advise the government in the management of the public debt and regulate internal credit and foreign exchange. So far as was possible by the management of money, the bank was to act to reduce fluctuations in production and trade, with their effects on employment and prices. It would require the chartered banks to transfer their gold reserves, take away from them the profitable privilege of the note issue, and it could influence interest rates by rediscounting the banks' commercial paper and by buying and selling securities on the open market. It was to be, in effect, a national bank of banks, a balance wheel on the economy.

Opposed or grumblingly accepted by most of the financial community, it was nevertheless a symbol of reorganization. R. B. Bennett, in the late days of his regime, was still on the rack of the depression and searching for means and men. In the matter of the central bank as a regulator of fiscal policy and in the man chosen as governor his search was well rewarded. The pulse-taker and decision-maker for much of the nation's business was to be Graham Ford Towers.

Towers was thirty-seven and an assistant general manager of the Royal Bank. The scion of an old Montreal family with an honours degree in economics from McGill University, he had had fourteen years as economist, inspector and supervisor of the bank's foreign business. Of central banking he had no experience at all, but he was a cool, flexible path-maker and experience was to be provided. J. A. C. Osborne, secretary of the Bank of England, was to be loaned to Canada to act as deputy governor for a period of five years. The choice of other officials was to be left to Towers himself.

He had already met Gordon at occasional meetings of bankers. The name began to figure in his discussions with the department of finance. Clifford Clark, the brilliant deputy minister who looked like a round-faced schoolboy behind his horn-rimmed spectacles, had heard the story of the withholding tax from his friend Fraser Elliott. W. A. Mackintosh, who knew much that went on in government and everything that went on at Queen's, had seen Gordon's papers in the bankers' examinations. It was Mackintosh and Clark who put the precipitating question: 'Why don't you go up to Toronto and look him over.'[14]

By late 1934 the first scouting was done. Towers and other emissaries had made three visits to the head office of the Bank of Nova Scotia, cleared their proposal with the president and begun overtures to Gordon. By the end of the year the tentative offer was firm: Gordon was wanted by Towers as secretary of the Bank of Canada.

Maisie's reaction was instant, definite and favourable: it was a chance too big to be missed. Gordon was not so sure. His salary of $5,500 a year would be a little better than doubled, but he liked Toronto and the Bank of Nova Scotia. He was already doing well, with the prospect of doing better. There was no reason why he could not aspire eventually to J. A. McLeod's chair. He had also heard the talk and shared the misgivings of bankers that he would be mixed up in Ottawa with a temporary political football. Most of his closer colleagues were of the mood of Tom Boyles: 'You're crazy if you take it, Donald.' All of them were overborne, however, by the influence pervading the home. On a January Monday morning, with his big bulk planted on Boyles's desk, the assistant manager delivered himself of a large, decisive sigh. 'Well, Tom, first time in my life I've ever done what my wife told me to. Maisie thinks I should go.'[15]

In the course of the next two weeks the Toronto house was disposed of, the tools and carpentry equipment brought up from the basement and shipped off with the furniture to a new address in Ottawa. On February 1, 1935, Gordon resigned from the Bank of Nova Scotia. It remained to transplant the family, which he decided to do by car. According to his son, Donald, the car was driven by Uncle Joe Barter, and according to Joe Barter it was driven by a luckless friend. At any rate it was old and broke down on the way, providing five-year-old Donnie with 'the first of a whole series of kind of blur memories of my father's rages . . . over his whole life he was in a state of war with machines'.[16] This battle was won, however, and the Gordons arrived in Ottawa. By the end of another week Donnie was installed in kindergarten, Maisie involved in home-making at 24 Clemow Avenue, and in the Victoria Building on Wellington Street the central bank's secretary was presiding over a birth.

CHAPTER 4

The Bank of Canada

There was less than a month to organize the bank for business, since opening day was scheduled for March 1. Across the street in the East Block Graham Towers and Osborne were mapping the lines of policy with Clifford Clark. Gordon's place, however, was on the third floor of the Victoria Building, where some twenty earlier arrivals were sorting themselves out. They worked to a clang of carpenters, were shifted about for carpet-laying and coped with the first of the paper-work beginning to cross their desks. Economists, accountants and auditors, they were all hand-picked men, but they were as new to central banking as the secretary was himself. Principles came over from the East Block and precise general instructions, but general they still remained. The routines for carrying them out had to be established, the jobs set and allocated and the methods and forms designed. The loose ends of the business had all to be pulled together, and most of the threads were soon in Gordon's hands.

The currency division of the office of the receiver-general was to be shifted over to the bank, with accompanying civil servants. The delicate matter of transfers and the establishment of new duties became part of the secretary's work. 'He was a pushy Scot and he stepped on a lot of toes,' as one of the survivors of early days remembers, 'but he didn't make many mistakes.'[1] Meanwhile routine took shape. 'I was deluged with phone calls from him,' says Tom Boyles, 'asking for copies of our forms, talking over our procedures, digging around for anything he could adapt to central banking.'[2] Never slow to ask, he usually got what he went for, even from other bankers who were not so friendly as Boyles. He arrived on some of their doorsteps involved in the business of gold.

The Dominion reserve of some $70 million was safe in the vaults of the East Block, to be taken over on the day the bank opened by the single stroke of a pen. In the vaults of the chartered banks, however, there was another $37 million which would have to be shipped to Ottawa. It meant an anguished parting in the case of several of the banks, since their gold was undervalued in relation to world prices and a good deal of it reserved for foreign commitments. Gordon came as the emissary of an unwanted central bank to impose terms that were disputed on many grounds. Yet he came back to be followed by the gold ingots with only the promise of some compensatory formula, later to be worked out, softening the price of surrender.

By March 1, Graham Towers and Osborne had moved over to the Victoria Building and were established in new offices. The secretary was installed in his own, and had installed the rest of the staff. The gold in the East Block vaults was well in excess of the 25 per cent reserve required to back the currency to be issued by the Bank of Canada. The new notes had been designed, with the figure of George V on the dollar bill, others of the Royal family on the bills from $2 to $100, and John A. Macdonald and Laurier to be glimpsed only by the affluent on the $500 and $1,000 denominations. The masses of government and chartered bank securities had been received, registered and stored, the multitudinous forms had arrived in time from the printers and the wheels of administration were geared for action. But there was no action yet. A reporter from the Toronto *Star* came up that day in the elevator to find an expanse of green broadloom carpet, an air of purposeful serenity and the imposing figure of Brooks, seated by the elevator door. A former Grenadier Guardsman who was now in middle age and looked much like R. B. Bennett in his black tailcoat and striped trousers, Brooks was to be a famous figure as the bank's major-domo. A legendary later banker, arriving to meet Towers, was to recall his first surprise at finding the governor 'sitting at that little table'.[3]

The reporter, taken to Towers, had found him at a walnut desk, slim, reserved, boyish, a little over six feet tall, with 'just the trace of a smile' behind his rimless glasses. 'His gaze is so steady it can be felt . . . the visitor has a peculiar feeling as if his head were transparent.'[4] Towers was the youngest in the world among governors of central banks, and he was surrounded in the reporter's opinion by a number of 'brisk young men'. Yet the brisk young men were actually sitting on their hands, awaiting an essential tool. The banknote company had not completed its deliveries to the offices of the receiver-general, which were now agencies of the bank, in all the nine provinces. To the exasperation of the secretary, the opening was ten days late.

When it did come, Gordon was soon on the move across the country. The bank's provincial agencies, inherited from the receiver-general, had all to be staffed and organized for the work of central banking. Some of them had to be moved and installed in new premises. During 1936 the secretary was much in Toronto, dealing as gently as he could with the alteration of a fine old post office which had been occupied by the receiver-general, 'Ionic in style, with three compartments intersected by Doric columns . . . with enriched oak and plate-glass letter-box'.[5] By 1937, with that experience behind him, he was facing a greater challenge. The new head office building had started to rise on Wellington Street, and he was in the midst of plans and contracts as a supervisor of the work.

Tough, confident and careful with money, he was as well aware of the depression as the bank was itself, and quite in harmony with its aims. The building as it finally emerged was a product of pared costs, notably lacking in frills or ostentation, but reflecting dignity enough in its austere classical style. There was adequate room for expansion and there had been some extra spending on efficiency after hot debate in the inner councils of the bank. It had resulted in posture chairs, excellent acoustics and lighting, and one of the first complete air-conditioning systems ever to be installed in Ottawa. From the tall windows fronting on Wellington Street seven bronze figures representing the seven major industries looked down on the ceremonies of opening day in 1938. The governor, the prime minister and a retinue of high officials looked up at them with pleased pride, which the secretary fully shared. He had not made the plans but he had seen that they were carried out, and within the limits of his budget.

Meanwhile the bank had earned the confidence of the country, and even of the chartered banks. While depression still hung on, it had cautiously maintained a flow of easy money, decreasing interest rates and smoothing the flow of trade. It was the guardian of foreign exchange, the marketer of the country's gold production, and by 1938 it was managing the public debt. Its staff had grown to well over 350; its research department, which had been a room of empty bookshelves at the time the bank opened, was a useful arm of government, and generally for the country's business it was a source of order and direction.

All this was in the high realms of policy, directed by Towers and Osborne. Gordon remained the administrator, the man of ways and means. He forged the appropriate tools, developed the required techniques, but there was never a doubt in any mind that he intended to rise higher. Still the pushy Scot, abrasive to some of the staff, he had established himself with all of them for exactly what he was. 'He arrived in February and I arrived at the beginning of March,' says J. R. Beattie, who was to end his own career as deputy governor. 'He was a really big man in every way . . . he had energy, a systematic approach, a really professional attitude to every damn thing he did. He set the tone, the morale, the pace . . . Gordon would have become the head of any organization because he had the guts to make a decision and be willing to be sacked if he was wrong.'[6]

By 1936, within the circle of the profession, the Bank of Canada's secretary was becoming an established figure. That year he was the man at the head table and the principal speaker of the evening when the members of the Bankers' Educational Association gathered in Toronto for the presentation of diplomas to students who had passed the examinations at Queen's. Gordon as a paternal figure counselling younger followers was not yet quite at ease. 'I think he was the most nervous speaker I ever saw in my life,' recalls R. M. Fowler, who was meeting him for the first time and was to see much of him later. 'He had quite clearly memorized his talk verbatim, and just managed to get through it with a lot of hesitations.'[7]

There was less hesitation in the onward march at home. Within a year of their arrival in Ottawa the Gordons had moved from the Glebe to 241 Hillcrest Avenue in Rockcliffe, the domain of the capital's elite. 'Maisie,' said her brother Joe, 'would never think of living in a house that wasn't up to their position', and she was as usual looking ahead. 'Never sell yourself short' was a long-familiar injunction, and whatever her husband's way-wardness he thoroughly agreed with that.[8]

He read everything he could lay his hands on with relation to economics and central banking, and what he learned he retained. Never slow to give out, when he had the information, he was as eager to take it in, from any source and on wildly assorted subjects. 'What's the good of a gold reserve, why don't we just get rid of it?' made the economist blink. 'Who the hell's this guy, Machiavelli?' turned the historian on, both to the benefit of Gordon. George Watts, who had joined the bank's research staff in 1936, was the target of many questions—'often damn fool questions, but he was never afraid to ask'.[9]

Donnie, by 1937, was entering Grade Three in the Ottawa Model School and had acquired a younger brother. Michael Huntley Gordon had arrived on October 19, 1936, to the accompaniment of some confusion since the parents returned from the hospital to find that thieves in a moving van had backed up to the door and removed most of the furniture. Confusion, how-ever, was not new to the Gordons and was quickly overcome. The house on Hillcrest proved to be a pleasant place, with wild strawberries growing in the backyard and room for children to play. Father was frequently with them, tinkering in his spare time. A swimming pool which Gordon began for Donnie was an early memory of Michael's as a pit half-lined with concrete that was gradually becoming a compost as it filled with autumn leaves. It was another of the secretary's shortfalls in the field of home improvement. 'According to him,' says Joe Barter, 'he was a great home carpenter', but little seemed to get finished and nothing worked if it was.[10]

Fortunately, perhaps, for the house the carpentry time was limited. Work was all-absorbing and steadily expanding in scale. Golf had returned as a desultory avocation, useful at least for meeting prominent people. Inept as he was himself, and little as he liked the exercise, Gordon appeared on the courses when the invitations came. There are no statistics as to how many were repeated, but his field of acquaintance widened. His golfing hosts came home with him, so did his friends in the bank, and more and more his friends in the civil service. Maisie was there, the piano and accordion were features of entertainment, and Gordon hospitality was as usual all-embracing. The Toronto evening singsongs began to be repeated in Ottawa, and the Gordon list of friendships as it widened out through the city included notable names.

'Gordon,' said Earle McLaughlin years later, 'seems to have been the right man at the right time in a lot of situations.'[11] He had certainly been lucky in the time of his coming to Ottawa. By October 1935, R. B. Bennett was gone and the Liberal government of Mackenzie King was back, still faced with the depression. It had, however, a valuable Bennett legacy in an expanding civil service. Oscar D. Skelton, deputy minister of external affairs, was the dean and the presiding spirit. Clifford Clark in the finance department, a graduate of Queen's and Harvard, was one of Skelton's recruits. So were Hume Wrong, Hugh Keenleyside, Dana Wilgress and Lester B. Pearson in the field of foreign affairs. Norman Robertson, with his bald dome and lank frame and enigmatic smile, was familiar in daily lineups at the Chateau Laurier cafeteria. By 1937 John Whitney Pickersgill was in the office of Mackenzie King. Most of them moved in orbits considerably remote from Gordon, yet Ottawa remained the centre, casual meetings were frequent and more and more he was part of a lively circle.

At the head of the bank's research department was O. D. Skelton's son, the brilliant Alex Skelton, who combined an appreciation of good liquor with a zest for life and work considerably resembling Gordon's. Ross Tolmie, an angular Manitoban and a Rhodes Scholar with a law degree from Oxford, was another kindred spirit. By 1938, a future governor of the Bank of Canada had arrived, in the person of James Coyne, and Robert B. Bryce had been attracted home from Cambridge. They were all men of brains and formidable education, and the condition of the country was attracting others like them. In 1937, out of the chaos of provincial claims and competing jurisdictions, came the Rowell-Sirois Commission on Dominion-Provincial

Relations. By the end of 1938, after a coast-to-coast tour, it had concluded its hearings in Ottawa, and W. A. Mackintosh, Alex Skelton, J. A. Corry, John Deutsch, R. M. Fowler and others who had been officials or had done research for the commission were working on the huge report. It exposed for the first time the whole web of constitutional and financial arrangements that tied the provinces together, and it went to the heart of most of the nation's problems.

They were almost equally problems of the central bank, and the men concerned with the solutions were frequently involved with Gordon. They came to the house in the evenings and discussion still went on, often with Donnie in pyjamas listening from the head of the stairs. He had the later impression, he said, that the Rowell-Sirois report had been written in his father's house, and however much that was exaggerated his father listened and learned. The knowledge he would one day need and the friends who would help him use it were beginning to come together.

Most important of all the relationships was the one with Graham Towers. 'Gordon and Towers,' said Louis Rasminsky, speaking after his retirement as a later governor of the bank, 'were complete foils to each other. I don't think I've ever known of a better or more unlikely partnership. Towers was a refined intellect; very, very penetrating, very subtle. At the same time he was a little bit withdrawn, a bit shy—I don't think I've ever heard Towers raise his voice, even when he said things that would raise other people's voices. Gordon on the other hand was a pretty rough diamond; he would pound the table and be pretty boisterous after hours and his formal education was very limited. These people who were most unlike seemed to me to be utterly dependent on each other—I think Gordon's attitude was verging on worship because Towers in a sense was everything he wasn't. But it was the same the other way round. Towers was the inside organization man— Gordon was the doer. Towers would leave it to others to take to the hustings and sell a program—but selling the program was a large part of the fun so far as Donald was concerned.'[12]

J. A. C. Osborne, the deputy governor of the bank, had come from England under the terms of a five-year contract which he was quite prepared to shorten. Able, affable and immensely valuable to Towers, he was nevertheless a Bank of England man, cast in the traditional mould. He was not easy with some of the ways of Canada or with some of the bankers around him. Alex Skelton was indispensable to the bank and equally so to the government in his easy mastery of federal and provincial problems. He was nevertheless a free-wheeling eccentric who worked with his own methods and lived by his own clock. He made his home at Cumberland, eighteen miles from Ottawa, and was unpredictable and nerve-wracking in all his comings and goings. His dress was a shock to Osborne and his car a public menace, with its doors held shut by baling wire, its erratic brakes and lighting, its dented, rattling chassis and its lack of a spare tire. It was remarkable, the research director had confided to one friend, how few parts of a car were actually essential. The chief of police at Cumberland had taken another view. When Skelton parted with the car it was for a price of $25 paid by the chief himself with the injunction that 'it was very important that the offer be accepted'.[13]

Congenial as he was to many of Skelton's ways, Gordon was not eccentric. He was rather too consistent in his thrusting urge to get on, his gathering of work to himself, his moving in on policy. He raised Osborne's hackles and there were occasional sharp clashes, yet the Scot could retreat when wrong, he was very often right, and he was a steadily growing man. He was obviously growing in his own eyes toward the post of deputy governor, and by 1938 Towers, Osborne and the finance department were all ready to concur. The death of Osborne's wife hastened his wish for retirement, and on September 12 he resigned. On September 15, formally confirmed in a seven year appointment, Gordon received his place.

The momentous change was celebrated a week later by a dinner at the Gordon home, with the governor and his wife attending. Donnie's contribution had been to help to set the table, and he was not yet quite familiar with the varieties of ware involved. At his own place Towers discovered a dribble glass, the private property of Michael, which he used throughout the meal. The politeness was characteristic but possibly the result of abstraction, for he had other things on his mind.

So had the deputy governor, as he settled into his office. The signature of Donald Gordon appeared on the country's banknotes, and there was a fine glow in that. There was a bigger salary and a new Buick car, with which he was at war as usual. He enjoyed showing Donnie the gold in the bank's new vaults. Late in the year, on a first return to Europe, he lunched with Montagu Norman, the governor of the Bank of England. He was finding his footing as an international banker, yet he came back unelated in a seething, darkening world. Hitler was on the loose, Czechoslovakia was threatened, and the money market was restless with the fear of approaching war.

The money problems of Canada had centred around mortgages, blanketing the farms of the west, imposing doldrums on the east and paralysing the lending companies under a partial moratorium. The scheme for a Central Mortgage Bank that would release a flow of funds, decrease rates to borrowers and generally relieve a dead weight on the economy was well along in the planning. Yet by 1939 it was gradually being superseded by another more urgent project.

'Hot' money was in motion around the world, some of it settling in Canada as capital fled Europe. Yet if war came, and Canada became involved, the outward flow would begin. The country's reserves would follow the foreign capital, mainly to the United States. There would be huge purchases of war supplies, requiring foreign exchange. With the current increase in imports the Canadian dollar was weakening in relation to the American dollar, and it was certain to continue sinking as the exchange deficit grew. How much of this could be tolerated and where it would have to stop remained the unanswered questions, not even asked in public. There had simply been no thought among average Canadian citizens or even their financiers of the vast restriction of imports and wild inflation of costs that might come with the great spending. One thing was certain: if war came and war supplies were to be purchased, every other transaction in the country's normal business would have to be watched and regulated to preserve foreign exchange. What that would mean in controls, bureaucracy and paperwork few men dared to think. It had, however, to be thought of, and the plans were under way.

From 'a glint in Towers' eye' they had become a secret shared by Charles Dunning, the minister of finance, Clifford Clark, his deputy, Sidney Turk, the chief of the bank's foreign exchange division in Montreal, and W. A. Cameron, the deputy chief in Toronto. Gordon was drawn in early, well before his promotion, since the secretarial department would be concerned with planning routine. He was more involved when he became deputy governor; and by that time the closed circle of the knowledgeable was beginning to widen dangerously because of physical needs.

One hint of the imposition of controls would set capital on the run, panic banks and businessmen and wreck the purpose of the plan. Yet the plan required machinery and the first tool, as usual, was a cluster of forms and instructions. By early 1939 that need was assessed. There was to be a series of thirteen forms, lettered A to M, each distinguished by a different colour of paper. Banks, post offices and customs houses, every outlet or inlet for the flow of goods or money, would require separate instructions. The instruction sheets could be multigraphed but the forms had to be printed, and the first run was estimated at five million. Forty tons, a quantity that was soon trebled, was set as the requirement of paper.

The next step was a series of discreet inquiries among several of the major printers. None of them could clear the press-time for a continuous and urgent run of five million forms, description still unspecified, in thirteen different colours. Neither could they find the stock. The thought of buying a paper mill began to concern the planners, but that subsided with the solution of the other problem. The banknote companies cleared their presses for action and somehow scraped up paper. Housed in an adjacent building, they could make deliveries without exciting comment, and they were used to working in secrecy. That part of the job, with a few more people involved in it, began to get under way.

The real test of security was within the bank itself. Through early spring and summer, as the forms began to come in, some forty members of the staff, each recruited on a 'need to know' basis, were at work in the lower rooms. Stenographers were typing and stencilling and clerks were sorting forms, while others assembled the instruction sheets that four duplicating machines were grinding out on a sixteen-hour a day schedule. For one man the mere loading of the hand-staplers became a full-time job. For all of those engaged in it the intent of the work must gradually have become obvious, yet never a word leaked out.

By July the 'unit shipments' were being put together and packed, each with forms and instruction sheets and each addressed to one of the country's three thousand bank branches or to post offices or customs houses. By August the unit shipments were being repacked in boxes, each carefully sealed and divided into separate groups. There was a group for each province, to be consigned to the bank's agency and accompanied by a sealed letter which the agent was not to open. Neither was he to open the boxes till he received word from Ottawa. When zero day came, if it actually came at all, he would be told by wire or telephone to open his sealed orders, unpack the unit shipments and dispatch them all separately to their various destinations. In the meantime he knew nothing and was not encouraged to inquire. By the late days of August the storage space of the bank's provincial agencies was piled high with freight, wholly mysterious in content, a continual source of intriguing speculation and taking up too much room.

Meanwhile, as the fear of war grew blacker in all the headlines, there was much holding of breath on higher levels. On August 27 Towers, Gordon and other senior officials sat in the bank's boardrooms with the general managers of all the chartered banks, who were there by invitation. There was not a clue from the governor of the work that was going on in the rooms beneath him. He had called the meeting, he said, to discuss financial difficulties that might arise in the event of war. There was a long and worried discussion that involved a number of issues and skirted only one. Towers touched it briefly. It would be well, he ventured mildly, to consider foreign exchange, with a view to husbanding resources. The bankers agreed that the question ought to be thought of, but were not themselves prepared. It was a technical matter for their foreign exchange experts who would be happy to be consulted. Monday, September 4, the Labour Day holiday, was suggested as the date for the meeting, and Montreal as the place. The Royal Bank's manager offered the facilities of his boardroom, and it was arranged that Turk and Cameron would attend for the Bank of Canada.

By the time the day arrived Hitler had struck at Poland, Great Britain had declared war and capital was in full flight. Foreign exchange control had been imposed in the United Kingdom, and both the *Wall Street Journal* and the *Financial Post* of Toronto had suggested the same for Canada. Yet the meeting that opened in the Royal Bank boardroom was still adrift in the days of laissez-faire. 'It fell to the Bank of Canada representatives to lead off,' wrote Sidney Turk later. 'It was pointed out that the banks in their exchange dealings would need to keep the national interest in mind even more than usual and accordingly would have to scrutinize all transactions carefully, particularly those involving transfers of funds abroad.' The banks fully agreed but they would have to persuade their clients, and they foresaw difficulties in that. 'Fear of offending important customers and perhaps losing business loomed large in their minds. Would it not be better if . . . ? Could we not do so and so? Official instructions should be given on this point . . . why does not the government give firm directions on that point?

'For two hours or more the luckless representatives of the Bank of Canada, inwardly sweating, were obliged to enter into serious discussion, to listen interestedly, to take note of suggestions, to parry this remark and turn aside that . . . and generally to conduct themselves as if no other course than voluntary cooperation had ever been thought of. Little wonder,' Turk concludes his recital, 'that when we finally broke away we asked each other "How did we do?"—"Did we show our hand?" There was no one else we could ask.'[14]

It was obvious ten days later that they had not shown their hand. On September 14 the chartered bank executives who had attended the second meeting arrived in Ottawa for a third. It was scheduled for the next day and it had been called by Graham Towers, presumably to continue discussion. There had, however, been intervening developments. On September 10 Canada had entered the war and the outward drift of foreign exchange was growing. The Canadian dollar had slipped to ninety cents in relation to the American dollar and was still on its way down. With every day's figures the sickening drop continued.

By that time there were new people in Ottawa, some of them at loose ends. Walter Gordon of Toronto, ensconced in an office in the East Block, was to be seen about the Department of Finance. The young David Mansur, an economist from the Sun Life, had been recruited by Clark and Towers for the Central Mortgage Bank. The plan for the bank, however, had been shelved in view of the war and neither Mansur nor James Coyne, the prospective secretary of the Mortgage Bank, was sure of his next job. Louis Rasminsky, the slim, elegant, cosmopolitan economist, was in much the same state. He had had nine years with the League of Nations in Geneva, gone from there to Mexico, from there on to Bolivia and eventually to the United States, where he had met Clifford Clark. As a result of that meeting Rasminsky had come to Canada, a recruit to the public service, for what he was not quite sure. He received a hint, which was soon transmitted to the others, on the afternoon of September 13. 'I believe I was in Clark's office at that time. The telephone rang and I knew it was Graham Towers telling how much foreign exchange we had lost that day. "Well, this is it," said Clark, and hung up.'[15]

Against this background the chartered bankers assembled at about ten o'clock on the morning of Friday, September 15. The surroundings, however, were not quite what they had expected. They were shown up, not to the bank's boardroom, but to a third floor above it which had been reserved for expansion. The room they entered was big, bare and undecorated, and seemed equipped for a rather dismal picnic. Graham Towers, Donald Gordon, Sidney Turk and W. A. Cameron stood waiting for them in front of battered lawn tables which had been hastily pushed together and a weirdly assorted row of folding chairs. There was no telephone in the room, no other furniture, and only a little washroom opened off. The one attraction for the eye, as the bankers settled gingerly around the tables, was a forbidding mound of paper in front of Gordon.

Towers stood up to deliver the usual greeting, and the thunderbolt followed the welcome with hardly a change in tone. The government, he said, had decided to introduce a system of foreign exchange control under the authority of the War Measures Act. It would be complete, compulsory and would be imposed within a few hours. Cool and immaculate as always on one of the occasions when he raised other's voices, he dealt for a while with the ensuing tumult of questions. Then he turned to Gordon. The deputy governor would supply the details of the plan, which was still before the cabinet. He himself would return to his own office to await word that the order in council had passed.

Outside the room there was a telephone booth, and as the governor left there were tentative moves to follow him. Gordon blocked them off. He saw Towers out, locked the door behind him and put the key in his pocket. The significance of the bare eyrie at which no elevators stopped was now apparent enough, but the deputy governor made it a little clearer. 'You're all my prisoners now. Nobody leaves and nobody uses the phone till the Order-in-Council's passed. But,' he added comfortingly, 'there'll be lunch served later on, and those that don't like sandwiches can have ice cream.'

There was little comfort for the bankers in the ensuing several hours. Before lunch, during lunch and after it they were introduced to the plan, informed of the arrangements made, and appalled at the work involved. Each with his clutch of papers from the mound in front of Gordon, they studied the thirteen forms, the thick pamphlets of instruction sheets and the copy of the long telegram to be sent at the appointed hour.

The chartered banks, the deputy governor informed them, were to become the agents of government in controlling foreign exchange. So were all the post offices in the country as well as all the customs houses. Not a dollar could leave nor any goods come in without official permission. The forms the bankers held were intended to cover both the inflow of goods and the outflow of money, and in all their wild variety the forms would have to be 'matched'. The authorized export form allowing a departure of capital would have to marry eventually with an authorized import form sanctioning the goods or services for which the money was spent. Nor was any business transaction, from multimillions for war supplies to fifty dollars for travel, exempt from the general rule. It would apply equally to all from zero hour onward and, as a final shock for the bankers, the tools had been prepared. The six-hundred-word telegram would go out to all their branches and following by the next mail from the central bank's agencies would be the shipments of forms and instructions.

It was a good day for a heart attack and one of the bankers faltered; he was feeling ill and was afraid he would have to leave. Gordon eyed him balefully, opened the locked door, and waved him out and into the arms of a burly nurse. There was no need to leave; the eventuality was prepared for; he could lie down in a room across the hall. Well away from a telephone, he seemed to recover quickly and was soon back with his colleagues. The afternoon wore on with grim discussion subsiding into black humour, and at five o'clock there was a call from Graham Towers.

Gordon took it in the booth outside the room, and returned shaking his head. The order in council was still before the cabinet and some of the wording had given rise to dispute. A fresh murmur rippled among the bankers, with even a note of hope. What would happen if the order was not passed? That, said the deputy governor, would be a serious matter. The eyes behind the spectacles swivelled the length of the tables with a solemn Scots glare. 'You see, gentlemen, since secrecy is absolutely essential it would become my personal duty to slit all your throats.'[16]

An hour later, however, the telephone rang again. This time, when Gordon returned from the call, the bankers were free to go and were launched on a sea of troubles. The order in council had passed, and zero hour was fifteen hours away. From the opening of business on Saturday the Canadian dollar stood pegged at ninety cents in relation to the American dollar. The telegrams, forms and instructions would be showering in on the branches. The Foreign Exchange Control Board, with Graham Towers as chairman and Donald Gordon as alternate, was about to commence its work.

On Saturday morning, September 16, a whole sector of the country's commercial life came to a shuddering standstill. Branch bank managers, with thirteen forms before them in thirteen different colours, were clawing through their instruction sheets and beginning to see double. Others were waiting for forms still in the mail, while enjoined by the peremptory telegram to do nothing without them. They could not pay drafts or cheques drawn from outside the borders, or authorize any transfer. Tellers at bank wickets were refusing to issue money orders drawn in American funds, and post masters and customs officers each in their own spheres were as suddenly uncooperative.

Since no money could go out to pay for foreign imports, the goods did not come in. At sidings below the border, trains were broken up, freight cars shunted off, and Canada-bound shipments consigned to a murky limbo. There was as much doubt about goods to be shipped to the Americans, since no one understood the effects of control. Amid a general roar of confusion, southward-bound newsprint, northward-bound fruit, eggs, fish, vegetables, tools, machinery, war supplies and cars of bawling livestock lay stopped in an enormous sprawl. While banks fought off their customers and prayed for the Sabbath silence, the phone calls, letters and telegrams began to descend on Ottawa.

The focal point of confusion was the bare third floor of the Bank of Canada building, where desks had arrived by early Saturday morning. Gordon was installed in an office and there were other offices on the floor, now equipped with telephones which were soon in frantic use. The bank, as agent of the board, had scraped together a staff of about fifty, including Coyne and Mansur and a number of its best men. Fortunately for them, it had also established from necessity a first working principle.

Since secrecy had had to be maintained while the country's business went on, the 'pre-zero commitment'—an order taken or given before controls were established—could be completed in the normal way. As the phones rang and the telegraph boys came panting in with their missives the screech of complaint resolved itself into one common dilemma. Almost all the business now trapped in the logjam had originated days earlier and was not subject to control. Yet it had to be released in form and there was only Form A, the General License to Export. It was no damn good, Mansur had complained earlier, since it covered everything and nothing and was practically a blank cheque. He proved to be quite right and the form was later discarded, but it was the saviour of that day. Mansur with all the staff was scrawling names till midnight on copies of Form A and firing off telegrams: 'You have been granted General License No. —.' By that time the telephone calls had stopped, 'possibly', as one of the frazzled staff recalls it, 'because we closed the switchboard'.[17]

By Monday morning the letters were coming in. The calls went out for staff and for the office space to house them. Fifty youthful lawyers arrived from Osgoode Hall, and were set to answering questions they had never thought to ask. Accountants were in high demand, clerks, stenographers and book-keepers all had to be found, and there was no time for training. Maxwell W. Mackenzie, arriving from Montreal, had a characteristic experience. A later friend of Gordon's who was meeting him for the first time, he was then a partner in an accounting firm which he thought could perhaps spare him. But he would have to go home, he said, to settle a few affairs and get some clothes and a toothbrush. 'You can get a toothbrush here,' Gordon decreed, 'and start work tonight.'

'So,' says Mackenzie, 'I walked into an office on the top floor of the Birks building and they handed me a copy of the Foreign Exchange Control Order and told me to go over in the corner and read it. I don't think I knew the difference between a Canadian dollar and an American dollar, but in half an hour they were back with a pile of letters. "Okay, you've read the order —now start answering these".'[18]

As the weeks went by and the banks mastered their paperwork, confusion settled to a steady din of problems. The staff in the Ottawa offices doubled and then redoubled. Across the country business had recovered from shock and begun its flow again, with every dollar for export and every item for import to be covered by a coloured form. As the forms flowed back on Ottawa each had to be matched or the search begun for a mate, and beyond that was the daily flood of petitioners and the mass of correspondence. An invalid required funds for a trip to an American hospital, and had to be proved sick; a man of affairs had business that required him in the United States and demanded dollars to get there. Thousands of exemptions were claimed, thousands of decisions protested while five hundred green young bureaucrats were still learning their jobs. Yet for all that the huge, maddening, cumbersome operation was somehow grinding on.

Gordon's name began to be heard in Canada, and the Gordon stories multiplied. He was not the chairman of the board and he did not set its policy, but he was the rude and massive genius who was making the machine work. Towers presided in the background but Gordon was well up front, obviously enjoying the limelight. He had his gift for making friends and for making the friends work and a way with the unexpected that enhanced a growing legend. Filtering up to his desk came the case of a Canadian travelling man who had had a lively holiday in New York before controls went on. The result he had left behind was an advanced case of pregnancy, and the lady's American lawyer was threatening suit for support. There had been, Gordon ruled, a 'pre-zero commitment'; Lothario would have to pay for it and the board would release the funds.

'First time I ever met him,' says Fraser ('Scottie') Bruce, later president of Alcan, 'I was down from the plant at Arvida with a peculiar problem on my hands. An elder of the church up there had come from the States, and he'd had the habit of taking American dollar bills out of the collection plate and putting back Canadian dollars. Nothing much wrong with it—till Foreign Exchange Control came along. Then all of a sudden it was illegal and the Mounties picked him up. I came looking for Gordon at the Bank of Canada to see what I could do.

'I had a long wait and then Brooks came along and told me Mr. Gordon would see me. He showed me up to the foreign exchange floor, and I expected a big office. But the door opens on this little cubbyhole with just room for one extra chair and a desk covered with papers and this great big bear of a man sprawled across it. He doesn't even look up. "What the hell do you want?—and the answer is no!"—that was the greeting I got. But I stayed there and he let me finish my story while he went on writing. When I finished he waved me off, "I understand, don't worry about it." And I went out not worrying—I knew it was all right. He was as big a man as he looked.'[19]

He was big enough by April 1940 to be elected president of the Canadian Club of Ottawa and deliver his current views. 'The kind of patriotism that we practise is nothing to be ashamed of. When we say that we are fighting for the British way of doing things we can hold our heads pretty proudly because, as we should know, all right thinking people of the world regard that statement as synonymous with the spirit of the Golden Rule and the spirit of true freedom.' At the same meeting he saluted the retiring president and presented him with a travelling bag, 'reinforced so as to defy the combined efforts of porters from the Maritime Provinces to Ottawa, with a right-hand side pocket that will hold four quarts'.[20] One could still be a little jovial, and a little confident and simplistic, in the haze of the phony war.

Then, abruptly, it was over. Norway went and Hitler struck at France. Disaster was complete abroad and it was reflected in the books of the country as vast purchases devoured foreign exchange. In spite of all controls the balance was slipping dangerously, and Towers left for Washington where the only relief lay. He was there on June 14, the day Paris fell and the remnants of the French government made their way to Bordeaux. He was still there on June 18 when a signal came to Ottawa—this time not a telegram—that plunged the deputy governor into action. The French cruiser *Emile Bertin*, Halifax naval authorities signalled the chief of staff, had just arrived in harbour with $305 million in gold consigned from the Bank of France to the Bank of Canada.[21]

The amount was considerably larger than the entire Canadian reserve, and there was an immediate rush of wired and phoned instructions. Space was cleared in the vaults of the Bank of Canada and in Halifax on a siding near the dock a string of empty passenger cars was shunted into position. They were intended to leave for Ottawa with some three hundred tons of gold ingots stacked along their floors, and at both ends of the line trucks, guards and naval and military authorities were placed on standing alert.

Yet there was no movement from the ship. By the next morning Gordon and J. L. Ralston, who had become minister of finance, were studying another signal. The commander of the *Emile Bertin* was not unloading the gold; he was awaiting further instructions. That immediately involved Rear-Admiral P. W. Nelles, chief of the Canadian Naval Staff, who was asked to hold the ship. By noon came a signal to Nelles direct from *Emile Bertin*: the captain had orders from France to retain his cargo on board and proceed at once to the French island of Martinique. The French ambassador in Washington had signalled that he concurred. That news sent Gordon back to Ralston, Ralston to Mackenzie King, and at one-thirty in the afternoon a meeting was convened which included King, Ralston, Nelles, Gordon, and C. G. 'Chubby' Power, the acting minister of national defence.

The deputy governor of the Bank of Canada and chairman (alternate) of the Foreign Exchange Control Board was now in the midst of the war on higher levels. He proceeded to make the most of it:

> I urged upon the Prime Minister that the vessel should not be allowed to leave in view of the very doubtful position of the French Government. . . . the Bank of France had sent the gold to the Bank of Canada

for safekeeping, and neither we nor anyone else had received any other instructions from the Bank of France. . . . To say the least the French government's position was uncertain and it would not be too exaggerated a view to suggest that it might be acting under duress—in any event we were entitled to take that view. I pointed out that leaving the gold in Canada was the safe course, and taking it out of Canada to Martinique could not but expose it to further risk. Furthermore, so far as I knew, there were no facilities in Martinique for storing of gold.

I further stressed that the only reason which could possibly be advanced for a change in the destination of the gold must arise from a change in the war position since the gold left France . . . we were playing safe by holding the gold if it later turned out to be detrimental to the British Empire interests if we allowed the gold to leave our shores. If any mistake were made it was best to make a mistake which could not prejudice the British Empire. I also pointed out the fact that the British Government had announced it did not propose to relieve the French Government of their treaty obligations as an ally . . . certainly it could be assumed that the British Empire in continuing the war proposed to avail itself of any available French resources in the form of the French navy, airships or military materials, and gold is most assuredly a weapon of war.

To all this, delivered in the Gordon manner and doubtless with more fervour than the later record implies, the prime minister was receptive. But he was abstracted by his other worries and he was against the use of force; someone should persuade the French to be cooperative. Gordon could call Halifax and dictate a letter to the agent of the Bank of Canada to be delivered to the captain of the ship. Ralston could send a telegram; and the meeting ended with that. Only Chubby Power, the fighting Irishman of Quebec, 'took the stand that we should not let the cruiser leave under any circumstances'.

By mid-afternoon confusion had become compounded. *Emile Bertin* reported herself as still determined to leave, but she was also waiting for instructions. At 7.30 in the evening Nelles called Gordon. He had been told by one of his liaison officers that the prime minister had authorized the ship's departure. Gordon took the officer's name, was immediately on the phone to him, and was given a revised story. Nelles's information had been less direct than he thought. An attaché at the French legation had told the liaison officer that the French ambassador to Canada had been told by the prime minister that the ship could leave Halifax at six o'clock in the evening. Just as Gordon hung up, the telephone rang again and it was Norman Robertson on the line, introducing a new diversion. He was speaking from External Affairs and he had been in touch with O. D. Skelton, the undersecretary. 'Doctor Skelton, in chatting over the matter with the Prime Minister, had mentioned the sum involved and the Prime Minister had expressed amazement that such a colossal figure was in question.'

Within the next few minutes Gordon, in touch with Ralston, had a re-revision of the story. The prime minister had not exactly said that the ship could go. He had been told by the French ambassador that it had left at six o'clock, and had then said that in that case there was nothing more to be done. With that word Gordon turned to the man who was of the same mind as himself, and discussion came to a point. 'Power said that as Acting Minister of National Defence he proposed to stop the ship at all costs, provided I supported him.' There was no doubt of the support, and by 9.30 the order had gone to Halifax that 'all necessary steps' should be taken to prevent the cruiser sailing.

By the next day (June 20), amid a tangle of cross-purposes and new conflicting stories, King was involved again. He had always been a little wary of the Bank of Canada, which he regarded as a Bennett creation, and he had been subjected to the deputy governor in the midst of crisis. 'Those people at the bank—they're mad,' he confided to Jack Pickersgill,[22] but he had steeled himself to his own form of action. From the prime minister to Commodore Reid, the naval commander at Halifax, went instructions 'to say to the captain of the *Emile Bertin* that the government of Canada did not wish him to leave, and that if he attempted to do so it would be regarded as an unfriendly act'. 'I did not remind him,' commented Gordon, 'that Reid was still under instructions, through Power, to "take all necessary steps" to prevent the departure.'

Later in the day came long, heated and less and less diplomatic wrangles between Skelton, Power and Gordon on one side and the French ambassador and his officials on the other. 'Our discussions were quite unsatisfactory.' France was collapsing, her government in chaos in Bordeaux, and the loyalties of her navy divided. None of the French officials was sure of his own authority or would give a direct order, but they were all of the 'opinion' that the ship should be allowed to leave.

Gordon had already turned in another direction. 'While the foregoing was going on I had sent two urgent cables to the Bank of England. . . . When I returned from the French Minister's office I found Catterns, Bank of England, on the long-distance telephone. Catterns apologized for several blunders which apparently had held up replies to my previous cables and informed me that an urgent message had been sent to the High Commissioner to be transmitted to the Canadian government. . . . "Please urge most strongly that immediate action, however strong, should be taken to prevent ship leaving Halifax for the time being".'

King, Ralston, Power and Nelles received that word from Gordon in a rapid series of calls. The high commissioner arrived in response to his cabled instructions and on the evening of June 20, as a result of many signals, the captain of the *Emile Bertin* agreed to a two-day wait pending agreement between the French and Canadian governments. At 8:00 A.M. on the 21st, however, Ralston called Gordon. Halfway across the world emissaries of the French government were being conducted through the forest of Compiègne to the sleeping-car where they would hear the terms of armistice. Out of Bordeaux, however, a signal had come to the commander of the moored cruiser. He was instructed to leave Halifax, forcing his way out if necessary, and he intended to obey his orders. 'The Prime Minister then refused to permit force to be used. . . . Ralston felt he was helpless and left it with me to see what other suggestion I could make.

'I then telephoned Hankison of the High Commissioner's office and permitted myself to become very annoyed. . . . I told him very emphatically that he should be on the Prime Minister's doorstep and also in urgent communication with his government . . . every minute counted.'

The fire was built under the high commissioner's office but it did not ignite King. 'At 9:30 A.M. Ralston called again to say that the Prime Minister still baulked at using force. . . . I urged that before we threw up our hands we should arrange an emergency meeting for one final try.' King was not available, but Ralston, Power, Skelton, Nelles and some senior military and naval officers were eventually huddled with Gordon. The bones of the question emerged. There would be much criticism from the still-neutral Americans if a French ship were sunk. 'The French navy might resent our action very seriously and might even attempt going into our harbour with all guns blazing.' There was only mild confidence in the shore batteries and other defences at Halifax. 'After discussion about ways and means to stop the boat it developed that the guns in Halifax harbour would probably be capable of tackling the job. In view of the opinions of the others Ralston put it up to me squarely whether or not I thought the ship should be sunk.'

The deputy governor of the Bank of Canada, with a question of high strategy imposed on him by the minister of finance, was a little inclined to weave. He would probably go for the sinking, and would certainly offer the threat of it, but he preferred to ask for instructions from the British government. Dr. Skelton, always the autonomous Canadian, disagreed with the latter suggestion and 'said that we should not ask the United Kingdom for instructions'. That point Gordon wriggled around: he was not asking for instructions but for an 'indication from our ally as to how serious she regarded the situation and how far she was asking for help'. The fine spinning of intricacies was quickly dropped, however, and the decision made was simply to maintain a bluff.

The meeting had hardly ended when there was another flurry of signals. *Emile Bertin* had announced that she was sailing in ten minutes. There was the immediate prospect of a French cruiser steaming out of Halifax harbour with all guns blazing and with return fire from shore. It seemed, however, that all sides were bluffing. Walter Gordon came into his namesake's office with word from his own naval sources in Halifax that the port's batteries were useless and that the cruiser could raze the city. The French captain, for his part, agreed in another signal to a delay of five hours. In that interval the British Admiralty entered the picture. Rather than stage a naval battle at Halifax the ship should be allowed to go. She would now be shadowed, however, by the British cruiser *Devonshire* which had arrived outside the harbour. At five in the afternoon the graceful, grey shape was at last in motion and the French ambassador was writing to the prime minister. The gist of the letter, Gordon noted later, with two exclamation points, 'apparently was that he, on behalf of the French Government, was prepared to relieve us of all responsibility for the safe custody of the gold!!'

It was clear, however, that no one was yet relieved. On June 22 Colonel Vanier, Canada's ambassador to France, who had made his way to Bordeaux, cabled that the French government was ordering the *Emile Bertin* to 'await instructions'. The same day the French ambassador in Ottawa ordered a return to Halifax. *Devonshire* from her shadowing position signalled that the French captain refused to obey his orders, and Admiralty signalled *Devonshire*, nervously cautioning against any impression being given to French naval officers 'that their loyalty was doubted'.

By the 24th Nelles was signalling Admiralty to request securing of the gold. Gordon was hammering Ralston to take steps at Martinique. What steps Ralston could have taken, even if he had had a mind to, seem highly problematic, but other action was developing round the island. On the 25th the *Emile Bertin* put in, while *Devonshire* lay off shore. *Fiji* hove in sight and a little later *Dunedin*, both of them British cruisers. They were polite, ominous and suggestive, but they did not impress the French. Admiral Robert, the commander at Martinique, was also polite but firm. The gold would not be allowed to return to France, but neither would it be handed over to the British.

On the 27th *Dunedin* signalled Admiralty: 'French assure disembarkation of gold ordered at Martinique. . . . I believe him and consider further pressure undesirable.' It was undesirable now for a number of reasons. A formidable remnant of the French navy was approaching Martinique. The aircraft carrier *Béarn*, the cruiser *Jeanne d'Arc* and a train of oilers and supply ships would be joining *Emile Bertin*. Proud and desperate French naval officers, embittered by defeat, torn in their loyalties and distracted by conflicting orders, might choose to fight it out. It was not a possibility that the British were prepared to consider and the thought of force subsided. By the first days of July *Emile Bertin*'s cargo was in storage at Martinique, far from the hungry vaults of the Bank of Canada.

The deputy governor had lost his naval battle, and was still smarting as he inscribed the record for posterity. Across the typed account, now in the Queen's University Archives, is an epilogue in pencil: 'I learned from Sir Frederick Phillips that my early cables did not reach Churchill's ear, and that if they had the result might have been different. Churchill was informed, but apparently it was too late to take action which might have been taken.'

CHAPTER 5

'His is the Churchill role'

Through the rest of 1940, as the allied countries reeled from the blows of the war, the Foreign Exchange Control Board was fighting a losing battle. The funds it was able to preserve by the checks of the new system were draining away in the face of huge demands. As factories came on stream and the flood of production mounted to supply the needs of Britain, tools, parts and a vast bulk of the materials were ordered from the United States. The outflow for payment, all in American funds, was scraping the bottom of the barrel.

By May 1940 every Canadian resident with gold or foreign exchange had been forced to sell his holdings to the Bank of Canada. From the bank itself the Foreign Exchange Control Board had received some $250 million. Another $650 million had been raised and handed over by the Dominion government, while at the same time the Bank of Canada had been quietly relieved through an order in council of the requirement to maintain a 25 per cent reserve in gold or foreign exchange against the currency. That was as well, for by July 2, 1941, the Bank of Canada's foreign exchange holdings were down to half a million dollars.

Roosevelt and the Americans, however, had already come to the rescue. On April 20, 1941, the president had placed his signature on the Hyde Park Declaration, affirming that 'in mobilizing the resources of the continent each country should provide the other with the defence articles it is best able to produce, and, above all, produce quickly, and that production programmes should be coordinated to this end'.[1] What this meant for Canada, with its production machine geared up, was some $300 million immediately in American defence contracts and the promise of many more. American funds would be flowing into the country, rather than flowing out. Beyond that, the Americans were to provide Great Britain under the lend-lease arrangement with everything she needed for supplies, equipment and munitions to be manufactured in Canada.

While Mackenzie King was adamant against Canada accepting direct lend-lease assistance from the United States, there was no such prohibition against material on British account. Canadian factories could now get what they needed for British war production without using up foreign exchange. In the long view the great dilemma was resolved; the Canadian production outflow would be balanced by an American inflow, and while the country would still have to conserve every possible dollar of foreign exchange it would not be threatened with exhaustion in the effort to supply Britain.

In the spring of 1941 Gordon was alternating between the problems of the Foreign Exchange Control Board and the problems of the Bank of Canada, with an occasional evening for diversion. The family had moved to 191 Buena Vista Road, Rockcliffe, and the master, as usual, saw a need for improvements. 'He was working like a madman,' recalls J. Douglas Gibson who was then an economist with the Bank of Nova Scotia, 'but he painted his house that summer—a funny red brick place—quite a large house and red fence out on the street going up from the yardway—he did the white trim.'[2]

The paintbrush was relaxation from the pressure of two offices and the impending shadow of a third. Deep as he was in the wartime councils on finance, Gordon was well aware of what was coming. More than a year earlier, in his travels across the country as foreign exchange controller, he had spoken to Toronto bankers and delivered his own view. He had talked of 'the giant symphony of the economic machine' that was tuning up in Canada and of what its working would mean: 'We are meeting here under the shadow of a catastrophe . . . only through public understanding of the potential effects of economic warfare can some of its later evils be prevented. We simply *must* plan so that those in authority will have the support of a *really educated* public opinion, for the pitfalls of half-truths are worse than the swamps of sheer ignorance.'[3]

They had been apt words that applied with more force now, and more directly to himself. With the Hyde Park agreement the problem of paying for war supplies was at least partially solved. Canadian productive powers could be developed to their full potential and the work of foreign exchange control would settle down to a routine. But with every new job and every piece of machinery consuming essential supplies the problem of inflation grew. The prospect ahead of Gordon was not one of release. We *must* plan, he had said; and he had meant more than he said. Sooner or later, as the war factories multiplied and the flow of wages and the shortages of goods increased, that 'giant symphony of the economic machine' would be entering on a new movement and requiring a new conductor. He could hardly have had a doubt as to who was the likely man.

The Wartime Prices and Trade Board had been established on September 3, 1939, under the authority of the War Measures Act. It was responsible to the Department of Labour and directed by civil servants who retained their other jobs. Hector McKinnon, the chairman, was also chairman of the Tariff Board. David Sim was commissioner of excise in the Department of National Revenue, and F. A. McGregor was commissioner of the Combines Investigation Act in the Department of Labour. These three, with half a dozen administrators and a staff which grew to about 175 in the course of two years, were to have supervision of rentals and 'to provide safeguards under war conditions against any undue enhancement in the prices of food, fuel and other necessaries of life, and to ensure an adequate supply and equitable distribution of such commodities'.[4]

It was a sufficiently large assignment, and the members of the board had had their lively times. During the fall of 1939, when ships from the West Indies were held up for convoy, they had clamped down on commercial users of sugar. In the summer of 1940, as thirty-four freighters streamed into Halifax escaping from French waters, the board had unloaded and distributed their cargoes of British coal. The German occupation of Norway, which cut off 75 per cent of the Canadian supply of fish oils, had led to the encouragement and development of an infant industry. Factories on the east and west coasts which had produced 56,000 gallons of cod liver oil in 1939 had almost quadrupled their output by 1941. Wool, fats and millfeed, all of them in short supply, had been produced with the board's help and channelled on to the users. Price control, however, had hardly entered the picture. The board had issued only some sixty orders, and fifty-one of these had concerned rentals. It was a supervising body directed at the source of supply, and the general public hardly knew that it existed.

Behind the board, however, was an array of formidable powers and the certainty that they would have to be used. By the early summer of 1941 the country was entering the zone of full employment and well embarked on inflation. Factories were devouring supplies, prices were chasing shortages and wages were chasing both. While Gordon painted his house the cost of living was rising at about 1 per cent per month, and moves were in train to stop it.

In August 1941 the responsibility for the Wartime Prices and Trade Board was shifted from the Department of Labour to the Department of Finance under James Lorimer Ilsley. At the same time the jurisdiction of the board was extended from the 'necessaries of life' to include all civilian goods. Ilsley, Clifford Clark, Graham Towers, Gordon and the rest of the senior advisers began a series of discussions which involved the members of the presently functioning board and widened out to include a steady stream of businessmen from all parts of the country and all sections of the economy. There was no question by then of the need for further controls, but there was much debate on method.

Goods were the primary factor in the cost of living, as imports, manufactures or produce grown on the farms. All passed to the retailer through the chain of distribution, and at every stage of the process costs were rising. At what point should the stop come and the ceiling clamp down? A first reasonable proposal was to control costs at the source. Tariff adjustments could affect the price of imports and reduce the nonessentials. Home producers and distributors could be required to market their output on new and approved bases. Along the chain to the retailer, as these measures took hold, the pressure of rising prices would be gradually phased out. That was the view of many of the senior businessmen, and the approach favoured by McKinnon.

The one flaw in the suggestion was that it would not work. At the first hint of controls the manufacturer would rush to cover his costs and provide for a substantial rise. Every wholesale distributor and every retail merchant would be in competition for stock. There would be a huge surge of demand with an accompanying surge of price rises projected months ahead. Wage demands would follow to increase the pressure on prices and install inflation as a permanent part of the system. Gradualism would lose the battle even before it was begun, and the recommended process was working in the wrong direction. What had to come, as it had with foreign exchange, was an instantaneous jamming-on of the brakes. It had to come, moreover, at the immediately controllable point and the ultimate point of impact. The brakes had to be applied on the retail price to the consumer.

Retail prices were as varied as the ways of Canadian merchandising and the habits of Canadian shoppers. The chain stores and the smaller stores down to the corner grocery all operated on separate and different bases, all justified regionally and all responding to volume in markups, costs, discounts and trading practices and terms. Could all these thousand differences be ironed out? They could not; and the attempt to do so would disrupt the structure of business. The only common factors in the retail trade of the country were the increasing scarcity of goods and the steady rise in prices. The freeze must deal with those, and it could change nothing else. The pressure of rising costs would somehow have to be absorbed, 'squeezed out' before the goods came to a warehouse, and the manufacturer and the producer would suffer most of the squeeze. There was challenge enough in that, but it was only part of the problem. Rents affected living costs and would also have to be controlled. Services took their share, and barber shops and hotel rooms, filling stations and restaurants would be under controls too. The difficulties appalled practical men and even theorists shuddered, but the bleak statistics were driving the planners on.

By September the men in the finance department and Towers in the Bank of Canada, with Gordon as a peripheral adviser, were prepared to support a freeze. McKinnon still dissented. An able civil servant, he simply could not convince himself that controls at the retail level could ever be made to work. Nor did he like talk of the 'Squeeze' or the bludgeoning of the business community into line with a dubious plan. On the other hand he could come up with no alternative that offered a chance of success and he was carried along with his peers. Late in the month the ever-present Bill Mackintosh of Queen's, who was now a special assistant to Clifford Clark, drew up a statement of policy. It passed the hurdle of Ilsley and went on to the greatest hurdle in the person of Mackenzie King.

King's fear of controls and his lack of interest in economics were both proverbial in the department. Mitchell Sharp, though he was not yet in Ottawa, heard later from Mackintosh of the prime minister's first startled reaction. 'He looked at the draft, read two or three paragraphs, looked up and said, "This *is* important, isn't it?"'[5] Then he dismissed Mackintosh, presumably finished reading the draft, and passed it along to the desk of Jack Pickersgill.

While the special assistant conned it there was a week or so of waiting. One concern of King, among the many crowding his desk, was James Garfield Gardiner, the minister of agriculture. The most ruthless politician in the cabinet, and at that time on a visit to his Saskatchewan constituents, Gardiner was dedicated to the raising of farm prices. He had good reason; the war demand and the costs on grain, milk and livestock were both steadily rising. When he came back from the west, stiffened by many meetings with prairie farmers, Gardiner was presented in cabinet with the draft of the new policy and announced that he reserved his position. He was prepared for ceilings on everything if they were 'flexible' on farm products. To anyone familiar with the ways of Jimmy Gardiner there was promise of trouble in that.

Still, Pickersgill records, the policy paper emerged from cabinet approved, though the dry wording of the economists was not admired by himself. 'It was a press statement prepared by a lot of people with technical knowledge and this is what finally convinced Mackenzie King who was very reluctant, under great pressure both by his own instincts and by a lot of his friends to resist this whole thing, but he finally agreed.' He was as cautious as usual, however, in taking the next step, and the momentous document lay on Pickersgill's desk. 'I kept looking at it and I could see the possibilities of the thing, if it was rewritten in English. I said to King—you know, you should never issue this as a press statement; you should go on the air and make a speech yourself—and by that time I had a text. I wrote the god-damned speech that Mackenzie King gave,' the special assistant concludes with typical modesty, 'and it was far and away the greatest broadcast he ever made.'[6]

It reached the country by way of the national network of the CBC on the evening of Friday, October 18, 1941. In the rounded periods of Pickersgill, intoned by the prime minister, Canadians learned that practically everything they used, ate, wore or were served by was subject to price control. The formal ceilings would be imposed on December 1; but from that date all retail prices would be frozen at or rolled back to the prices prevailing in the four-week 'basic period' from September 15 to October 11, 1941. The ceilings would apply to rentals, while wages and salaries would be 'stabilized', with the prospect of a 1 per cent bonus for every 1-point rise in the cost of living. The battle with inflation was joined. The country was embarked, said King, on an experiment 'hitherto untried on this continent, and perhaps having regard to its depth and variety, hitherto untried by the will and consent of any free people anywhere'.[7]

The Wartime Prices and Trade Board was now expanded in functions, but it was a skeleton with a reluctant head. Hector McKinnon knew everything there was to know about the country's tariffs and trade. He was familiar enough with businessmen to know what it would mean to deal with them in administering the new controls, and he did not relish the prospect. He was not equipped, he felt, for the huge job of recruiting that would be required to staff the board, or for the endless hours of cajoling, threatening and persuading that would go to the unravelling of problems in the glare of the public eye. Neither were Sim and McGregor, his two closest aides, but all three were in agreement that they knew a man who was. Finally they went to Pickersgill and Pickersgill went to Ilsley. 'We've got three civil servants who are going to quit,' he said, 'if you don't get Gordon for the Board.'[8]

That was already a prospect but it was stopped short, for once, by an obdurate Graham Towers. He had looked forward to the return of his deputy governor as the work of foreign exchange control settled to an easier routine. He was swamped with problems himself, and when Gordon's name had surfaced during the discussion of price control he had flatly refused to release him. He still refused Ilsley, and for a week the finance minister and the governor of the Bank of Canada politely locked horns. Then there was a call from King, an urgent and protracted interview, and Towers emerged from the meeting deprived of his right-hand man.

As the subject of all the discussions, Gordon was cool toward his prospects. Ilsley's proposal, as it came to him, was that he would act with Hector McKinnon as associate chairman of the board. Sketched out as a plan of organization was an expanded head office which would include former officials with the addition of several others and would set general policy. Under that, distributed across the country, would be a web of Commodity and Trade administrations, each one supervising a specific trade or industry. About sixty or so administrators would be required and each of the men, ideally, would be a leader in his own field, convinced of the need for the price policy, able to convince his competitors and fully aware of the intricacies and tricks and loopholes of the trade. Finally, under the administrator and facing the general public, there would have to be a nation wide network of regional organizations and local field offices, none of them now existing.

This was the hopeful chart for the maintenance of the price wall, holding the line for the consumer and squeezing the costs back to be absorbed in the productive chain. Manufacturers and processors, packers, distributors and farmers were all part of the chain, and they would all be loud in their complaints. There would certainly be cases, moreover, where losses would be unacceptable, whatever the amount of squeezing. Nobody could control the price of imported goods, and some of these were essential foods and supplies. Tariff reductions could mitigate the squeeze here, at the general cost of the country. At the same general cost there could be subsidization of farmers and of hard-pressed manufacturers who could establish legitimate claims; and a last resort in some cases would be bulk purchase of supplies. All these functions, under the wing of the Prices Board and supplementing its work, were to be handled by a Commodity Price Stabilization Corporation which would allot subsidies, regulate tariff changes and handle the bulk purchases made on government account.

The whole was a formidable prospect, and the ramifications and necessities of the Wartime Prices and Trade Board were expanding day by day. Moreover, of the two heads now proposed for the monster, Gordon wanted no part of it and McKinnon was unconvinced that it would work at all. 'He really believed,' says Jack Pickersgill, 'that it was a kind of madness.' On November 6, when Ilsley rose in the Commons to outline the workings of the price policy, he was still a harried man. The dragooned Gordon was unappointed and rebellious, while the unhappy Hector McKinnon was as dubious as he had ever been. Both men, however, were being swept along by events. There was much work going on and much tentative recruiting; every train to Ottawa was emptying out its businessmen and telephone lines were jammed across the country. The board was gathering its materials and it had to be given shape. On November 10 Ilsley informed the House that Gordon would join McKinnon as associate chairman of the board. Ten days later, however, to the grateful relief of both men, that arrangement fell through. Well as they got along and much as they liked each other, McKinnon could not be teamed with Donald Gordon. As a tariff expert, moreover, he had found his natural place. McKinnon, Ilsley announced, was to become chairman of the new Commodity Price Stabilization Corporation. The Wartime Prices and Trade Board, in the person of Donald Gordon, was to have a single head.

Ten days earlier the telephone had rung in Ross Tolmie's office in the legal department of Finance. Gordon as associate chairman had already accepted his fate. 'Ross,' he said, 'I'd like you to send me a list of a dozen lawyers across the country, lawyers who don't give a damn about the law, just want to get things done, like you.'[9] The same day there had been a brisk exchange by telegram with Douglas Dewar of Vancouver, a wealthy retired accountant, a Scot and a bosom friend: 'Douglas, I need you'—'When and where?' —'Here and now.' By the next night Dewar was on the train for four years' service in Ottawa, all totally unpaid since he refused even expenses. The gathering of an official clan, by all means and emissaries, had preceded the official job.

The results, by November 20, were filling Ottawa hotels. Administrators, as the section heads of industries, had been the men in most demand and the men most difficult to get. They had also posed an early and major problem. The leading man of an industry, if he could be lured away from his private wartime troubles, would still be partial to his own special field. He would know all the tricks of the trade and he might well be charged with favouritism. On the other hand, the impartial civil servant, drafted away from other work to head an industrial sector, would be months in learning the bare rudiments of his job. And there were no months to be spared; the decision made quite consciously was to go for knowledgeable men and to drive them hard and trust them.

It was hardly seen as a favour by any of the men concerned. Very few were convinced as yet that price controls would work. Each one, as a leader of private enterprise considering his own business, had little to look ahead to but restricted lines and profits. He had less to look ahead to as an official servant of the board, even if it proved successful. He would be a meddling nuisance to competitors who would be forced to open their books, justify their costs and methods and reduce or stop the production of nonessential goods. They would certainly dispute his rulings and consign his name to anathema at every turn of the screw. Over the chosen men, however, was the whip of national necessity which most were prepared to bend to, and there were other inducements. One captain of industry, flatly refusing an approach, had announced that he would not touch the job with a ten-foot pole. Too bad, said the silky David Sim who was acting as Gordon's emissary; would he name his next competitor? 'You mean he'd know all my costs?'[10] That he would, said Sim, and the alternate name was dropped; the board had gained an administrator.

All means had been employed and all moods were in evidence on the morning of November 20 when some fifty of the just-appointed administrators assembled in the railway committee room of the House of Commons. At the head of the long table, flanked by his other officials, was the new chairman of the board. Whatever his earlier feelings he was price controller now; and, true to himself, he was headlong into the job. It spread out before him wide as the map of the country and confused as the country's mind, which still remained to be shaped. He had to convince, convert, organize, bully, wheedle and exact, but the first of his tools was words. He launched the work with a flood of them that went on for the next ten days.

'Gentlemen,' he told the administrators, 'we are meeting here as members of the General Staff commanding an army, consisting of every citizen of Canada, about to go into action against the disaster of inflation.' Many of the men before him had proposed alternative plans, all of which had been rejected. He ran over the reasons. Gradualism would not work; there could be no concession to costs. The only possible policy had been an immediately imposed ceiling on all retail prices. What did that mean? It meant that 'business through our Administrators can work out the adjustment of the "squeeze" back from the retailers through intermediate processors and suppliers to the primary producers . . . the adjustment must be financed primarily by the business groups concerned, not by the consumer nor by labour.'

With that cheerful prescription he handed out to the administrators the dozen typed pages of a preliminary statement of policy. 'You may digest this material during the quiet tranquility which is likely to be your lot in the immediate future . . . we are having a pretty hectic time . . . but keep pressing us for action because the man who yells the loudest at a time like this is the one who is heard.'[11]

On the night of the 21st he took to the radio network to define the battle for the people:

> As a nation at war we must spend huge sums of money—our taxes and our war loans—to buy the materials of war. We soon begin to bid against ourselves for materials and commodities which we have to have, both for war and for ordinary uses. We bid against ourselves and prices begin to rise. Since one man's prices are another man's costs, each price increase generates other price increases, leading on to wages and salary increases.
>
> This starts the vicious circle. As wages and other costs rise in the chase after prices we have more money to spend in bidding against ourselves and we thus force prices higher and higher. Wages and salaries are bound to lag behind prices. We soon have disputes and confusion, with hardships falling more and more unfairly on people of small incomes and modest savings. We begin to find that our dollar of savings has shrunk to a fraction of its value in terms of living costs. We have a country seized with fear and disruption. In such a state no country can hope to wage war. Such a state means defeat of the war effort and, in the aftermath, it means a swift toboggan slide to a state of collapse.

There had been little need with businessmen to hammer at the danger of inflation; they all knew it and feared it. Gordon's major war effort, and his obsession for the next six years, was to convince the average man and the average woman. That night, by the time he finished his talk, he was off to a good start:

> No further increase in prices can be permitted. Starting December 1, the level of prices must be returned to and maintained at the level which prevailed in the period of September 15 to October 11. . . . I can give you fifty reasons why this policy will not work. But, outweighing all these, there is one imperative and impelling reason why it must and will be made to work. The reason is necessity—national necessity, urgent, dire, undeniable—for the survival of this country and your homes and families.[12]

During the next week, in a tumultuous office in the Birks building, contending with the yells of the recruited, recruiting or stealing others and chewing cough drops madly for the benefit of his failing voice, he found the time to contract an important alliance. Charlotte Whitton, who was then the director of the Canadian Welfare Council, brought together in Ottawa the presidents of most of the national women's organizations. Gordon stalked in on them, beefy, husky, harried but unmistakeably in earnest, and outlined the dimensions of their job. They were the shoppers of the nation, they would have to supervise prices; much of the success of the control board was ultimately in their hands. He had gained the promise, by the end of the afternoon, of a million and a half assistants.

On Thursday, November 27, again in the railway committee room, there was the most crucial meeting of all. Everyone had agreed from the first that only the general public, a convinced general public, could really enforce controls. The program would have to be sold, over and over again, and above all to the press. On the 27th, with the prime minister beside him, Gordon faced some three hundred editors, columnists, radio broadcasters and assorted moulders of opinion from across the country. His essential arguments were unchanged but he was dealing with knowledgeable, potentially dangerous critics who might erode his support. He had been told as a boy, he said, that it was no use trying to teach your grandmother to suck eggs; she knew all about it. He assumed that the press knew all about inflation and was well aware of its dangers. He expected and would take criticism, but he had been placed in his job to apply the policy of the freeze. He could not do it without the help of the press, and it had to be a convinced press:

What of the plea that a sharp stoppage will cause as much if not more chaos and ruin as inflation itself? Gentlemen, that contention is ridiculous. It is based upon a conception of the price ceiling policy and its administration which assumes an unimaginative, bureaucratic application which will disregard the very difficult adjustments which have to be made. No one who has played any part in the formulating of this policy has ever played down the difficulties. There are a great many of them—even at this stage—which appear insoluble. But the difficulties, when resolutely faced, begin to show themselves as involving for the most part equitable adjustments between groups of businessmen. . . . Here is the biggest opportunity which business has ever had to demonstrate what it can do in self-regulation in the general interest.

That would go out to businessmen in a hundred columns the next day, and there was more for the press itself:

This problem of controlling inflation we are attacking is basically a problem in human relations and where goodwill, cooperation and above all understanding exist, cannot long remain unsolved. That is the tremendous part the press can play in this campaign—the education of Mr. John Public to a realization that he and his family are the soldiers in this battle. . . . I say to you seriously that never has the press of this country—never has a free press anywhere—been called upon to shoulder a heavier responsibility or perform a greater duty.[13]

On Friday, November 28, he was back on the air again, repeating his call to the people. 'Can we do it? Can we make the price ceiling work? I say, *Yes, we can*. Prices must not exceed the prices which prevailed between September 15 and October 11. *Do not pay higher prices*. That is where the women of Canada, who do most of the household buying, are so important. Every woman must be a guardian of the price law. If you find some bootleg dealer who wants you to conspire with him to break the law, you must not only refuse; you must let him know in unmistakeable terms that he is an enemy of his country.'[14]

By December 1—'the day we go into battle'—his voice was almost beyond the relief of cough drops. From administrators in the field the yells were rising in chorus, and the home and regional offices were a turmoil of mobilization. But the general had sounded his war-cry, the troops were being deployed, and some at least of the first auguries were good.

'Day by day,' wrote Frederick Griffin in the Toronto *Star*,

a corps of administrators has been built up. They are the direct supervisors of the various branches of business: manufacturing, merchandizing, wholesale and retail; food, clothing, shoes, jewellery and the like . . . top-ranking businessmen who know all the answers, men versed in the costs, practices, channels and devices of their own particular trades.

These men, most of them executives or technicians of business, were drafted. All the instincts, training, background of most of them were against control. Many saw only failure, grief, chaos ahead. But the country's need, the public good and Gordon's magnetism enlisted them. Now he has won their enthusiasm and devotion . . . his is the Churchill role of overall inspiring, directing and executing. Around this headquarters nucleus has grown gradually but quickly and in brief time the big, varied, widespread, deep-reaching business administration necessary to put the plan into effect. Don't ask anyone how it has been done. But it has been done.[15]

CHAPTER 6

'God bless daddy's ceiling'

By Sunday, December 7, 1941, thirteen regional directorates had been established across the country, from Charlottetown to Vancouver. On that day, the directors arrived in Ottawa. All local businessmen, most of them dragooned for their jobs, they were handed manilla envelopes with thick sheaves of instructions which they were not given time to read. Controls had been in effect for a week, the hard hands of the administrators were clamped on the productive chain and the whole length was a writhing mass of problems. At the same time on the distributive front, in the holding down or rolling back of prices, there were retail problems and consumer problems of infinite variety and detail, each requiring its solution on a strictly local level. But there were not yet local offices; there were only the thirteen men, responsible for whole regions and blankly ignorant of their jobs. They would have to go back and learn them, they would have to establish a web of local offices, and somehow in the meantime they must cope with what came up.

'Your immediate problem,' Gordon told them that Sunday morning, at about the same time that Japanese aircraft carriers were retiring from the smoky ruin of Pearl Harbor, 'is to deal with the local grief which will arise and the questions which will come to the surface. . . . Don't say, Cripes, I don't know! . . . say, the matter is under consideration.'

Beyond that he had few prescriptions or answers. The rolling back, the adjustment and the justifying of prices would be an infinite series of difficulties, but the line was going to be held. The regional directors, like the administrators, would be largely acting on their own, making their own decisions. They would require the patience of Job combined with the wisdom of Solomon, and a sense of humour would help. Business, which had been very sceptical, seemed to be rallying round; and he had great hopes that women, who did nearly 85 per cent of the retail buying in the country, would maintain a watch on prices. He also shared with the directors a crumb of higher comfort, offered by his son, Michael. 'My youngster is a little dubious about the whole thing—he is only four years old—but when he was saying his prayers—God bless this, God bless that—I was really touched to hear him include—"and God bless daddy's ceiling".'[1]

The regional directors left and the head office in the Birks building began to fill with its recruits. They overflowed to other offices, scratching for desks and telephones, crowding each other for elbow room and trying to find their feet. The administrations in the field were squeezing back the costs, the embryo regional directorates were clamping the ceilings down and the country squirmed and blustered in the grip of the new constraints. The ad hoc solutions imposed on commodities and regions created a swarm of problems for the men in head office. Everything required direction they were not prepared to give, but directions had to go out. The daily stream of letters, telegrams, phone calls and urgently protesting visitors was to be dealt with, Gordon decreed, by 'spontaneous ingenuity'. In his own office, besieged by agitated callers, he practised his other arts. There was no use, he informed one noisy meeting, in taking him on in a yelling match, 'because, as you can see, I am equipped to out-yell you all'.[2]

Beneath the yells and the squirming there seemed to be a general flow of public acceptance. The hard, set jaw and the thick-lensed spectacles of the 'Price Czar' glowered from every newspaper, and he remained the delight of reporters. Gordon, said Grattan O'Leary, was enforcing the control of prices as he had of foreign exchange. 'Starting out with the absolute edict that the thing is necessary, that it is a vital war need, he has simply said to business: "There is the ceiling; you work under it." He hasn't said or pretended that he knows more about business than businessmen; he has left it to businessmen themselves to make their own adjustments. In other words, he has tossed them the ball.'[3]

To that grand simplicity there were still some serious objections. 'Price control,' Gordon told a meeting of university economists on January 2, 1942, was 'a screeching creature barely a month old, afflicted with all the weaknesses of infancy and thoroughly disliked by anybody who has anything to do with it. . . . For myself, I refuse to believe that any one child could be so troublesome, and I am convinced that the little brat is really quintuplets multiplied by mirrors stretching into infinity.'

The humour was a little heavy because the audience was a little cold. The authoritarianism of the Prices Board repelled the academics, and the chairman met their comments in a somewhat waspish mood. 'Do not suggest that we strangle the monster . . . it may be that we will replace him with another monster much more dangerous if you suggest that price control be cast into the nethermost pit from which it sprang.'

> There is a very important job to be done, and I cannot for the life of me see why the professors and economists of this country should not regard this as primarily up to themselves: why these men in far-off fields should not go out into the highways and byways and preach the doctrines and try to make the explanations to the people . . . we have to go forward, right or wrong, and what is needed is a forthright person to go forward, after as much consideration as possible, and say, 'This is what we are going to do and how we are going to do it.'[4]

Whatever his effect on the professors the forthright person went on. By March 1942, seventy-five local offices were functioning in the thirteen regions, and more were scrambling for staff and finding quarters. The administrations were set and maintaining the flow of production, and the work of the regional directors was winning the retail trade. The confidence of women had been won and they were already a powerful field force. The Commodity Price Stabilization Corporation and three subsidiary companies, all under the Prices Board, were grappling with the problems of imports, tariffs and subsidies and channelling essential goods. Supplies were short and manufacturing in turmoil as it coped with thousands of adjustments. Nothing was working smoothly and the flow of complaints was endless as semi-autonomous administrators and scattered regional directors imposed rulings in their individual fields. The machine was a massive makeshift but it was somehow grinding on, and it was receiving better direction from an expanding head office.

Many of Gordon's friends, begged, borrowed or stolen as the best men to be found, were now part of the staff. Sim and McGregor had remained when Hector McKinnon left. James Coyne, brilliant, young and difficult, had been brought from Foreign Exchange Control, and so had Max Mackenzie. W. A. Mackintosh was standing in for Finance. Robert Fowler had been lured from his Toronto law office, Douglas Gibson from the Bank of Nova Scotia; and there were able dollar-a-year men, with some equally able women, from business and the civil service. They were all swamped with a mounting mass of problems but they were settling into their jobs. The board had an office in Washington, another office in London and could at least claim to be accepted now at home. It had been called an experiment, said Gordon, in an aside to Mackenzie King, 'but we refused first of all to consider it an experiment . . . we were so deliberately and offensively rude to everybody who used that description that we have not heard the word applied to our effort for some time'.[5] The price ceilings were holding and the graph of the cost of living was almost a flat line. The hand clamped down on the country was still rough but it was firm.

Ilsley, as minister of finance, was the man responsible to Parliament for all the work of the board. Clifford Clark was the indispensable deputy, and by early 1942 there was a new and notable assistant in the person of Mitchell Sharp. A young westerner from Winnipeg, Sharp was close to the grain trade, but he was soon as close to the board. His job, as it took shape, was to act as general liaison man between Ilsley, the tall, sandy-haired, ascetic-looking introvert who was directing financial policy and the booming, burly Gordon who was making the daily news.

It proved to be fairly easy, for in spite of their glaring differences the two men liked each other. The ramifications of price control were endless, Gordon's authority was awesome and as a potential trouble-maker he could have terrified a politician. Yet Ilsley measured his man and took what he saw on trust. In their own way Gordon's political antennae were as sharp as Mackenzie King's. 'If he hadn't started wrong as a banker,' said Grattan O'Leary, 'he would have made a great chieftain for a party.'[6] He was not chief of a party and he was not minister of finance, and he did not mistake his role. There was a clear, fine line between the responsible civil servant and the responsible man in cabinet, and Gordon never crossed it.

For all that, he was well exposed to the public as a part of basic strategy. The Prices Board, in its ultimate possibilities, invaded every field of the country's life. In addition to controlling prices it could restrict civilian supplies, regulate distribution, forbid the manufacture of nonessential goods and even affect the supply and use of manpower. But it could not do any of this, even through an army of enforcers, without public acceptance. The monster born of government would have to be sold by government through the work of a master salesman. Ilsley at first was hesitant, disliking the whole process, but he was brought to see the necessity and there was no doubt as to the man. 'A decision was made very early,' says Mitchell Sharp, 'to personalize the board, and therefore they built up Donald Gordon.'[7]

It was not difficult to do, for the subject responded with zest. He had already travelled the country, making himself known. Boards of Trade, Canadian Clubs and a dozen assorted service clubs had all heard his message. Around him in his own office under the skilful Frank Prendergast, drafted from Imperial Oil, was a public relations section that was well ahead of its time. As the Information Branch, it was actually prepared to supply information; it was forthright, possessed of humour and it generally told the truth. A poll of Ottawa newsmen credited it with frank and complete pronouncements about 85 per cent of the time, an astounding record for any government agency. In response, the cooperation in the building up of the chairman was at times almost lyrical.

Frederick Griffin of the Toronto *Star*, welcomed to the board's offices and invited to attend a meeting, emerged with this assessment:

> Here, in a wide, plain Canadian sense, is a brain pool. Here is a democratic mobilization. . . . Donald Gordon is a big, black-visaged buddha of a man who speaks with a rumbling Scots burr. At a meeting he presides with a kind of hierarchical ease. Where this dark Gordon sits is the head of the table. . . . Perhaps it's the Gael in him, but his power is mystic. As he presides a clan spirit develops . . . a leader but no fuehrer, he dominates but does not dictate . . . this large, dark, brooding man with the range-finder mind sits with his shoulders hunched over the table. . . . In logical, graphic, homely, sometimes salty language he reasons and he clarifies. He listens quietly, does not appear to hurry, though alert intensity shines through the veil of his eyes. . . . He goes through an agenda like a piece-worker on buttonholes. He tosses off decisions like a batter hitting flies . . . the wheels in his head seem to click to a conclusion— 'Right—what's next?'[8]

To anyone around Gordon, he was hardly a brooding buddha, but his capabilities and his magnetism were opening out to the full. He was surrounded by sharp minds, he was getting the best to be had from them and he was making sure that he kept them. 'In the wartime atmosphere they could get just about anybody they wanted,' says Robert Fowler,[9] and the story of his own coming was characteristic enough. Called down to Ottawa for 'maybe three months', he was to be there for four years. As secretary and general counsel of the board, he was close enough to the chairman to be less impressed than newsmen but he was still responsive to the spell. So was Douglas Gibson at the head of the research department, another of the right-hand men. Like all the others he was hugely overworked—'awful hours, just awful—that's where I learned about sixteen-hour days'. Gordon's hours were as long, however, and Gordon's leadership effective. 'He never looked over your shoulder—never criticized the little things—but if the results weren't good you got hell.'[10]

Some of the women in the office were to be as well remembered as the men. Guarding the approach to Gordon, disciplining the staff round him and occasionally disciplining the chairman, was the tall, slender, fortyish Nan Young. She had been his secretary in the Bank of Canada and had come over with him to the Prices Board as one of the indispensables. Completely dedicated to the work and completely devoted to Gordon, she channelled the flow of visitors, distributed the flood of paper and reduced the chaos of his desk. In a place of daily crises and of frantic searches for documents she remained the finder of everything and an enduring rock of order.

One woman on a higher executive level had had more experience than Gordon of the ways and workings of his board. Phyllis Turner, who was later to become Mrs. Frank Mackenzie Ross, wife of the lieutenant-governor of British Columbia, was then a widow in her thirties. She had two children, of whom the elder was John Turner, a future minister of finance. She herself, as an economist who had graduated from the University of British Columbia, studied at Bryn Mawr and taken a degree at the London School of Economics, had joined Hector McKinnon as an early recruit to the Tariff Board. She had gone with him to the Prices Board, experienced the first of the sugar crises in 1939, and embarked in 1940 on the search for cod liver oil.

For several months, hip-booted and oilskinned, the glamorous young widow with the stamp of Bryn Mawr had toured the ports of the Maritimes persuading sceptical fishermen to save the codfish livers they had usually thrown away. With that done, and some processing plants opened, she had gone to the west coast. In those waters were the dogfish with livers high in vitamin content urgently required in Britain, and the first time Gordon met her she was still involved in the quest for them. 'My God, I didn't even know a dogfish had a liver,' was the chairman's only comment, and it was about all he ever learned.[11] Though she and her future husband were to become his lifelong friends, Phyllis Turner, as Oils and Fats administrator, was left to her own devices because she knew what she was about.

Byrne Hope Sanders, the personable editor of *Chatelaine*, had much the same relationship as head of the Consumer Branch. 'There's a big job to be done,' Gordon told her at the beginning, 'go ahead and do it.' Travelling across the country, with her tracks criss-crossing Gordon's, she was soon as familiar as he was to thousands of Canadian women. In each of the regional directorates, banding together the local organizations, she established the Women's Regional Advisory Committees, famous within the Prices Board as Byrne Sander's WRACs. Under them grew up, as the real spine of price control, a widespread army of sixteen thousand women. Each one, prominent in her own locality, was equipped with a little blue book. She was to record prices in the book, report on any discrepancies and generally maintain a watch on local conditions. To complaints about her 'army of snoopers' Sanders had one reply: 'We're just appealing to women's good sense—they're not reporting on *someone*, they're just reporting their own weekly purchases.'[12]

If it was makeshift logic and practice, it was characteristic of the board and it was generally working well. The local snoopers and the retailers seemed to be getting along, and up to June 1942 the official enforcers of the board had conducted only 147 prosecutions. By that time, moreover, another problem was looming that enlarged the function of the WRACs.

Gordon had fought rationing as a hopelessly cumbersome process that could not be made to work. By June, however, he had been forced to change his mind. 'We have reached the conclusion,' he informed Ilsley, 'that we should no longer delay an outright preparation for ration by coupon.'[13] The dreary prospect was the issuance of applications and the mailing out of ration books to millions of the country's households. Worse than that, however, was the fact that the first rationing was planned to apply to sugar.

Byrne Sanders had discussed the move with the WRACs, and foresaw a near-disaster. 'I went up the line telling all the people—it's the big jam-making season—you can't ration in June. But they wouldn't do anything about it—the women would just have to go with less jam or something. One idiot suggested they make jelly without sugar—typical male approach. Finally I got to Jim Coyne, the deputy chairman, and he said—okay, Byrne, I'll try to take it up with Gordon.

'Ten minutes later the door opened and it was Gordon. He stalked in in his shirtsleeves, turned a chair round, flung a leg over it and said—I hear you've got a problem. Well, I told him the problem—he nodded and walked out—and sugar rationing was put off till the next September. That was typical of the man. He listened to women and respected them, and the women always responded.'[14]

It was well they did, for they were as essential a part of the rationing process as they were of price control. Tea and coffee were rationed in August 1942, sugar in September, butter in December, and the applications for the ration books went out through the hands of women. Thousands of volunteers, fifty to each group, knocked at the country's house-doors and set the plan in motion.

As a journalist among economists and industrialists at the meetings in the chairman's office, Byrne Sanders was sometimes swamped in words. So, it seemed, was Gordon, but never for very long. 'He'd sit and listen with those great hands of his like big hams on the table, looking very dour, and an administrator would finish his story and Gordon would lean back and say, "Well now, I'm a little corner retailer, or I'm a housewife in her kitchen and I can't understand a word of that. Put it to me in plain English".'[15]

By the middle of 1942, as U-boats slaughtered the convoys and the war devoured supplies, the strains of a thousand shortages were making themselves felt. Materials had to be allocated to the country's manufacturers, and their lines trimmed of the nonessential products. Manpower had to be conserved, consumer credit restricted, and the waste cut out from delivery and distribution. There were to be no new cars or stoves or refrigerators or electric irons; the double-breasted suit was abolished to save cloth and there were to be no cuffs on trousers. The price problem remained, but there were even greater problems in deciding what could be made, how and where it could be made, and how got to the consumer. From steel and oil and newsprint to dress-goods, shoes and socks, and from the factory door to the storefront the same imperatives prevailed; everything had to be streamlined, everything had to be simplified and stripped to the bare bone. 'Did you know,' asked Byrne Hope Sanders, 'there are seventy-five shades of black? We cut them to five.'[16]

With all this there was more control and direction from the departments of head office. Policy covered the field and invaded the domains of the administrators, who were used to acting on their own. Edicts disrupted industries, and the industrialists roared in protest. As the daily delegations and the reports and complaints came in, more stenographers and secretaries and senior and junior experts dealt with the retail problems and the varied griefs of the consumer. The paper flow was enormous and much of it probably useless, but few form letters went out from the board's office. From Gordon on down, at whatever cost in hours or strain on personnel, correspondence was read, specific answers were given and they were answers to be understood. The country had to be assured that it was dealing with human beings, that the monster had a head and heart.

In Gordon's case the assurance was easily come by. A friendly press was building his image in the country and he remained the builder of legends in all his personal encounters. Under the wide aegis of the price board there was a normal quota of blunders, and the effects of the worst came back on the chairman's office. He is remembered on one occasion, for once with his head down, trapped at the big table in the face of an outraged industry. One of the board's orders, in the eyes of the delegation, was not only a confession of ignorance, it was an affront to common sense. How could Gordon have authorized it—how did he propose to execute it—and what in the name of God had he had in mind? The battering went on for an hour and the chairman took it all, visibly, pathetically shrinking. 'His head went lower, his shoulders pulled in, his chest was practically resting on those great big hands—my God, but he was an actor! Then when they'd finished everything and sat there waiting for an argument, he just looked up and grinned: "Gentlemen, I was wrong." That did it—they went out of there his friends, sympathizing with all his troubles.'[17]

The wild variety of his problems required varied techniques. By November 1942, as life grew spartan in the grip of the new restrictions, fears developed of more. The notion had got abroad, Gordon informed Ilsley, that the board was planning to close some 20,000 retail stores, standardize all production of food, shoes and clothing and distribute through its own outlets like the GUM stores of the Russians. It was totally impracticable totalitarianism, but the rumour spread like wildfire. On a grey morning in the last week of November Max Mackenzie was called to Gordon's office. In the committee room on the next floor below, some hundred and fifty retailers from all across the country were waiting to have it out.

'I'll be delayed for a bit,' Gordon told Mackenzie. 'You go down and chat with them till I come.'

It was an impossible chat for Mackenzie, and he was not the man desired. He could take his lumps from the retailers and absorb a little of the first heat of the blast, but he could not dispel the overshadowing nightmare. The men convinced that they were about to lose their businesses were after the head of Gordon.

After an interminable quarter-hour the man himself walked in, apologizing for the delay. He shambled down the room and turned to his hostile listeners, a bear absorbed in thought. 'Gentlemen,' he began softly in the warm, narrative burr reserved for special occasions, 'I was thinking on the way down of the story of a young lady . . .'

She had been, it developed, a lonely young lady, perhaps a stenographer or a secretary, living in her own apartment where few came to call. On one evening, perhaps because she was lonelier than usual, she divested herself of her clothes, drew a bath and lay long in the warm and scented water. She washed her hair, did her nails, put on her sheerest nightgown and settled into her bed. The clock ticked somnolently away.

The door opened and a young man stepped in, tall, lithe, magnificent. He picked her up in his arms, carried her out of the apartment and down the stairs to the street. A Rolls Royce was waiting, they drove for half an hour under the light of a full moon and came to a little wood—the burr evoked the scented night-time silence and the soft murmuring of the trees. Then the girl was again in the young man's arms. He carried her to a grassy knoll, laid her gently down, bent over her. She looked up at him with wide, luminous eyes as the whisper parted her lips: 'And—now what?'

'Lady, it's your dream.' The chairman glinted at the businessmen, letting his point sink in, and the nightmare broke in a roar of relieved laughter. Mackenzie watched as another crisis blew away with the wind.[18]

There was no such ease for Gordon in his dealings with James Gardiner. The Prices Board and agriculture had been at war from the beginning. All farmers were convinced that prices were too low, and their official voice in the cabinet was the most convinced of all. Wheat stood pegged at a ceiling of ninety cents a bushel, and Gardiner fought continually to raise the price to a dollar. He was as difficult on all the grains and the rationing of farm products, but his fiercest wrestlings with Gordon were around the question of meat.

By September 1942, hours of Gordon's time and reams of his office paper had been devoted to convincing the country that meat rationing must come. Along with that, in the case of beef cattle, there would have to be an embargo against sales to the United States. Shortages loomed in Canada, there was a huge demand from Britain and a steady flow of exports was draining away supplies. American prices were higher than the ceiling prices in Canada and the cattle were going south. Gardiner maintained, moreover, with all the authority of a cabinet minister and in the face of Gordon's statistics, that they must be allowed to go. He capped everything in September with a flat statement to the press. There was no need of rationing, no need of an embargo, and if either came the farmer's course was clear. Since he was clamped under a ceiling that was set by eastern interests, he should hold his beef from the market and wait till the ceiling gave.

On September 19 Gordon exploded to Ilsley in a seventeen-page letter. The board, he wrote, concluding his screed of battle, was placed in an impossible position when it was 'subject to the veto, direct or indirect of the Minister of Agriculture . . . when a member of the government sets out to destroy public confidence and advise one class of citizens to resist the administrative efforts of a board to carry out declared and widely publicized Government policy'. He wondered, he said, what would happen if the minister of labour urged workers to strike for higher wages, or the minister of finance advised them not to buy government bonds till they paid higher interest.[19]

For all the eloquence, however, nothing could move Gardiner. Nor would Mackenzie King move him. The war between board and cabinet minister was potentially a war of votes, which the prime minister dreaded. Carefully

absent himself during a series of confrontations, he was spared the departure
of Gordon from one in Ilsley's office: 'Jimmy Gardiner, you're a stubborn
little son of a bitch!' In the strained silence that followed Ilsley looked at
Gardiner.

'Don't you resent that?'

'Well,' said the prairie minister, 'where I come from, stubborn is a sign of
strength and son of a bitch is more a term of endearment. But I do kind of
resent him calling me little.'[20]

On December 7, 1942, the chairman of the Wartime Prices and Trade Board
was able to come on at one of the commercial breaks in an Imperial Oil
hockey broadcast and inform the country that not only were ceilings holding
but that there would be a reduction in the prices of coffee, tea, oranges and
milk. It had been bought at the price of subsidies and there were more
controls ahead, but even with the western farmers the board could make
some claims. Douglas Gibson and Gordon, in one of their tangles with
Agriculture, had been blasted by a Gardiner aide: 'You guys got one thing
absolutely in common—you're both damn Eastern bankers!'[21] There was a
reply to that, however, and Gordon made it to Ilsley. Farmers had been
generously subsidized on much of their own production. 'Total farm income
is now at an all-time high . . . there is a floor under nearly all farm prices.
The prices of things farmers buy have been strictly controlled . . . both in
his capacity as a producer and in his capacity as a consumer, the farmer's
position in the matter of prices and goods has been substantially improved.'[22]

West and east through the country there were still the unending strains,
the everlasting disputes, the thousands of minor tangles. The worst of them
flowed back, developing as major problems, to the desks in head office. The
clerks, stenographers and secretaries were being worn out with overtime;
and the senior staff with its sixteen-hour days was often following Gordon
in his taste for noisy nights. Liquor was hard to come by in a strictly
rationed country, but there were somehow always means. 'The head of the
Statistics Centre had sixty girls working for him and he organized them all
and paid for their permanents and they'd each get their 13 oz. per month
and bring it back to him and he'd buy it . . . surprising how many of the
girls didn't drink in those days. . . . Nan Young too . . . she had quite a few
people organized to supply the boss.'[23]

There was no more painting of fences at Buena Vista Road. Father was
seldom at home and when he came it was with the big black bag, loaded
with night-time work. Thirteen-year-old Donnie was becoming a lonely boy
and Michael's prayers, if they were said, were usually said to the maid.

Maisie Gordon was as totally absorbed as Donald in the capital's wartime scene. With Molly Towers, the wife of Graham Towers, she had organized three canteens, raised the money to finance them and recruited a staff of Red Cross vounteers. Serving as the local president, and first of the volunteers, she shopped daily, wrote out all the menus and saw to the preparation of 1,800 meals. Up each morning usually ahead of her husband, she was out of the house by six and often away till midnight. Life for both the Gordons was an obsessed, exhausting, semi-competitive routine, only relieved by the parties.

Most of them seemed to be staff parties where anyone came who was handy and talk was always of the board. Yet hardly a national figure, industrial, political or financial, was outside the Gordon circle or a stranger in the Gordon home. Inseparable from every evening was the generous flow of whiskey, the display of Gordon capacity and the Gordon lust for song. 'One of the sights of Ottawa was to see him and Davy Sim, each with his accordion, bellowing out what they called the price board hymn: "It's me, it's me, O Lord, standin' in the need of prayer".'[24]

'I was a very poor but dedicated piano player,' says Robert Fowler, 'and what probably turned into one of the most painful acts in Ottawa was me playing the piano and Donald singing. As the evening wore on he tended to get louder and louder, and my difficulty was that since I played entirely by ear I couldn't hear the piano.'[25]

There was no piano for Gordon at the Five Lakes Fishing Club, but there was David Sim's accordion and a clutch of his favourite friends. The low, rambling clubhouse was set on one of the lakes, twenty-odd miles from Ottawa by an execrable gravel road. Clifford Clark had discovered it in the folds of the Gatineau hills and had mobilized thirty friends, mainly from the civil service. He had persuaded them each to put up a thousand dollars for a communal country place which they could reach by pooled cars, saving on rationed gas. Gordon had persuaded Maisie and the two were often there 'with Maisie harping at Donald', as one of the members recalls, 'that he shouldn't drink so much'. The chairman caught no fish and was not a swimmer, but there was always a memorable party on the evenings Gordon came.

With his widening reputation and his extending responsibilities came the delights of wartime travel. In September 1942 the chairman was invited to Washington with other members of the board. Wyn Plumptre, the able Toronto economist who was the representative there, was encountering a mass of problems as the Canadian and American war efforts melded closer together. So was Leon Henderson, the American price controller, and the

Canadian John Kenneth Galbraith, who was Henderson's right-hand man. There was an urgent need on many fronts for high-level discussions and time, as usual, pressed. Gordon, who hated flying and avoided it whenever he could, found himself with Robert Fowler and others of his delegation in an oddly-appointed plane. On one side of the interior was a row of seats for passengers, while stacked up on the other side was a line of heavy boxes, soon discovered by their markings to contain high explosive.

Hedge-hopping with its overload, the plane lurched down to Washington and the shaken group from Canada finally reached its hotel. There had been money passed, however, in a familiar wartime way, and their reservations were 'lost'. The bland clerk, in return for a consideration, directed them to another inn. Gordon and Fowler found themselves at the end of a harried trip in a sleazy, smelly cubicle with sagging twin beds whose sheets retained the warmth of the last occupants and with bath and toilet the length of the hall away. Amid a blue haze of profanity Gordon settled on one bed and Fowler climbed over him since there was no room to go round. Opening their bags and briefcases, they prepared themselves in that state for what proved to be a useful mission.

For Gordon, during the week that followed, there was a personal interview with the president of which no record remains. Well recalled, however, is one of the convivial banquets that closed a day's proceedings. The expansion of the Canadian war effort had been given generous praise, which required a suitable answer. He was reminded, Gordon said, of the story of a prairie sailor torpedoed in a Canadian corvette. He had been brought to hospital to be examined, and the examiner was a hard-faced matron who found him to be much tattooed. 'Tattoo on chest,' she had proceeded to record on the chart, 'JANET-ELOISE—tattoo on right arm a heart—tattoo on chest a serpent—tattoo on penis (lengthwise) the word SWAN.' A day later, however, there had been administrations at the hands of a pretty nurse, including an alcohol rub. There would have to be a change, she said, bringing the chart to the matron. 'That word SWAN is really SASKATCHEWAN.'[26]

The drink, the partying and the story-telling were all a part of the job, and the man was happy in his work. 'He always had to believe that whatever he was doing at the time was the most important thing to be done,'[27] and it was easy to drive ahead with that conviction. There were complaints now in the formerly docile press of the Price Czar 'who is responsible to nobody and is understood to have consulted with nobody before telling the public— do this or else'.[28] It was not true; he was as loyal as ever to Ilsley and he had Ilsley's total trust. It might be true, as the same journalist complained, that

'War is doing something to government in Ottawa. It is driving a coach and four through our old concepts of the meaning of parliament.'[29] If it was doing that—and it was—Gordon was not responsible and the critics were still few. The general feeling of the country was assessed by another man:

> The fact that he is going after the Canadian people without gloves demonstrates his willingness to make the sacrifices he demands of others. He is willing to run the risk of losing all his popularity, to be looked at even as an ogre, in order to serve the one compelling necessity, to make Canada do enough to win the war.[30]

Besides, it was worth a few knocks, after all, to have the job he had been given, to stand as high as he did. 'I remember one day,' says Mary Jukes, who was an assistant of Byrne Sanders, 'when the prime minister and Ilsley and Howe were all down in Washington for a special meeting. Somebody mentioned it to Gordon as I went by his door. "You know," he said, "that leaves me the top man. *I'm* running the country!"—and he gave that wonderful whoop of delight.'[31]

CHAPTER 7

War Machine

B y the middle of 1943 the Wartime Prices and Trade Board had some 5,300 people distributed across the country in its head office, its regional and local offices and its directorates and administrations. Widespread as it was, it was tightening up at the centre. With more officials at more desks in Ottawa, there was less of spacious freedom for the businessmen in the field. Though the original thirteen offices had been increased to fourteen, local offices had been consolidated and equipped with larger staffs. Of sixty-four administrators, some fifty-odd were grouped in 'Co-ordination' of closely allied trades, while larger basic industries remained separately controlled. The five satellite companies functioned as before, arranging for essential imports, regulating bulk purchases, allotting production subsidies and channelling scarce supplies. Munitions and the tools of war were outside the board's control, but there was hardly a peacetime product and hardly a peacetime habit that it had not restricted or changed.

The huge, sprawling bureaucracy had been somehow pulled together and was taking shape at the top. Supply, pricing and major industrial problems were now assigned by divisions to some of the senior men. As experienced early-comers, they were the men closest to Gordon. James Coyne, still in his early thirties and intent on active service, was one loss to the Air Force. Douglas Dewar remained, however, along with Max Mackenzie, both as deputy chairmen. Fowler, Gibson and some of the senior coordinators were part of the central group. All had separate duties, and rather more than they could handle, but they had assumed a formal status as the board's executive committee. By nine o'clock on most mornings of the week they were gathered around the chairman at the big table in his office and policy was determined there.

It passed down to the regions through Price and Supply representatives, who were the senior authorities in each and acted in the chairman's name. The heads of the local offices were clustered under them, and in direct touch with the public were the local office staffs. As consumer representatives, information officers, investigation and enforcement officers, retail, wholesale and service trade specialists and specialists in household needs, they were the receivers of all complaints, the proposers of local solutions, the explainers, advisers, advocates and trackers-down of offenders. Most of them drawn from the community and in touch with community affairs, they were the eyes, the ears and the fingers through which policy worked.

As an always-toughening policy, it was receiving a harder sell. Around Byrne Hope Sanders in the indispensable Consumer Branch was an able group of some seventy-five women which included Mme. René de la Durantaye, a distinguished journalist and publicist, as second-in-command for Quebec, Mme. Albert Sénécal as director of the French language information service for women, and Kate Aitken of Toronto and Irene Gougeon of Ottawa as widely travelling senior representatives. Under the whole group, which was distributed coast-to-coast, the allied army of sixteen thousand women was steadily widening its field. By mid-March 1943, as textile shortages threatened and clothes rationing was talked of, 'spontaneous ingenuity' had come to be applied again.

Launched in Ottawa under the slogan 'Make Over, Mend and Make Do', a 'Remake Revue' began a tour of the country that was to go on for three years. Forty complete wardrobes of women's and children's clothing, each assembled from makeovers and worn by local models, were displayed in all the cities and many of the larger towns. Similar displays, designed by local women, went into the windows of department stores, were featured at fall fairs and written up in the newspapers wherever they came on view. Prices Board representatives, modelling their own hand-me-downs, addressed groups in the regions, traded patterns and designs and organized 'Remake Centres'. It was the beginning of a long campaign that would ransack the nation's clothes closets, open its old trunks, recover its forgotten zippers, buttons and fastenings and actually help to forestall the rationing of cloth.

Men's discarded suits, ripped apart and turned, mended and reassembled, appeared as suits for the children and skirts or suits for the wives. Old flannel pyjamas became children's underwear or nightclothes. Father's shirt with the frayed cuffs trimmed away became a blouse for the daughter, and mother's worn-out sweater, with the buttonholes changing sides, a cardigan for the son. Holed socks, opened out and mended, were sewn together as warm woollen bathrobes, and colourful assortments of neckties transformed as new kimonos. Nightgowns came from suit linings, new hats from old hats, and tablecloths and window drapes became yards of usable fabrics that were cut to smart designs. By the end of the year thousands of women in hundreds of local centres were remaking the family castoffs, making the children like them, and proudly wearing some of their own productions. In one case a white and shimmering evening dress emerged from the silk of a parachute that had been sent home ripped and muddied from a shooting-down in France. Mending and making over, as a new branch of the war work, was becoming high fashion.

At the same time, and in all fields, the Wartime Prices and Trade Board campaigned for public acceptance. The Consumer Branch and most of the other departments had speakers for every audience and for every variety of occasion. In the national magazines there were hundreds of persuasive stories, hammering the message home. On 'Soldier's Wife', the most popular of English-language soap operas, the household counsellor of the board dealt with consumers' questions, and L'Ami du Consommateur on a similar radio serial performed the same function in Quebec. The *News Weekly* of the Consumer Branch went out to all the regions and their women's organizations, bright, informative and occasionally self-deprecating with neatly acid cartoons. Prices Board films produced by the National Film Board made the round of the schools; and for three years the board's coverage in the newspapers averaged from one million to two million lines a month. The chairman, dominant in everything, dominated much of the space, and rose to the height of eminence in a comic strip cartoon. Facing the demons of inflation, he stood with outthrust fist, delivering the board's injunction: 'We CAN control prices! . . . Eat it Up—Wear it Out—Make it Do!'[1]

Among the daily parade of his visitors there was always the inquiring press; and to Gordon Sinclair, one of the most inquiring, he seemed on top of his job:

> They say that this black Highlander of the clan Gordon has the biggest hands and the biggest job in Ottawa. . . . You go to see him and find neither fuss nor fancy surroundings. No panelled and plushed office holds Boss Gordon. No old masters add colour to his walls. His desk might be the desk of an assistant accountant in a bank, which Gordon once was. He engulfs your hand in a massive yet gentle grip, adjusts his thick spectacles once, avoids the usual polite nothing talk and asks what you want to know.

There was a good deal that Sinclair wanted to know, and the resultant sparring was brisk:

'Today you, in this office, have a finger on every shop, factory, burial
ground or peanut stand in the entire country. You tell us what to do and
what not to do. That's foreign to all we were told by Dominion Day
orators back through the years. Will it go on?'

'I don't know. The Government of after-the-war will decide that, and
in my opinion they'll decide to revise or abolish these restrictions . . . I
don't think this can go on forever.'

'What's been the one big headache?'

'Organization.'

'Does any great crisis lie over the horizon—can you see that far?'

'Maybe yes, maybe no. If we see what looks like a crisis coming we
head it off, or try to.'

'Do you admit you are, or were, licked on the meat situation?'

'No, we don't.'

'What percentage in the cost of living do you think you have saved
the people of Canada?'

'Don't put it that way. I hate talking in percentages. Percentages of
what? They don't get anywhere. It's enough to say that I and the rest of
us here are satisfied that a price ceiling is necessary . . . it's a case of price
control or economic suicide.'

'Now here's a fake economy. Because I can't buy trousers with a
watch pocket, I have to go out and squander my money on a new wrist
watch. Why don't your tailoring experts cut out one of the hip pockets
instead of the watch pocket?'

'There now—you stuck your neck right out. The watch pocket was
abolished, yes—but there were others like you with pocket watches, so
it was restored. You see we are a flexible unit.'

'You cut the cuffs off my trousers—but you're wearing cuffs on your
own.'

'Sure I am—because they're an old pair.'[2]

For all the confidence of the chairman, the board was still a bureaucracy
with its tentacles reaching everywhere and some characteristics of the breed.
Involved lines of authority were subject to frequent tangles, and centraliza-
tion produced its quota of thickets. One notorious order wound its way to an
administrator calling for standardized tombstones. In another case a manufacturer of rubber goods applied for permission to market synthetic washers
at three for ten cents. During an eight-months passage through the labyrinth
of head office the order went from the Heating and Plumbing administrator
to the Hardware administrator, to the Chemicals controller, to Oils and

Fats as a derivative product of soy beans, and finally received its approval from Sundry Items.

There were crossed wires between head office and the administrators, between the administrators themselves and the too-eager enforcers, and between procurement and supply. Allotments were made or rescinded without sufficient notice and with much resultant uproar. The Information Branch complained to the executive committee about unannounced decisions or abrupt changes of policy that left it out on a limb. Letters came in that nobody knew what to do with, and passed from desk to desk:

> I am a farmer raising some cattle, also veal to help supply meat for the market. I have to head my cows with a sire animal, but my own pays no attention to my cows but is nearly always in some part of the field by himself—in other words he is no good as a breeder. . . . I have a near neighbour and I made a liberal offer to him to turn his sire in with my cows . . . however, I wish to say he refused. . . . Can this neighbour prevent me from raising veal for market during wartime?[3]

If there was an answer to that question it remains lost in the files. There was, however, spontaneous and effective action in response to another query:

> I would be pleased and much appreciative if you would direct me where to get a toilet vase or chamber vase, medium size for children. . . . I have a two years old baby and a little Chamber vase is needed two or three times daily and often during the night, and it requires a medium size one. I am told they are not making them any more. These are things you just cannot go without in the country . . . and I wish to be directed where to get same.

The letter came one morning into the hands of the executive committee, and in the afternoon there was a memorandum for Gordon. Roy Geddes, one of the senior administrators, had used his lunch break well:

> Have located and obtained at the Superfluity Shop a brace of vases, J. C. Newman model, McMaster steel, enamelled in pale Bracken blue, unchipped, uncracked, uncomfortable but wind, water and soundproof, interchangeable for day and night duty—fitting seats, sir, for the present small bottom of a future Chairman, Coordinator or Supply Chief, because who knows from what small seats large bottoms have begun? I await your instructions.

He would suggest, replied the chairman, that the articles be forwarded to the complainant 'with request that she now let the matter drop'.[4]

As the board grew the chairman was growing with it and developing in his own way. The booming Scotch burr had a harder ring of authority; he was no longer a deputy-anything but the man in sole charge. He was carrying too much weight and he always drank too much, but he had a great exemplar in that. Winston Churchill's photograph hung on his office wall, the one self-conscious ornament of the baldly functional room. He liked to think of Churchill and of himself as linked with Churchill; his speeches echoed many of the famous phrases. Quite as obsessed a warrior and as sure of his own cause, he had the same impatience with obstacles and frequently as short a temper.

His feud with some of the bureaucrats had begun with his coming to the board and was only a little alleviated by the presence of Fred Stone. The chief of personnel, acquired from the CPR by way of Munitions and Supplies, was a lean and salty railroader with a long career ahead of him in tough and demanding jobs. The Prices Board job, however, was the toughest he would ever know. Arriving amid the expansive chaos of 1941, he found a blackboard list of administrators appointed by order in council but there were no hands to help them. 'The Chiefs had been designated; now we had to beat the bushes for hundreds of Indians.' Normally for the employment of civil servants there was a procedure of application and examinations which took about sixty days. The first memo from the chairman to his chief of personnel made short work of that: 'Staff is to be provided on 24 hours notice. If you are unable to comply, please advise.' Stone read the order and promptly tore it up, but there was no escaping the assorted urgencies of Gordon or the growing clamour from the field. Stolen from other departments or snatched from private companies, clerks, stenographers, bookkeepers, office boys and secretaries were rounded up and hired. Some were dumped by the taxi load or shipped by train or plane to the empty offices of administrators who had neither chairs nor desks. Sometimes, amid a confusion of demands and orders, two lots of staff would arrive for the same job and be instantly redistributed without official sanction. Stone's mode of procedure, though it made its bow to the Civil Service Commission, reversed the normal practice: 'We put somebody into a job and then submitted his application for processing. If it took longer than sixty days we were in trouble.'[5]

Trouble was the name of the game in getting around officialdom, and some of the circumventions went on at a high level. James Stewart, president of the Canadian Bank of Commerce, was Gordon's invaluable administrator in the board's Toronto office. When an order in council drafted him away from that work to head a government tribunal, Gordon took to the telephone, 'yelling so loud,' Stewart told Stone, 'that he hardly needed the phone. But I said—now Donald, calm yourself. I knew you wouldn't like that appointment, so I got out of it. I simply looked up the telephone directory and found several James Stewarts, one of whom I knew to be a man of discretion, tact and good judgment, so I sent him the order in council and he is acting now.'

'Donald Gordon,' says Stone, 'thought highly of this arrangement,'[6] but he was not always so lucky and he lost his share of battles. He could not dictate to some of the stiffer mandarins or change many of their ways. Brushed aside as the board was knocked together, they gradually began to reassert their grip. Staff appointments were delayed, salary cheques withheld and promised promotions blocked. The travel expenses of mobile high executives were one of the running sores, overtime was questioned and supper money for juniors produced a three-months' quarrel. The free hand of the chairman was being locked in paper handcuffs, and at least to one protagonist his response was loud and clear:

I am sufficiently aware of your methods of opposing anything which does not meet with your personal agreement, and recognize very familiar tactics. Unfortunately, I have neither the available time nor, I must confess, the patience to engage with you in a battle to see which one wears down first. . . . I consider it necessary, among other things, to provide for payment of supper money, amounting to 75 cents, to members of the staff required to work not less than three hours overtime . . . accordingly in my personal responsibility as Chairman of this Board I am today authorizing the comptroller of the Board to issue necessary instructions.[7]

Through the whole of 1943, as staff overflowed the Birks building and scrambled for other quarters, Gordon was engaged in a battle to provide the board with a home. He had suggested a site on Wellington Street and agreed to an alternative on Sussex Street, only to have both rejected. By February the Department of Public Works, after due and lengthy study, had decided on the renovation of an older building. To that the chairman reacted in a familiar Gordon way. 'Our position is clear. We either have the Sussex Street site or revert to the more expensive one on Wellington.' By March 4 he was noting on the copy of his letter, 'Advised Sussex approved', but he was still far from a home. In July he was informing Ilsley that the 'anxiously awaited' building which was to have been ready by June 1 would not be completed till October. By the last week of November, with 'my patience about exhausted', he had heard that the new building was to be given to the Department of Labour. That rumour died, preventing a further explosion, but it was late in the next January before the doors could finally be opened and the staff of the board assembled in the long, barn-like structure with its echoing bare floors. There were to be no rugs in any office of the Prices Board, and the one amenity for the chairman was a catwalk into his office by a door from the side street. It allowed him to reach his desk and the morning's quota of trouble without first running the gauntlet of those who were bringing more.[8]

The daily parade stretched the routine of his days, often into hard nights. 'He'd go down to the Chateau,' Douglas Gibson recalls, 'to meet some guys that had come in with a special problem, and they'd produce a bottle and go on into the small hours. But there was one thing about Donald—if you were at a party with him the night before and were five minutes late in the morning he'd cut you down. And there were no jokes about anything that had gone on. He'd look at you as though you were a damn fool—you're working now—that stuff's gone.

'How he stood it I don't know—he never took care of himself, never took any exercise, but he had such enormous vitality. And there were so many sides to him—he'd get upset sometimes, and you'd suddenly realize he was upset. Sometimes it seemed the orders started him off—all those orders we were signing and sending out. "You know, people are just damn fools to get into this thing and push other people around. They don't know what's happening to them. Making decisions—affecting all kinds of people's lives— how do we know what they want?" He'd get quite humble at times—I don't know—I think he worried about a lot of things.'[9]

'I got word one day,' says Byrne Hope Sanders, 'that a little woman on my staff had been going into a tavern and trading her ration stamps for beer. So of course I got on my high horse, very indignant, and called her in—told her I was extremely sorry but I couldn't have a member of the Consumer Branch trading ration stamps in beer parlours and she'd have to go.

'She went out, weeping, and two or three days later I got a call from Gordon. He was very gentle—he always was very gentle when he wasn't mad. The little woman had somehow got past Nan Young and in to see him. She'd had some reasons for what she was doing, I guess, and I hadn't asked her about them, but he had. "I just wanted to tell you," he said, "that you were right in letting her go from your department, but I'm going to find a job for her with somebody else".'[10]

The Price Czar and his authority were well respected in Canada and admired in the United States. Leon Henderson was openly and sincerely envious of the success of Canadian controls. Early in 1943, when Gordon spoke in Chicago, he had an audience of the same mind. 'It gives many of us in the United States a certain feeling of security,' recorded the Chicago Better Business Bureau, 'that over the border, not very far away, is one whose leadership in a vital economic realm is not only pleasant to listen to when described orally, but in the crucible of experience found effective.'[11]

He himself was informing Ilsley by August that 'I consider our organization today as more or less established'. He had to add, however, that 'any glamour which may have surrounded our early organization has worn off, and our work has settled down into established routines and procedures'.[12] The honeymoon with the public was not exactly over, but it was settling into a marriage.

With the retail, wholesale and distributing trades and with most of the country's industry the board generally had close and good relations. Thousands of small retailers not only accepted but almost welcomed controls, as reducing competition. The large chains, though they submitted their weekly price lists and were always well watched, had freedom enough to merchandise and adjust prices seasonally at the general level of the ceiling. Industry and manufacturing, for all the variety of problems and all the wailing about losses, were contributing to the board's direction through many of their own leaders. It was businessmen and industrialists who headed the administrations, fought, argued and compromised and shared rigours with their peers. Controls, standardization and the vast variety of adjustments were being worked out in concert at the hands of knowledgeable men.

With Jimmy Gardiner and agriculture there had never been that harmony. Cattle prices and grain prices sustained a long debate that enlivened prairie politics and exploded in King's office. Gardiner sniped at meat rationing which had to be imposed in May, and fought as stubbornly and insistently to break the ceiling on wheat. Paul Martin, as a parliamentary assistant and an observer of the prime minister, recalls one of the occasions when King was pleading for peace. 'Well, Mr. King,' Gordon summarized the discussion, 'there's no sense trying to keep the peace as long as your minister takes the position he does. I'm here to control prices—that's why you put me here. If you want me out—fine!'[13]

In the fall the closing of the Grain Exchange removed a bone of contention, but there were others near at hand. Labour had accepted controls and the stabilization of wages, but it had never been a whole-hearted associate in Gordon's war on inflation. He could not fully convince the leaders of the major unions, for he did not share their views. The banker worked with businessmen in an obsessed concern for controls, for the maintenance of the cost of living in relation to real wages, essentially for the status quo. The essential drive for labour was to change the status quo, and it had been suspended only in the interest of total war. The workingman was tired, sick to death of controls, and he was sure now that the war was going to be won. Officially he was better off—statistics could prove that; but they did not prove that he was sharing equally with business or would in the postwar world. He was part of a common effort and had been promised much for the future, but he wanted some of it now.

As that wave washed the country, stirring up other ripples, Gordon took to the rostrum with a long and formidable speech. The war front, he told a convention of the Canadian Weekly Newspapers Association in Toronto in August 1943, was beginning to look promising, but it was not so on the home front. Wartime controls were losing public support, and the pressures of inflation were growing. 'If the dam breaks, then God help us, because the flood waters will spread far and wide and bring endless suffering, misery and bitterness.'

He seemed to see nothing anywhere but new auguries of trouble: 'thousands of wage increases being demanded . . . labour is militant and demanding wage adjustments all along the line . . . food prices are creeping steadily upward as the agricultural industry insists upon and obtains higher prices . . . business and industry keep their eyes on profit margins and jealously protest any move to limit or control them . . . black markets are commencing to develop'. He was speaking at least partly for the benefit of King's cabinet which he felt was weakening behind him; and he was not inclined in the heat of that sultry evening to spare anyone else:

There is too much emphasis placed on the burdens, dislocations and so-called sacrifices of war. The plain fact is that the great majority of Canadians living comfortably at home are better off right now than they ever were before the war. Is it reasonable to expect Utopia while fighting a war, and particularly a war that is referred to as total war? . . .

What will the wage-earner gain if his wages double but the purchase price of his food, his clothing, his rent—everything—trebles or quadruples? . . .

If only one simple thought could be thoroughly grasped by the country I believe much of the struggle would be over. It is this—of what use is it to labour, to agriculture, to the shopkeeper or any person to obtain more money if the purchasing power of money melts faster than the original amount received?[14]

The editors of the Canadian weeklies went home with their heads ringing, and in the daily press of the country there was much concerned support. But it was not as general as usual, and there was a threatening counter-wave. 'Mr. Gordon,' said the Peterborough *Examiner*, 'spoke in his usual somewhat angry tone and we think he alienated the sympathy and respect which he should command by so doing. His statement that the majority of Canadians were better off than they ever were before the war may be statistically true, but it merely rasps the feelings of thousands of white-collar workers who are decidedly worse off.'[15] By September 1943 a convention of the Trades and Labour Congress had heard Gordon labelled 'the Number One Nazi in this country';[16] Col. Tom Kennedy, the Ontario minister of agriculture, had given him equal rank as the enemy of the country's farmers; and the *Country Guide* was exulting over 'tremendous pressure on the price ceilings'. Still more dangerous and authoritative was the view of the *Financial Post*. Under the heading 'Cabinet to Ditch the Ceilings?' it reported that 'The sand in the hour-glass of Canada's price ceiling policy is running very low' and speculated on the possibility of 'the retirement from the Wartime Prices and Trade Board of Donald Gordon and a dozen or more of his associates'.[17]

There was no such thought in Ilsley's mind and he was as firm as ever in his public stand for Gordon. 'We went to him in 1941,' he told the Commons, 'and requested him, almost pleaded with him, to take on the most difficult of all jobs, the most thankless of all jobs, one of the most, if not the most important of all jobs, the administration and enforcement of the price ceiling policy.'[18] Gordon was going to stay, so far as Ilsley was concerned, and the policy was still successful. The rise in the cost of living which had sparked the summer's uproar had been held to 1 per cent, and it was flattening out by the year-end with other signs of relief. 'In the supply picture,' the board was able to report, 'the beginning of the end of shortages is starting to emerge, though still somewhat dimly.'[19] There was a little canned salmon that had long been off the market, a little more tea and coffee and a reduction in the price of milk. But the interminable work went on amid a running fire of criticism, and in the mood of a bleak December the chairman had had enough.

'For some time,' he wrote to Ilsley on December 10, 'I have had in mind raising with you the question of my returning to my regular duties as Deputy Governor of the Bank of Canada. . . . I have been hoping that there might develop an appropriate point at which I could expect to be relieved. I believe that the present time is as appropriate as it is likely to be in the future.'[20]

The time had not come; there was never a chance that Ilsley would agree to release him and he was hardly serious himself. For all the pricks of the barbs he was a towering public figure, supported throughout the country by a generally admiring press. He was talked of for the cabinet, even mentioned occasionally as a potential prime minister, and he was one of the inner circle directing the country's war. Mr. and Mrs. Gordon had dined with Mackenzie King and the exiled Queen of the Netherlands. On December 27 he was notified that he had been awarded a companionship in the Order of St. Michael and St. George; he was to be Mr. Donald Gordon, CMG. He had come far from the first beginnings at Old Meldrum and he was in the middle of his biggest job. He could not let go of the machine, nor would the machine let him go.

The price of it all was high, and rather more for the family. Maisie continued her war work at a pace as frantic as his own, and with all her husband's energy she had much less of his strength. She complained of his continual drinking but she was with him at most of the parties and she was beginning to follow suit. There were other evenings at home that would be part of some painful memories for thirteen-year-old Donnie. 'Just the year before I left I became aware that he drank a lot—when father drank things got a little tense and I can remember disappearing as quickly as I could . . . in convivial circumstances with contemporaries he was enchanting—I think he was the kind of person I would want to drink with—there would always be good stories, but he never stopped and sometimes he was put to bed and it was pretty messy.'[21]

The boy adored his mother, yearned for closeness with his father and saw too little of each. 'She was off before eight in the morning and back about six, father would get home around seven and that's when I saw them, basically. . . . They were hard-driving, dynamic and in an odd way, I think, both haughty individuals who competed with each other hammer and tongs —at one moment you would see them arguing and almost physically fighting each other . . . and when you turned round they were all sweetness and light. It was absolutely baffling—devastating . . . when they were having sort of flat-out conversations she would maintain that what she was doing was as important as what he was doing, and she had to believe that.'[22]

The great days for the boy, and occasionally even for Michael, were when Maisie took them along to share her work. On the expeditions of the six-year-old he usually sat on counters or played with clerks in warehouses while his mother bought supplies. Donnie, as the senior brother, was given a larger part. 'I remember days of her on the phone getting orders, and I worked for her as busboy, dishwasher and so on, and everybody there knew her . . . she devised all the menus, checked over the steam tables, told people what to fix and not fix—the whole works. She was like father in that—a driver, an inspirer—she could give people this enormous desire to please.'[23]

The Gordon home was ruled by a paternal Scot, often short-tempered and with a brusque view of discipline. 'Most of his spankings were reasonable and fair,' his son Donald recalls, 'but one Sunday morning I went into his study and there was a pen or pencil missing. He asked me what I'd done with it and when I said I'd never had it he spanked me with his razor strap, which he didn't use very often. It was unjust and I was furious and I lost my temper and abused him, so he spanked me again for impertinence. You know, I can feel it to this day . . . if there ever is a heaven I'm going to face him with it because, god-damn it, that's the kind of thing you never forgive.'[24]

For Michael discipline was lighter and the main sources of authority were Olga and Harold House, the one the housekeeper-cook and the other Gordon's driver. For all her outside efforts, Maisie herself took over the weekend cooking and there was not much time for the boy. 'During the war I saw very little of father and very little of mother. . . . I would be sent over to play at Government House—Queen Juliana and Princess Beatrix were living there with the family and other foreign children—at the time I didn't think it was such a big deal.'[25]

Sometimes, like Donnie before him on the evenings when there were important visitors, Michael perched in his pyjamas listening to discussions below. 'I can remember when the decision was made to ration meat. I used to love hearing shop talk and I would sit at the head of the circular staircase listening.' He had less enthusiasm for the Victory Garden which became a family project, reinforced by an order:

> Everyone was supposed to have one and father and I were to be an example, and the result of that on my small life was that I had to drag my little red wagon round the street following the bread and milk wagon horses and pick up the manure for the garden. In Rockcliffe, back and forth from school, there used to be fights between the English and French kids—not very pleasant. I remember getting cornered and no help around, but I had my wagonload of horseballs and put the enemy to flight—the first clearcut victory for the Anglophones over the Francophones in Rockcliffe. This was the only good to come out of the bloody Victory Garden as far as I was concerned.[26]

In the course of that hot summer of 1943 there was one relief for Gordon, important enough to be mentioned to his son and heir. 'I paid today the last of what I owed from the 1929 crash.'[27] It was a rare confidence and it was remembered, because in Donnie's case there were not to be many more. As the strains grew on his parents and the early August heat was searing the streets of Ottawa, word came that the family was to have a break. For his own sake and Maisie's the chairman was taking them away, as far away as possible. He would be at Frye's Island in the Bay of Fundy, he informed Ilsley: 'no telephone—can be reached by telegram through Black's Harbour, New Brunswick. . . . Miss Young, my secretary, will be able to get me back on short notice.'[28]

The jubilant boys were embarked on the Ocean Limited, given their supper in the dining car and Michael was put to bed. Donnie, however, stayed on in the compartment, by arrangement, he soon sensed, for his parents had made a decision. Little by little, as they talked to him, the holiday glow faded and his small world fell apart. 'Up until then my parents had been able to operate a household for myself and my brother—well, they acted as parents. I was just going into Grade Nine at Collegiate and I was one of a group of twenty or so kids and was enjoying everything, but they said to me—look, we can't handle it—you're going away to school. I particularly didn't want to go to boarding school, but they argued with me till two or three in the morning and that was it. I went to Lakefield and did the standard Tom Brown sort of thing, crossing off hours till the next time I'd get home. It was never the same after that. I was pretty well funded till the time I was twenty or so, but I've always thought that I was basically on my own at the age of thirteen.'[29]

CHAPTER 8

'Foggy shores of peace'

In January 1944, though Gordon did not know it, he was the subject of an irritable note in the diary of Field-Marshal Viscount Wavell. In Delhi as commander-in-chief of the British forces in India, Wavell was reorganizing his Defence Council and having disputes with London:

> War Cabinet have proposed an unknown young and apparently, from the description given by the Secretary of State, tactless and ambitious Canadian as Finance Member. . . . Cabinet's lack of imagination in dealing with India is sometimes astonishing. They turned down my recommendation for an Indian on plea that they must appoint man of 'acknowledged and outstanding qualifications'. Person now proposed is certainly not this. Surely you cannot suppose that selection of young and almost unknown Canadian whose name does not appear in any book of reference and who has no experience of India will be easy to defend.[1]

No defence was necessary, since London deferred to Wavell and Gordon remained at home. The ambitious, tactless Canadian who did not figure in any of the general's reference books had quite enough on his domestic plate to inhibit foreign adventures. With C. D. Howe in the ministry of Munitions and Supplies he was dividing the resources of the country in support of total war. The civilian sectors of all business and industry responded to his direction. He was setting the nation's living standards and making the people like them. At forty-two he was no longer quite so young as Wavell seemed to believe, and as a substantial public figure he was acquiring a private girth. In April, when he was called to Government House to receive his CMG, there was distressing evidence of that. 'On this Saturday afternoon,' he reported to Douglas Dewar, 'the Governor-General will engage his bauble around my neck. It is a sad commentary on the performance that I have had to take the "troosers" to the tailor and have him fill in a gap of seven inches.'[2]

He was writing to the deputy chairman because Dewar's health had failed him and he had gone home to Penticton. They talked of rest and a return but Gordon scarcely believed it; he was privately convinced he had lost the invaluable Scot. It was another of many worries following him across the country and trailing him up the catwalk to the problems piled on his desk. Most of them he could shrug off, douse in a wet night and face fresh in the morning with all his old élan. But the greatest of the private problems, for the man who was never sick, was one he could not cope with.

Maisie had not been with him when he went to receive his bauble; she had been lying in a Toronto hospital. A series of fierce migraines, continuing for several months, had put an end to her war work and brought her close to a breakdown. Diagnosed as sinus trouble, they had led to an operation and a cruelly prolonged treatment in which nasal bones had been crushed. She had fought the weeks of agony as she had fought the earlier headaches with drugs, denial and rebellion and with no concession to pain. She had not won when she came home; she was never again to be a wholly well woman, but neither she nor Gordon would admit that life had changed. Pain would haunt Maisie, idleness would be even worse, and she would turn to liquor and Nembutol to find a release from both. Gordon forever after would damn the work of the doctors and rebel as fiercely as she did against the effects of pain. But he could not transmute his sympathy into understanding of his wife; his own angers in his black and liquorous moments were inclined to turn on her. The quarrels became more shrill, the reconciliations more strained and tense and temporary, and home too often a place where the boys went round on tiptoe.

Donnie came home for holidays, a subdued and wistful stranger, somehow subtly a reproach. There had been something wrong in his going, something badly done; the father was aware of that. He resented the sense of failure and could not be blind to its cost. Always generous with money, there was an old, invaluable nearness, the sense of a sure relationship, he was unable to buy back. Nothing yet, however, had been able to subdue Michael, and in the developing young hellion there was relief from other thoughts.

An uninvited Michael had been fished out naked, at the height of a summer garden party, from the swimming pool on the grounds of the French embassy. As a great admirer of Donnie he had extended his admiration to Donnie's first girl friend, and in all innocence had presented her with a bouquet of goldenrod, inducing hay fever. Like every little brother he had acquired some curious lore. 'I'm not sure if it was Donnie or some-body else, but whoever it was told me that the foam on the Ottawa River came from people urinating in it. I remained firmly convinced of that till I went down to the Maritimes in 1954.'[3]

On one day at the Prices Board when the chairman sat at his desk, guarded by double doors, with Nan Young outside them, and beyond her by an RCMP constable, a grubby trio of 'Daredevils' led by his youngest son stalked in to confront him. He was about to be held up, Michael crisply informed him, and produced the tools for the job. 'Father played along with the joke and was very good about it, so we tied him up to the chair, put a gag on him and then went out and forgot him. I suppose they couldn't hear him outside on account of the double doors and nobody came to disturb him . . . how long he remained like that I don't know, but he wasn't too damn pleased.'[4]

If he was depressed by the loss of Dewar, there was some relief for the chairman in the arrival of a new aide. Malcolm Wallace McCutcheon had been a school teacher, an insurance salesman and a lawyer, and was by then chairman of the board of the National Life Assurance Company. With James Stewart, president of the Canadian Bank of Commerce, he had been one of the pillars of the Prices Board in Toronto. As hard-drinking and convivial as Gordon, he was also as hard-headed, with the same affinity for work. 'I wonder,' Gordon wrote, tactfully hinting at replacement to the absent deputy chairman, 'if it would not be wise to move McCutcheon down as soon as possible.'[5] By early summer Fowler had gone to Toronto to apply necessary persuasion, and in August McCutcheon came.

'The first time I met him,' Donnie records hauntingly, 'was the day after he had driven a car through the gates of the Mint with my father on their way home from the Chateau.'[6] Yet the man who was to succeed Dewar was more than a boon companion. In the long, hard days that preceded the chairman's nights, and even more in his blackest hours with Maisie, he would find McCutcheon at hand.

Through the summer of 1944, as the Normandy landings came and the allied armies moved in from the beachheads, the war demands on the home front were entering a new phase. Control, discipline and sacrifice were all to result in victory; that much seemed sure. But beyond victory, what? At the heart of a thousand questions was the fear of unemployment and the thought of the great depression that had followed the earlier war. Both had threatened government and the base of the established order, and the threat would come again. If it were to be staved off this time, the thrust of postwar planning must be directed to one end: security and a better livelihood for the family of the average man.

That thought in Britain had produced the Beveridge Report. It was followed a year later, in 1943, by the Marsh *Report on Social Security in Canada*. The latter work was engaging the thoughts of the government, of the National War Finance Committee which was chaired by Ilsley himself, of officials of the Bank of Canada and the civil service and of Gordon, Gibson and Mackintosh. The group had begun to form before the war and it had been pulled together and added to by many of the later stresses. It was, according to one admirer in *Fortune* magazine, a sizeable collection of brains:

> Canadian officials are less tradition-bound than their colleagues in Whitehall . . . they are not so deep in the mêlée of everyday politics as their colleagues in Washington. They know the U.S. and the United Kingdom better than the best American and British civil servants know any country except their own. Some were educated at California and Harvard, at Oxford or the London School of Economics. All are compelled —as men of affairs in a large country are not—to know and understand their neighbours. Ottawa is small; Canadian leaders meet often and easily to exchange ideas, achieving a coordination of policy that, to an American, seems little short of wonderful.[7]

Some effects of that smallness were less appealing to Gordon. For all his own fiats, the supper vouchers for overtime were still routed around him to the desk of the minister of finance. His relations with Jimmy Gardiner were a running ripple of friction and those disputes continued. He still ranted at a Treasury Board which had changed none of its ways: 'Why do matters have to be made so difficult . . . why is it necessary to place so many hurdles in the way of an administration which is striving to discharge an almost impossible task?'[8] Yet it was still good to be one of a close-knit group and to be near the levers of power in maturing large plans. For large plans they would have to be, and in one way or another they affected the Prices Board.

By August 1944, as a first nibbling at the Marsh Report, Parliament had approved the system of family allowances; the Baby Bonus was a Canadian institution. To the warm-hearted it was a help for struggling parents, and to the cold-blooded it was a shoring-up of purchasing power against a time of later need. To Graham Towers it was 'not only socially desirable but also a very useful piece of insurance—partial insurance—against the dangers with which we are likely to be confronted'. Yet 'partial' was the operative word; there was a great deal more to be done, and Towers, writing to Gordon, took a long look ahead.

After the war, with the return of people from the forces, there would probably be some 4,700,000 Canadians wanting work, about 50 per cent more than those presently employed. That prospect should be the background for all planning. 'Policies should be tested to see whether they are sufficiently bold, not whether they are sufficiently conservative.' Exports, foreign loans and trade treaties, tax structures, interest rates and huge investments for housing occupied the banker's mind. He approved the plans for veterans as liberal, wise and necessary. Yet the base for all plans was a redivision of income and a better social order. Old age pensions, a continuing national disgrace, would certainly have to be improved. Health insurance was coming, though it was delayed by wrangling provinces, and even 'regional disparity' was becoming a live issue. The discrepancies in living standards between the rich and poor provinces had been a theme of the Rowell-Sirois Report and were again a theme with Towers: 'It is, I think, very difficult to maintain the thesis that very material and serious variations will be tolerated indefinitely.' There was great change in the making and business would have to conform. 'Passive resistance or lack of interest is likely to result in business getting the worst of both worlds.' To all plans, moreover, there was one formidable proviso:

> If, in addition to other things which must be done, we had to search for
> a completely new level of wages, costs, prices, interest rates and so forth,
> our troubles—and by the same token, our internal quarrels—would be
> multiplied. As it is, we have prospects of emerging from the war in
> better order, from this point of view, than any country I can think of....
> I hope it is becoming more and more clear to the public, and certainly
> to those who have participated in the anti-inflationary work, that the
> benefits are worth all the toil and effort which have been put into this job.[9]

To Gordon the words of the favourite mentor were the sum of all his challenges. He believed in the established order and he was working for the average man; it was a combination of convictions that had made him what he was, and put him where he was. The war effort was one thing and he had been one of the great organizers; he could fairly claim that. There was a new and added stimulus in the thought of building for peace.

Yet the average man at home, and the average woman too, were changing as the war moved on. They might be faced with the prospect of unemployment, but that was years ahead. For the moment there were plentiful jobs, a controlled cost of living and more money in the savings banks than there had ever been before. There were worn-out cars and stoves, refrigerators and electric toasters, clothes, shoes, underwear, the hundreds of indispensables and other hundreds of frills, all requiring replacement. Peace seemed to be near, nearer than it really was, and the housewife and her husband were impatient for some of the fruits. With some $6.5 billion of new purchasing power dammed back by controls, a huge wave of demand was building up. If it were allowed to break now, or even to break soon, there would be no resources to cope with it in the way of labour or supplies. Inflation would sweep the country, wreck the base of a readjusting economy and threaten the postwar plans. The average man and woman had endured control in war and accepted the word of their leaders, the Price Czar among them, that it would lead to better things. They would have to be shown, in spite of the nearing victory, that there was still a while to wait.

Through the autumn of 1944 the supply picture was a dizzying series of changes. As the U-boats went to the bottom or headed in for their harbours, the sea lanes were reopened and more goods came in. Metals, materials and food products not required for the war began to arrive in quantity under relaxed controls. Yet the basic needs were the materials that the war was still consuming, and there was no end to the destruction. The first slackening of war orders closed some of the munitions plants and reconversion began. But it was only reconversion and not yet production. There was more tea and coffee but less butter and sugar; the liberated countries of Europe were creating a new demand. They would soon be demanding meat and other foods and essentials; the dribs and drabs of abundance were only a fiction yet.

Businessmen and industry squirmed in the grip of controls, eager to get back to 'normal'. But normalcy was another fiction and it was soon clear that there was to be no early peace. Shell factories reopened as reverses occurred in France, rationing came and went with the shift of war requirements, and there was no return of armies. Instead, in the late fall, horrified by savage battles and the mounting casualty lists, the tired, divided country was face to face with conscription.

Gordon, unlike Ilsley, did not support conscription. For all his Scots blood and all his Churchillian ways, he believed it had come too late and could not be made to work. When King's half-measures led to the departure of Ralston he did not have much regret. 'I am inclined to the opinion,' he confided to Douglas Dewar as the crisis peaked in November, 'that the solution found was the best in all circumstances at this stage of the war.' In any case there was not much he could do. While the storm raged in the House he sat apart from it in the Wartime Prices and Trade Board, holding the ceilings down. 'At the moment of writing the fog over Parliament Hill is thicker than ever. God knows what is going to come out of it, and in the meantime the Bureaucrats have to carry on under their own steam.'[10]

The carrying-on was always a little more difficult and a little more complex. 'I believe,' he had said in October, 'the hardest part of the struggle lies before us, both because wartime pressures are still very heavy and because of a premature and quite false assumption fostered by favourable war news that our problems are over and done with.'[11] They were not over and they would not end with the war; there was a long way to go in the face of a changing mood. For the most part, however, he seemed to have convinced the country that he was still sure of his directions. A journalist in *Saturday Night*, writing of the 'horizon-hunting heart of the master mariner', put it in nautical terms: 'Donald Gordon never had a thought of turning back. We're headed for a berth in a better post-war harbour. . . . What it all means for you and me as passengers on the good ship CANADA is that we are in Donald Gordon's hands again as we head in for the foggy shores of peace.'[12]

There was that much reassurance, considerably overblown. On the bridge of the ship, however, it was getting a little lonelier than it had been on the voyage out. As peace and reconversion threatened a thousand changes, businessmen at the Prices Board were thinking of their neglected companies. Max Mackenzie, who had arrived five years earlier without a change of shirts or a toothbrush, was back in Montreal. He had had to be allowed to leave to rescue a depleted partnership, drained of men by the war. Careers were calling others and so was the civil service as new imperatives arose. Gordon's November letter, as it went to Douglas Dewar, continued a tale of losses and resignations: 'We gave George Britnell a sendoff yesterday . . . Edgar Burton tells me that he will have to leave us at the end of the year . . . Langford came in to resign the other day . . . Croft of Services Administration also wants to get away . . . I have had to agree to let Kemp go . . . the Bank of Nova Scotia are pressing me for Doug Gibson . . . I heard that Howard Foreman is likely to be the next applicant for release . . . and so it goes.'[13]

On January 1, 1945, the chairman climbed up to the roof of his house on Buena Vista Road to cure a New Year's hangover by shovelling away some snow. It was probably a good vantage point from which to survey his problems. Weight was certainly one, drink was said to be allied to it; but resolutions in that regard were not likely to be kept. Gordon's efforts at reform remained brief and spasmodic. 'I'm on the wagon this week—I'm only drinking gin.' Urged by a concerned doctor to lose twenty-five pounds, he emerged depressed from the interview but soon recovered his cheer. 'He said I could have a drink if each time I had one I gave up a potato . . . yesterday I gave up twenty potatoes.'[14]

At home life was tense, but there were often easier periods when Maisie seemed to be well. 'There is no question in my mind,' Michael records of the time, 'that there was a very great love affair between my mother and my father, because I saw between them moments of great tenderness and devotion.'[15] Though Maisie could not work there was a great deal of going out, and if some occasions were disastrous there were better times at home. One evening of bridge, passed in the company of the Clutterbucks, was admiringly witnessed by Donnie.

Sir Alexander Clutterbuck, the British high commissioner, was a warm enthusiast of the game. His wife's bridge, on the other hand, left a great deal to be desired. So, as usual, did Maisie's, but the formidable chairman of the Prices Board, whose poker and bridge were excellent, maintained a forgiving calm. 'No complaints, no scoldings, nothing but kindness and encouragement. Sir Alexander, of course, was suffering it like a British diplomat, but I thought sure there'd be an explosion from father.' When the explosion came, however, it was at the end of the long evening and not from the expected source. 'Do be careful, my dear,' Clutterbuck said to his lady as she came down the Gordon stairway trailing a long coat, 'or you'll break your god-damned neck.'[16]

The Gordons could laugh at that, and there was still much else that they shared; were both determined to share. As hungry for life as ever, neither would relax the pace, nor concede that it should be relaxed. They remained inseparable and competitive in the working out of problems. 'Even in her worst times he would talk to her about things he was wrestling with and she would give him good, tough advice.'[17] Yet it was advice, all too often, that came from a sick woman, an incoherent woman, at the end of a dragged-out party or in the midst of a flaring quarrel. For all the appearance of recovery Maisie lived with pain, and liquor followed by Nembutol remained a dangerous crutch.

It was the largest problem for Gordon, facing the new year, and he could not find or would not accept a solution. 'Father had a great deal of sympathy for any creature that was hurt, any kind of sickness, and he wanted to help mother very much but he didn't know how and he reacted with anger in not knowing how, anger partially at himself, partially directed at her and a great deal at the medical profession. . . . I suppose if she had been walking round with a broken leg or a broken back he could have handled the thing better, but he couldn't handle that.'[18]

For the Prices Board the most imminent and worrisome questions were of supply, labour and production and the pace of decontrol. The year ahead would see the end of the war, probably the return of armies and the tumult of reconstruction. It was going to be a year of money, superabundant money, with millions in war gratuities and reestablishment credits added to civilian savings. There would not be unemployment; there would be a continuing shortage of labour, with factories clamouring to reopen and produce civilian goods. Housing demands would be enormous, so would the demand for every household article, for foods, textiles, long-curtailed services, the equipping of new businesses and the supply of new machines. All of it was quite legitimate and there would be increased resources to meet it, but other demands came first. There would have to be a sharing of food, and of all essential supplies, with a starved and devastated Europe.

That was elementary and more than humanitarian; with the world-wide fear of communism it was a fact of political life. What it meant for Canada and the Prices Board was another year of controls, perhaps longer than that. Plenty gleamed on the horizon but goods would still be scarce, far scarcer than money. Every factor of inflation was enlarged rather than reduced. Only the grip of the price ceilings could ruin production in, direct and divide supply and prevent a scramble in scarcity with all the resultant chaos. The chairman's word to the country had still to be 'hold on'.

By February 1945 the board's mass of administrative work was lessening a little at the centre. Production controls were being lifted as materials became available, and with each change there was less need of direction. More men could be spared, more were anxious to go, and the result at head office was consolidation and departures. McCutcheon, Roy Geddes and Ken Taylor, who had been the first secretary of the board and later the food coordinator, became joint deputy chairmen. By March Robert Fowler was preparing to take his leave, but there were things to be seen to first.

'On the first day I arrived at the Prices Board office,' he recalls, 'I was handed a file to study about a critical problem in the newsprint industry—it was something to which somebody with a legal training could contribute and I was the only one Gordon and Max Mackenzie could think of that is really how I got into the paper business.'[19] He was well and truly into it during the ensuing four years, and involved with fierce competitors who had been tamed at least for the duration. Newsprint, as the fodder of communications and the base of a free press, was an essential tool of war. It had been produced by a pooled effort under the board's control, with points, quotas and allotments and a joint sharing of returns. For many mills the pool system, with its guaranteed production for an inexhaustible demand, had been a saving fact of life. Yet the controls and the compensation had been everlasting disputed, and now, with peace looming, they were still more fiercely fought.

'I remember,' Fowler says of one of his last missions with the board, 'Donald and I came down to Montreal and summoned the Newsprint Advisory Committee—it consisted then of every newsprint produced in Canada—and we concocted a plan which Donald carried out. We told them we had decided they were being so difficult, so troublesome that there were better things to do and we were going to scrap the compensation plan forthwith, as of next month. They could squabble among themselves as to what would happen—so be it—we were fed up with them. You never saw such consternation on the faces of a group of people in your life. They realized that the controls of the compensation plan were the only thing that had brought them through the war at all, and the thought that we were going to withdraw horrified them.'[20]

It was one example for the chairman of the changes brought by war that he would have to reverse in peace. In flour milling, meat packing, leather goods, textiles and hundreds of smaller industries the lions of private enterprise were lying down with the lambs. They lamented the fact continually but they had almost come to like it. All restricted jointly, they were all protected jointly, with controlled profits and production and an effortless, assured sale. Competition had been exorcised as the great industrial driveshaft, but the time was fast approaching when it would have to be put back. Producers facing consumers, without the shelter of a Prices Board, would once again be scrambling in an open market. Not only John Civilian but a quarter of a million homecomers demobilized from the forces would be demanding that, and soon.

By midsummer of 1945, with the war in Europe over, the country seethed in the throes of demobilization. Between July and December some 240,000 men and women from the services were travelling back to their homes, beginning the search for new homes and looking about for jobs. To cope with the rush of traffic the board commandeered hotel space, ordered the cancelling of conventions and limited civilian travel by train, bus or air.

Gordon had come home on an evening in late June to find an earlier arrival. Joe Barter, in the uniform of a sergeant-major, was sitting with a towering stranger and a depleted plate of fruit, watched by the admiring boys. 'Joe went over with the 49th Artillery,' Michael remembers, 'and he didn't go through the regular demobilization. He hitched a ride on a ship leaving Italy with a group of Americans and got to New York and landed on our doorstep. I was there with Donnie and we didn't know who this Mutt and Jeff combination were—Joe was a short little fellow and the other guy, a corporal, was at least six-feet-six. They landed in on us and they wanted oranges—just sat in the living room, eating oranges.'[21]

The arrival of Joe was welcome, but it had not prevented a departure. Maisie was gone for the summer and perhaps for longer still. She could not cope with her headaches, she could not cope with her husband and she had reached the end of her resources. She leaned on Wallace McCutcheon, who was now a family friend, but he could change little in Gordon and he was unable to help her. With another breakdown coming, the lesser evil was a period of separation and McCutcheon had arranged that.

There had been gruff concurrence from the husband in the plans made for his wife. She would be at Inglewood, near Toronto, and close to Mc-Cutcheon's family. McCutcheon would look in on her whenever he went to Toronto, and Gordon himself could visit her when the mood between them improved. She would be living in a small cottage converted from an old schoolhouse, and she had liked the place when she saw it. She could have the boys with her, there were fields and water near, and for the drained and haggard woman it offered a hope of rest. It was the best McCutcheon could do, and it was more than Gordon had any means of offering. He had to agree to her going and remain in an emptied home.

Through the hot summer in the diminishing head office he wrestled with the demands of the job. They seemed to be changing daily as the pressures of demobilization and reconversion were added to other strains. The broad central problem was the pace of decontrol, and it was narrowing down to a matter of supply and labour. Steel was still short, and textiles shorter still. Pulp, paper, newsprint, lumber, coal and oil were all in demand everywhere and still had to be controlled. Yet the demands of demobilized people for housing, goods and clothing, for the starting of small businesses and every form of assistance, had all to be given priority and all were local needs. As the head office contracted the regional offices expanded with larger staffs than before. They were administering board orders that were a constant shift of expedients, but they were holding the ceilings down.

The Price Czar faced the public as the image and personification of the continuing grip of the board. He was hammered at by business and besought by the big merchandisers to do away with controls. He was praised by small retailers, dreading the competition, for keeping controls on. He was the 'boss Gordon' who gave or withheld goods, delayed the opening of a factory or stood in the way of trade. He loomed up in the newspapers, roundly damned by women, when he threatened the rationing of rayon stockings and girdles. He discovered some grateful husbands when the board maintained restrictions on dinner jackets and tails. 'Man's best friend,' said one of the relieved men, 'can no longer be the dog but Donald Gordon.'[22] Throughout it all was the background to the hot glare of publicity and the gabble of complaints and frills. The chairman's policy was made for him by the labour shortage in Canada, the shortage of other essentials and the demands of necessitous Europe. Set up by government as the man on the lonely bridge, he had now to persuade the country to accept his course and pace.

At home he suffered from loneliness, and was rougher, cruder and more boisterous whenever he sought relief. Needing Maisie desperately, he often came down to visit her, refusing to admit a break. It remained a fact, however, and he could sense the growing apart. McCutcheon was the only link, the only one he could talk to who could also talk to her. He could discuss nothing with the boys, and it seemed to him that even Michael was beginning to grow away. For Donnie the great occasions were the times when McCutcheon came. 'He was closer to being a father than my father ever was. He talked to me as a human being.' The friend was good for the boys and he was good for Maisie and Gordon; easily and unobtrusively he was trying to reknit bonds. Yet it was a hard thing for the husband to admit that he could not help. He resented that, and the resentment was another barrier between himself and the sick woman. He went back to the desk in Ottawa, a man estranged from his wife.

On other Saturdays, in another mood, he would take off for Five Lakes. The 1939 Buick was showing signs of wear and it was not helped by his driving or the rutted gravel of the road. He had his usual profane resentment of the ways of all machines. He could not swim, he was always afraid of water and he was not built for canoes. During his whole time as a member of the Five Lakes Fishing Club he was known to catch one fish: 'sat on the wharf with a drink, not even looking at his line, and the damned thing jumped out at him.' Yet he needed the friends at the club, the shrugging-off of worries and even the thought of Maisie. The long, loud evenings were hardly a normal health-cure, but they were rest and release for him.

At the end of one of the longer, louder sessions he sat with David Sim. The accordions had been played out, the last of the other members had taken himself to bed and the two mellow lingerers were subsiding into philosophy. On the mantel over the fireplace there was a long and varied array of the evening's bottles, and they induced profound thoughts. 'You know, Davy,' Gordon reflected, 'there's a lot of unfairness in this world. Some have and some haven't—look at all those bottles. Some have a lot of this and some a lot of that—they ought to be all even.' He got up ponderously, swayed over to the fireplace and proceeded to make things right, delicately pouring gin into a depleted bottle of rye. 'He had the apothecary's hand,' Sim remembers admiringly, and they carefully levelled the contents of all the other bottles. With that done, the two proud levellers felt the need of an audience and the bottles' owners were summarily hauled from bed. There was much sound and fury but it soon changed to empiricism, and a first sampling of the mixtures went on to free consumption. 'Well,' Sim says believably, summing it all up, 'it was a late night.'[23]

With or without Maisie the late nights went on, but the giant constitution stood up to the hard days. Gordon was a hurt man, an angry, self-accusing and wholly baffled man when he returned to his empty home. But Mc-Cutcheon was often there and some relief and encouragement came with the endless talks. Maisie was improving with the summer—he had to believe that—and she would somehow come home well.

She did come home in October, and they were at least together again. Yet the abrasive months had put their mark on the chairman, and he showed the strain in his work. At head office more of his friends were leaving and he was beginning to resent departures. There was reason for most of the goings and the volume of work was declining; in his good hours he was prepared to acknowledge that. Yet he had his bad hours too, when he talked of rats who were scurrying to leave the ship and threatened to 'pull the plug'.[24] For all the lessening of detail, there were still difficult decisions; and in the thinning corps around him there were fewer to give advice. He showed, at least in one case, not only the loss of his old and valued experts but of some of his old skill.

Meat rationing, reimposed to meet the demand from Europe, was fought as usual by Gardiner on all political fronts. Accompanying that was another minor uproar. Beginning in southern Alberta and spreading to British Columbia, some ten thousand coal miners went out on a wildcat strike, not for money but for meat. As men in an essential industry and at particularly hard labour, they refused their new allotment and demanded a double ration. If Gordon disputed the need, they said, he should come down and work in a coal mine.

He refused the invitation and at first derided the claim. It was 'a lot of fuss and bother'. Meat rationing would hold and so would price controls until the danger of inflation was past:

And don't let us make the mistake of feeling terribly virtuous if we do make our intelligent contribution to the relief of the suffering people of war-devastated areas and if in the process we find it necessary to put ourselves to some inconvenience as we are doing with meat rationing.

Rather let us thank God that this fortunate land is given the privilege
of helping, remembering that it was the exertions of others which saved
us from the horrors and brutalities of active combat on our own soil.[25]

It was true enough but the words had been heard too often, and in
another vein he had said too much himself. Never quite appreciating the
claims of western agriculture, he had been ham-handed in most of his
dealings with Gardiner. He was more so now with the miners. He dismissed
the wildcat strike as not supported by the union. It was an illegal trial of
strength between the board and a few 'agitators'. First claiming that the
double ration was unnecessary, he offered to reconsider if the men went back
to work. But they would get nothing more 'unless they come up with a
better argument than they have so far used', and he asked with a new
rhetoric and a new touch of pomposity, 'Is there a government in Ottawa
or are the miners the government?'[26] They were all the words of a tired and
harried man, but they brought some stinging rebuttals.

The new meat rationing, said the Vancouver *News Herald*, 'is a black
mark on a white record . . . adopted without adequate consultation with
those whose interests were most vitally affected. . . . Frankly, we prefer Mr.
Gordon in his capacity of public servant conforming to popular will than the
new Mr. Gordon in the capacity of autocrat trying to override public
opinion.'[27] 'Upon what meat doth our Caesar feed?' misquoted the Sydney
Post Record from the other end of the country. 'Mr. Gordon himself must
be feeding on a peculiar quality of meat to reach such heights of self-
importance and imagined authority.'[28]

The spat was one of many and was soon over. In ten days the men were
back at the mines and eventually with increased rations. The chairman could
feel generally, in spite of the spurts of criticism, that he held his ground in
the country. 'Given a decent break,' he reported to Ilsley in October, 'there
is sufficient momentum behind the present public support and understanding of the anti-inflation controls to carry over for some months.'[29] Yet ninety
per cent of the war factories were already closing down, and hundreds of
these and others were tooling up for peace. There would be goods demanding to be sold, money demanding to buy them, and soon as well as inevitably
something would have to give. Over the whole range of production essentials
and nonessentials would have to be sorted out, demand matched with resources and priorities of release established for all civilian needs. Some
ceilings must hold, others would have to be adjusted and others lifted
completely in the face of assured supply. The country was tired of controls
and beginning to strain at the leash; the task ahead for the Prices Board was
gradually to withdraw its hand.

That work faced the chairman, another maze of complexity, as he came to the end of the year. There had been more domestic change after long discussions with Maisie. The address of the Gordons was now 25 Cartier Avenue; they had left the comfortable home on Buena Vista and settled into an apartment. There would be less room for the boys, but less room was needed, with Donnie working in the summers and Michael leaving for a boarding school in Toronto. 'I didn't resent being sent off,' he remembers, 'because mother, God bless her, made it into a really big deal—there were marble-coated halls and it was a palace and all the rest—but I resented it after I was there on account of the school itself and I got into a hell of a lot of trouble.'[30]

That much could be expected from Michael's earlier record, and it was one more thing to think of. It was clear, too, that Donnie would be seldom seen. 'I came home for Christmas, I had a week or ten days at Easter and I worked in the summer . . . one summer I worked in British Columbia for Douglas Dewar—picked fruit and raised chickens for him—and another summer I worked in the Bank of Nova Scotia.'[31] The father could find the jobs and was always generous with money, but the gap between himself and his son seemed to be widening. The boy was devoted to his mother but he was forming his own ideas. 'I don't think either of them could really run a home.'[32] There was that question for the parents and there was the question of their life together, with the strains of work opposed to the strains of idleness, and the old, uneasy pattern haunted by pain and illness threatening them both again. The shores of peace, as they loomed up round Gordon, had still their patches of fog.

CHAPTER 9

'He may leave now'

B y January 4, 1946, the Prices Board had mapped out policy for the year
ahead. It was faced with a dwindling staff, an increasing volume of
production throughout the country and a growing pressure of demand.
Some supplies were adequate, others would soon become so, and in the case
of nonessentials the effort to restrain the purchaser would be more than the
work was worth. In the United States, moreover, the rickety structure of
price ceilings was threatening to break down. If that happened and American
prices soared there could be disastrous effects in Canada. With the Canadian
dollar pegged at 91 cents in relation to the American dollar, import costs
might rise to unbearable levels while Canadian-made goods required for the
domestic market would inevitably be drawn south. An artificial scarcity
produced by the gap in prices would complicate every problem.

On that question nothing could be done by the board, but Gordon writing
to Ilsley delivered a broad hint. 'Short term considerations could probably
lead to the conclusion that on the basis of relative price levels the Canadian
dollar is undervalued in relation to the United States dollar. Obviously, also,
an appreciation of the Canadian dollar would greatly ease many pressures
on domestic ceilings . . . however, the Board does not press this point of view
but suggests that the question is one calling for consideration as a matter of
high government policy.'[1]

The chairman's policy for the Prices Board was 'that a limited list of
articles of a non-staple character be exempted from the provisions of price
control . . . as early as feasible in 1946.' He proposed to give way first in
areas where the work of maintaining controls was disproportionate to the
results; secondly on goods and services where supply seemed to be adequate,
and thirdly on items which did not greatly affect the cost of living. He was
not sure of the results; he was feeling his way as usual, but 'some risks must

be taken in the interests of making a beginning and also in view of our declining ability to meet the problems of administration'.[2]

On the whole he was optimistic. Canadian decontrol would have to be very gradual, and it would be paced to some extent by developments in the United States. If the ceilings could be held there, and labour disputes avoided, a massive reconversion would soon be increasing output. 'It can reasonably be assumed that with the rapid expansion of civilian production the peak of the inflationary pressures will pass within, say, six months.'[3] The worst, he thought, might be over by the second half of the year.

It was a hope to be considerably deferred, though the process began well. In February the board issued a list of several hundred items in the fields of drugs, cosmetics, jewellery, tobacco and some services on which controls were removed. Accompanying the list as it went to the larger retailers was a personal plea from the chairman. Canadian merchandisers were not to leap to increase prices; they were to continue the cooperation they had given through the years of war. 'With the same public support, with the same long-headed self-interest and with the same patience it ought to be possible to meet the inevitable difficulties of the transition from war to peace with a similar measure of success. Will you help?'[4]

The merchandisers were cooperative, and there was no great bulge in prices. In April the board issued a second list, again of several hundred items, on which ceilings no longer applied. There was more good news in May with the lifting of controls on all capital equipment, and again in June on milk. In July, moreover, though the American ceilings gave and American prices climbed, the worst of the effects on Canada were removed by decisive action.

Following the polite suggestion in Gordon's letter to Ilsley, there had been work behind the scenes. It had involved James Coyne, who was again with the Bank of Canada, and some executives of the board. 'We felt that our prices were such that we could very well afford to put the dollar back to par,' says Douglas Gibson. 'Gordon, Coyne and myself saw Ilsley and Clifford Clark, and then Ilsley took us to the Prime Minister and he approved. Ilsley said, "Do you want to discuss it in cabinet tonight, Mr. Prime Minister?" and King said, "Oh no, that would be like publishing it—we'll announce it first".'[5]

With that momentous announcement the purchasing power of the Canadian dollar was increased by 10 per cent in relation to the American dollar. Yet if it was a sorely needed change and a defence against American pressures, it was far from being enough. In a United States that had burst from under its ceilings a wave of industrial disputes was delaying all production. Money was chasing goods, inflation was growing with shortages, and the second half of the year promised to be worse than the first. Nearer home, moreover, and for some of the same reasons, the chairman's tidy blueprint had gone considerably awry.

Ceilings had been lifted formally, or simply allowed to lapse, on thousands of minor articles. The board, by July, had reversed its former procedure and instead of stipulating specific decontrols it was issuing a list of items on which ceilings still applied. The new list, however, was twenty pages long, included most of the necessities and was not promising to diminish. Almost every staple and article of household use was still gripped by controls. The Price Czar, no longer relaxed or relenting, had checked the course of release. He was citing 'unfavourable developments', he was again at odds with labour, and he was thrusting up in spite of himself to a new status in the country.

The trouble had begun in the United States in January with a strike that shut down steel mills for a matter of seven weeks. A coal strike had followed, restricting the supplies of coke and again idling the mills. The result north of the border was a shortage of American steel, and imports declined by some 75 per cent during the first six months of 1946. In the meantime, as American strikes were settled, the contagion moved to Canada. The steel mills were struck, then the textile mills and finally the largest of the chemical plants that supplied industrial producers.

By mid-July, with production stoppages everywhere, a parliamentary Committee on Industrial Relations was studying the whole problem. On the 26th Gordon was summoned to appear. He had nothing to do with wage control but wages affected prices and strikes affected supply. Ten days earlier he had written to the minister of labour, giving his own views, and the letter was read again before the committee. To an impressively bleak summary he had much to add in person.

The country, he said, was in the grip of what amounted to a general strike. 'I don't think the completely disastrous effect of the strike situation has been fully appreciated . . . its effect on the whole Canadian economy is absolutely startling.' Within two weeks, he predicted, all housing construction and all commercial building would have to be shut down. Foundries would be closed in a month, bringing the production of agricultural machinery to a full stop and seriously affecting the railroads. The textile strike would cut the production of clothing, already in short supply. In men's suits there would be a bare 6 per cent of the normally required volume; the shortfall in babies' diapers would be 42 per cent, and next fall, he warned the members of the committee, when they were looking around for shirts they would find them hard to get. Added to all this would be the effect of strikes by chemical workers. They had already cut in half the production of soap, rayon, pulp and essential petroleum products, and they threatened within two weeks to close down the Canadian glass-making industry and such plants as Eldorado Mines, Noranda Mines and International Nickel.

The committee heard him out, and there was a depressed silence at the end. In such a situation, one of the members asked, would it not be wiser to let controls go and take a chance with inflation? That, Gordon replied, would be even more disastrous. Had he any other remedy? He had no specific advice and he was not the controller of wages, but he ventured an observation. At the Prices Board, in the case of essential commodities, when some manufacturers had gone 'on strike' because they did not think they were making enough profit 'we forced them back into production'. It was true enough but it embodied a dangerous suggestion, and there were many reporters present. His words grew as they reached the evening papers. 'The implication was,' said the Ottawa *Journal*, 'although he didn't say it in so many words—that if "striking" manufacturers could be "forced" back into production in the "national interest" so could labour.'[6]

There were more implications in considering specific strikes. How did Gordon feel about the steelworkers' demand for an increase of 15 per cent per hour? He answered flatly: 'If the steel strike is settled at the magnitude of the increase demanded it would have such an impact on our whole economy that I doubt seriously whether it would be worth while for the price board to struggle any longer with control.'

'At what point, on the basis of an hourly wage increase, could the impact be absorbed by the national economy, and at what point would you be forced to throw in the sponge?'

Gordon did not know.

'At 10 cents?' the inquiring member persisted.

'A 10-cent increase would put a pressure on price control which would be practically unbearable. I would be very much afraid that it might be the beginning of the end.' Would he concede that controls would have a fighting chance of surviving if there were a 10-cent increase? He conceded the 'fighting chance but no more', and again the pencils of the reporters transmuted the words into print.[7] The 10-cent basis haunted future discussion as the pivot point of the dispute.

In late August it was the starting point for a settlement which was to range upward by instalments, but there had been some side-effects. Gordon, obsessed with inflation and the rising cost of supplies, had been drawn into the wage field by the rising cost of labour. He had been cast in opposition to the able Charles Millard, the director of the Steelworkers' Union, and Millard had made some points. Gordon was clinging to wage controls in the face of his own figures; since the beginning of the year and the beginning of decontrol the rise in the cost of living had been nearly five points. There was justification in that of the demands for increased wages, and there would be still more in the effects of a good settlement. Gordon was forgetting the increased volume of production that would absorb increased costs and he was also ignoring the settlements that had been made in the United States. Did he expect to go on indefinitely with a differential of 33 cents an hour between American and Canadian wages?

On August 20, Arthur Smith, the Conservative from Calgary West who had originally sponsored the parliamentary investigation, rose in the House of Commons to deliver a summing-up. He had kind words for Gordon and his appearance before the committee. 'We were all greatly impressed by him. I was particularly impressed by his fearlessness and his power. I am afraid that—at certain times only—I was not equally impressed with his logic.' From the beginning of decontrol, Smith pointed out, there had been a gradual increase in the prices of manufactured articles. 'Yet when labour asks for more than 10 cents, anything beyond that is inflation.' The Prices Board chairman, he thought, was too isolated from the problems that concerned the Department of Labour. 'We find the Wartime Prices and Trade Board operating in another airtight compartment and no practical liaison between them. Just how we expect to hold the price ceiling, admitting that wages enter into that ceiling as part of the cost, without these two elements coming together somewhere is something I have been utterly unable to understand. The government must accept responsibility for that.'[8]

By October Gordon himself was offering another prescription. Government, he wrote Ilsley, should give up the attempt to fight the battles of industry by maintaining wage controls. It was being placed in a false position as the great opponent of labour. There was no question that wages would have to advance and that price increases would follow. 'To my way of thinking the events of the last six months have demonstrated quite conclusively that effective wage control is not possible. . . . I feel very strongly that the best thing to do is to give up a lost battle and do the best that we can to minimize the increase in prices.' Such a policy, while it maintained and defended control of major staples, would have 'at least the merit of being logical and comprehensible'.[9]

With that policy accepted, he took to the radio in November. In five 15-minute talks broadcast nationally he lectured an impatient country on 'The Realities of Price Control', 'Your Bread and Butter', 'The Shirt on Your

Back', 'A Roof Over Your Head' and 'Facing the Facts'. The facts were, as he explained them, that controls were not giving way, nor was the guiding hand removed. That hand, however, was easing, modifying and withdrawing as conditions made it possible.

The lectures were good-tempered and were generally well received. The chairman's reduced publicity staff was still alert to his quirks and helpful in using some of them to develop supporting copy. Word was leaked to the newspapers of a sentence in one speech that had provoked internal discussion. Gordon, in dealing with several 'nonsensical' complaints in a first draft of his speech, enjoined the country to face facts and not be like the ostrich that buried its head in the sand. Ostriches didn't bury their heads in the sand, one of the researchers informed him; that was a popular myth. People *thought* that ostriches buried their heads in the sand, Gordon retorted; the sentence would stay as it was. The purists pressed him harder but were ordered out of the office; the chairman was still obdurate and he liked his figure of speech. 'Then, the way those things happen,' reported the Montreal *Gazette*, 'word of the ostrich reached the chairman's attractive wife. She picked up the phone. If the sentence wasn't changed and the chairman insisted on making himself ridiculous over the air, there would be no dinner served in the Gordon household that evening.' As a result, concluded the report, 'a new version of the sentence went out on the airways and the people of Canada heard the rich brogue of the chairman make the point this way: "That sort of nonsense is symbolized by the fable of the ostrich hiding its head in the sand." P.S. The chairman ate a hearty dinner.'[10]

There were other reflections, however, of a changing image. He seemed to be becoming the mouthpiece of much more than the Prices Board. 'Gordon Slated for the Cabinet,' announced the Montreal *Herald* in a banner headline, and went on to voice its conviction. 'With the price board nearing the end of its career it is not likely that the government will permit Mr. Gordon to slip back into private life . . . his recent appearances on nation-wide broadcasts have increased his importance . . . any political party would like to get him, the Liberals particularly.'[11]

Conservatives were of much the same view, but differed strongly in shading. The rising John Diefenbaker had a plea for equal time. Gordon had been given five periods on a national network to present the case for 'controlled readjustment'. He was not just giving the facts of government policy; he was speaking on a most controversial issue and giving decided opinions. 'There are many able Canadians who do not share Mr. Gordon's view . . . yet there is no forum like that afforded Mr. Gordon by which their arguments might be put before the people. . . . Clearly this is a case of the people being denied freedom of the air, which is inseparable from freedom of speech.'[12]

Even friendlier voices were manifesting new concern. 'The question in our mind,' said the Ottawa *Journal*, 'is whether the defence of price control and rent control which he is making should not have been undertaken by a member of the cabinet. . . . Mr. Gordon, as we have said many times, has done magnificent work in a post of extreme difficulty. After public service of that sort it would be a pity to see him involved innocently in political controversy as control approaches its inevitable end—involved as a defender of government policies for which the government itself must take full responsibility.'[13]

'The question,' said the Montreal *Gazette*, 'is really not one of whether Mr. Gordon may or may not be safely entrusted with functions that exceed the normal methods of government. It is the question of whether or not a precedent is being set that may prove undesirable in time to come.'[14]

The Prices Board and the man built to personify it were becoming political issues. Gordon could sense the danger, and he was in a more exposed position. In early December an exhausted Ilsley gave up the ministry of Finance for the easier post of Justice. Douglas Charles Abbott became Gordon's new minister. The two men liked each other and worked well together, but there was no replacing the relationship with the friend of five years. On the 24th of the month there was a Christmas present of sorts when the Winnipeg *Free Press*, the most authoritative voice on the prairies, voted Donald Gordon 'Man of the Year'.[15] But there were to be no more major addresses by the chairman of the Wartime Prices and Trade Board, and his advice to senior officials also invited to speak was, 'When in doubt, don't'.[16]

In January 1947 a flaring row with Gardiner inaugurated the chairman's year. It was concerned as usual with meat, and involved some of the packing companies who were supporting the minister of agriculture. 'There are interests in Toronto,' Gordon burst out at a press conference, 'trying to blow the price ceilings by creating the impression that the black market is rampant and the meat situation in a mess.'[17] The dispute was different from hundreds that had gone before it only in the fact that it was nearly the last. The meat situation was tight and still subject to controls, but it was certainly not in a mess. Nor were price ceilings being 'blown' through any concerted pressures; they were being lifted flexibly and responsively in relation to supplies and costs.

The board's annual report for 1946, which came out on February 15, 1947, and included all developments to February 1, made this claim for its policy:

> In returning to a free price structure and in re-establishing the peacetime flow of external trade, growing recognition had to be given to the effects of higher costs at home and higher prices abroad. While the continuing threat of disorderly price advances was vigorously combatted, it was no part of the emergency program to seek to avoid the realities of higher costs by expanding or unduly prolonging economic controls which were temporary in their objectives and in the powers on which they were based.[18]

By the time the report came out, subsidies had been eliminated on all but a few staples, ceilings were being lifted on major household items, automobile production was creeping back toward normal, and all restrictions had been revoked on consumer credit. In prices as well as wages the free market of the country was rising to a higher level, but inflation had been contained. Looking back over the period from October 1, 1941, to April 1, 1945, just before the end of the war in Europe, the rise in the cost of living had been 3.2 points or 2.8 per cent. Since then, with wage increases and the relaxation of controls, it had risen by 6.5 points or 5.4 per cent.[19] By contrast, in the same postwar period, the American leap forward had been nearly 20 per cent, and the rise in the United Kingdom and other countries of Western Europe a great deal more than that. Canada was being returned to the hands of its producers and consumers in a healthier financial condition than any other country in the world.

There were still many controls, administered with increasing difficulty by the board's diminishing staff. But they were narrowing down to the great essential staples governed by world demand. Iron, steel, coal, vegetable oils and cotton still had to be imported and channelled to the large users. Foods had to be conserved to supply demands from Europe; rentals would have to be controlled while housing remained a problem. Yet most of the Canadian economy was beginning to run free. The Wartime Prices and Trade Board was reverting to its earlier functions and the time had arrived when the chairman could think of stepping down.

There were newspaper rumours in January that he was returning to the Bank of Canada. By February 3 there was harder news reported in the Ottawa *Journal*. He was 'really tired' and was planning a vacation in the south. Mrs. Gordon would be with him, 'now bothered by a sinus condition which a change in climate is expected to improve'.[20]

When they came home after a three-weeks stay under the palms and oleanders of Biloxi, Mississippi, he was well rested himself and Maisie seemed alert and cheerful. She was, she insisted, on the way to full recovery, and he was more than willing to believe her. He had to believe, too, that his own departure from the Prices Board would make for a better life. Between the two there was much of the old closeness and something of the old excitement in the thought of change again.

On March 6 he wrote formally to Abbott, requesting to be relieved of his duties. On the 19th Mackenzie King rose in the House of Commons to announce the resignation, effective April 15. 'I believe,' said King, 'I can speak on behalf of the Canadian nation when upon his taking leave of us I present to Mr. Gordon our thanks for the inestimable services he has rendered our country during the years when it needed them most. . . . He may leave now; the best interests of the nation will not suffer.'[21]

'Never in our time,' said *La Presse* on March 20, 'has any Canadian figure been accorded such whole-hearted, genuine and sincere tribute as has Donald Gordon in the editorial columns of all the English press.'[22] Letters, telegrams, magazine articles and radio broadcasts followed the newspaper comment with few dissenting notes. Across the breadth of the country there was a wave of applause and thanks. The *Toronto Star*, which had first christened him Price Czar, apologized freely and handsomely and withdrew the baleful name. He had not been a blustering tyrant; he had been a devoted public servant.

In the House of Commons M. J. Coldwell on behalf of the CCF praised and endorsed his work, though Conservatives sat on their hands. In the Senate Norman Lambert concluded a long eulogy with the hope that freedom from the Prices Board and relaxation for the chairman would provide more time for his songs. 'I know that in this city there are still many roofs able to withstand the reverberations of his lusty baritone voice when he chooses to raise it in praise of Scottish lore and story.'[23] Leon Henderson scribbled a note from Washington: 'I still feel you are the best damn price controller in the world. Even if you weren't you'd look like the best just by reference to the folly and suicide we are committing down here.'[24]

The French-Canadian press was quite as generous as the English, and more so than it might have been for many familiar reasons. The French Canadian in Ottawa had still a difficult time, and Gordon's rapport with

Frenchness had not been one of his strengths. Always fair, he had come down hard and instantly on the suggestion of precedence for English in the text of board orders; the French translation was to be considered equally official. Yet translations had often been bad, often issued late; there had been failures in communication and difficulties for French officials that he had been very slow to adjust. He had not found, because he had not made time to look for it, a solid working relationship with his personnel from Quebec. Yet that was overlooked now in considering the man and his work.

'The Canadian consumers owe him more than they can repay,' said *Le Canada*.[25] 'Donald Gordon,' said *La Presse*, 'is now almost a legend. From one end of Canada to the other people who do not know him curse him or bless him. . . . It is to be regretted that all Canadians did not have the opportunity to see Donald Gordon at work . . . this extraordinarily dynamic man has the knack of electrifying anyone coming near him and of winning him over to his cause. . . . Those who have characterized him as an almighty and Machiavellian czar behind a Kremlin from where he would have directed the wheels of a controlled economy have erred from end to end. No one is more capable than this great Scotsman of understanding the human side of economic life.'[26]

The first of the ceremonies of departure took place in his own office. On March 27, Ken Taylor, who was to succeed as chairman of the board, marched in at the head of the senior staff. He was, he said, about to present a motion 'without precedent in the history of this Board, in that it is something *you* don't know anything about, has not even been discussed with you and probably won't meet with your approval. The rest of us, however, are unanimously and enthusiastically in favour of having placed in the official minutes something that will indicate to future generations that at one time in the proceedings of the Wartime Prices and Trade Board its members had courage enough to tell the Chairman frankly what they thought of him. . . .

'I wish we could have said bluntly what we all genuinely feel, that there is not another man in Canada who could have done the job you have done. You can knock off now with a sense of personal satisfaction that your fellow citizens throughout Canada are infinitely better off than they would have been if you had not been looking after their interests.'[27]

On April 14, the day before he was to lumber down the catwalk for the last time as chairman, there was a staff party on Sussex Street, with gifts and speeches for himself, a bouquet of roses for Maisie and another for Nan Young. The climactic affair, however, was reserved for two weeks later. On May 2, at the Royal York in Toronto, four hundred guests from the elite of government, industry and the business life of the country gathered for a banquet in his honour. Douglas Abbott, presiding at the head table, sum-marized his own experience. 'One thing I can say for Donald Gordon: he never left those who worked for him holding the bag, nor did he ever leave his political chiefs holding the bag.' Then he held out the keys to a new car, a presentation of the gathering, and the chairman offered his reflections. The price ceilings on the industry had only been lifted in April, 'and a month later they are giving away automobiles free'.[28]

Among the many speeches of the evening there was one threatened oration from returning brother Jack. Gordon had not seen much of him during all the years in Ottawa, but this occasion had brought the wanderer out. Now working at Sarnia and obscurely involved in leftish union activities, Jack retained to the full not only his taste for liquor but his sense of free-and-equalness with any living man. Uninvited to the banquet, he had some-how found a seat and acquired appropriate dress. As the mood of enthusiasm waxed he sprang up to enhance it, not to be checked by scowls from his younger brother. Simultaneously, however, the stiff boiled front of his dickey shot from his rented vest to be stopped short by his nose. Jack's intended eloquence, much to the relief of the chairman, was lost in a Bronx cheer.[29]

Gordon's reply to other speeches carried a familiar ring. 'Sure I did a good job. I claim it and I'm proud of it.' They were words that appealed to copy editors when the speech was reported later, and went out as the best remembered. Yet the two following sentences conveyed another nuance and were equally characteristic. 'I couldn't long have travelled in the company of the working force at the price board if I hadn't. Teamwork did the job.'[30]

It was Ilsley's words, however, that brought the evening to its peak. The tall, greying, worn-out minister of justice was now free of Finance, but he was not free of its memories. Through five years and hundreds of meetings with Gordon he had sat making his notes, doodling his wry cartoons, ab-sorbing his own impressions. He gave some of them now in a speech that was long remembered as the best he ever made.

He went back to the late Thirties and traced the despair of the democ-racies as they gave way step by step before Hitler and Mussolini. 'Our fears were that the peace-loving peoples might not have the capacity to organize their men and resources into effective resistance. . . . If you will pardon a personal reference, I remember my own doubts. . . . It is not my purpose tonight to say anything about the way in which Canadians organized them-selves for war on the battlefields, on the high seas, in the air and in war production. The record is there so that he who runs may read. But there were other tasks of immense importance to be done. The financial and economic activities of the nation required organization as well, organization

without which Canada could not have carried on her part in the war.' He
went on to the selection of Gordon, first for foreign exchange control and
then 'to do what appeared to be almost impossible, that is, to make an overall price ceiling work'.

It had been made to work; and why? 'My suggestion is that Donald
Gordon succeeded because he was and is a great democrat. He never would
have succeeded had he sought to live up to the reputation which his
detractors gave him, the reputation of a dictator. . . . What the public got
from Gordon was not dictation but leadership. . . . He went through this
ordeal without the slightest financial benefit or advantage to himself. He
could have stayed in the Bank, where there was abundance of useful work,
and by-passed all the grief and headaches of price control. The fact that he
did not, the fact that he was able to surround himself with persons who
themselves took on trouble gladly without getting paid for taking it on,
reflects credit—I almost said glory—on Canada. Gordon has the qualities of
a true leader. Those under him swear by him. And as for those not under
him but who were associated with him during the war years and afterward
—we regarded that association as an inspiration.

'It buttressed our confidence in Canadians, our devotion to Canada. It
strengthened our faith in our democratic form of government. It showed us
that when the nation is in trouble there are men with the courage and
capacity to solve its problems and meet its difficulties. It proved that our
form of government is equal to any emergency. It proved that democracy
can really be made to work in a crisis. For this strengthening of my faith in
our institutions and in my fellow-Canadians I wish to express my gratitude
to Donald Gordon.'[31]

There was not much left to ask for from an evening in a man's life, but
more was added at the close. As soberer guests departed and busboys started
on the clearing-up of tables, one of the sedate lingered, encircled by a
Gordon arm. It was Jimmy Gardiner who neither drank nor sang but was
smiling like a Cheshire cat, enveloped in waves of sound. The chairman
was leading the last of his trusty stalwarts in 'There'll Be Blood on the
Prairie Tonight'.[32]

CHAPTER 10

'Donald Gordon, Gentleman'

By the beginning of May 1947 the returning deputy governor was installed at the Bank of Canada. The surroundings were more luxurious than the ones he had just left, he was trailed by flattering offers from private banks and businesses and there was a quick succession of other honours and appointments. He was, ex officio, a director of the Industrial Development Bank which was a subsidiary of the Bank of Canada. He stepped to the world stage in September 1948 when he was elected a director of the International Bank for Reconstruction and Development, with a gratifying, tax-free honorarium of $17,000 added to his yearly salary. His old friendship with Queen's University, cemented by work in fund-raising, had also brought its reward. At Convocation in 1947 he was presented *honoris causa* with the degree of Doctor of Laws.

None of it changed him much, or answered some surrounding questions. 'He was at home and welcomed back,' says Louis Rasminsky, 'but, having had this enormously important wartime job and having done it so supremely well, one wondered how long Gordon would be satisfied to be the Number Two man in any organization.'[1]

Graham Towers was above him, admired, respected and congenial, but a man in the prime of life for whom retirement was far off. Rasminsky himself, too big for the diminished functions of Foreign Exchange Control, had far more training than Gordon as an international banker. James Coyne, only a step below as secretary of the Bank of Canada, was a Rhodes scholar, a lawyer, a master technician of banking and a brilliant, coming man. They were all friends but they were a formidable collection of talent; too formidable at times for the high school education and the two diplomas from Queen's. As the ad hoc methods of wartime gave way to long-range planning, the master of the brusque solution was occasionally at a disadvantage.

'Donald was a very specific thinker,' Rasminsky says, 'quite capable of absorbing central ideas . . . but I don't think he was an originator. I don't think it came to him naturally (as it did to Towers) to figure out things except on a pragmatic basis. . . . Graham's thinking was more conceptual than Donald's.'[2]

There was still need of the pragmatist and he was supreme in his own field. To Beaverbrook, who met him on his visits to London, he was 'the most interesting man in Canada'.[3] He was often in the United States, preaching cooperation in the era of the Cold War, and he was aware of the Third World. One of his last messages as deputy governor of the Bank was addressed to an audience in New York: 'Those undeveloped areas of the world that are still outside the iron curtain must be assisted to increase their production, raise their standard of living and build up their economic and social defences against the aggression and domination which threaten them.'[4]

On one theme, which was conceptual enough, he had strong domestic views. 'We've got all this wealth,' he complained to Douglas Gibson, 'and all these people that are well educated and what the hell are we doing with them?—fighting and struggling at minor material issues and we don't have any real sense of purpose.'[5] With his imagination fired by the stir of the late Forties, he had rebukes for the faint of heart:

> Out of the explosive new technological developments afoot in the world today no country stands a better chance of benefit in things both material and spiritual than this richly endowed and happy land of Canada. Nowhere on earth is there less reason to distrust the future or to doubt our capacity to meet the challenge.[6]

He could still command newspaper space whenever he opened his mouth, and he had not forgotten the Prices Board or any of his old commitments. One, made to the flour millers, emerged as a case in headlines. F. A. Mc-Gregor—'Baptist Fred' to some—had been one of the original colleagues when the board was formed. More gifted as an enforcer than a negotiator and with an inborn antipathy to the ways of big business, he had had to be taught, in the words of Robert Fowler, 'to be a little tolerant of human frailty and occasionally give the benefit of the doubt even to a large concern'.[7] By 1948, returned to his old function as commissioner of the Combines Investigation Act, he was in more congenial work. The flour millers, he discovered, were setting prices jointly under the terms of an old agreement for which no record existed. He pounced on them, with loud surrounding commotion, for action in restraint of trade.

Gordon was out immediately as the advocate for the defence. The agree-

1. John Gordon, Donald Gordon's father, at the time of his marriage.

2. Margaret Watt Gordon, Donald Gordon's mother.

3. Donald Gordon with his parents and sister.

4. The Gordon family in 1914 shortly after their arrival in Canada, Donald on his mother's left.

5. The young Donald Gordon with his brothers Jack and Jim.

6. Donald Gordon as a young man.

7. Gordon, the young banker.

8. Gordon with sons Donnie and Michael.

9. The Gordon retreat at Luster Lake in the Gatineau hills.

10. Gordon with Maisie, his first wife, and their two sons, Michael and Donnie.

11. Norma and Donald Gordon at a children's Christmas party in Central Station, 1959.

12. Norma and Donald Gordon with their son, Campbell, at Jasper Park Lodge.

ment had been made, he said, at the time controls were lifted, and was quite specific in its terms. He had said to the millers 'Watch it'—because the board would watch them. 'If you start jacking up prices beyond what we think reasonable, you go back under controls.' The millers had been reasonable; after much internal squabbling they had scaled their demands down. They had agreed jointly on increases, informed Gordon jointly, and the chairman had approved the rise. It was a verbal business arrangement made in good faith, and Gordon was unequivocal in his attitude to Mc-Gregor's suit: 'I'll fight all down the line to make good the assurances we gave during the war . . . we had legislative authority to give the assurances. Finance Minister Ilsley knew and approved of what we were doing. In fact the entire war cabinet knew. It was government policy.'[8]

On the line here for Gordon was his own trust in business and the businessman's trust in him. For Stuart Garson, who was then minister of justice, there were two deciding factors. In the first place, McGregor must or should have known that the millers were operating under the authority of the board. Secondly: 'For the Government, in the face of these assurances, to prosecute an industry because it did not have formal, written authorization for all of its actions, would leave that industry and all other industries with the impression that if we ever required their cooperation under similar circumstances again, they would have to deal with the government at arm's length.'[9]

In the upshot the case against the mills was dropped. McGregor's resignation was accepted with an appreciation of his services that did not include regret, and Gordon remained on the field. Whatever his new position, he was a formidable public figure.

He could be equally formidable in private, since his old ways were unchanged. Ian Mackenzie, who was approaching the end of his term as House leader and minister of veterans affairs, was one of the boon companions of many of the late nights. Paul Martin, then one of his colleagues, is the authority concerning one evening when the minister stayed at home.

He was told by Maisie, Martin recollects, that she was reading quietly in bed when her husband slammed in, an aroma of Scotch around him and the light of purpose in his eyes. He threw his coat on the floor, walked over to the phone and grabbed the receiver from the hook. He used to have the habit of writing on the wallpaper in pencil some of his important telephone numbers. The first number he could see was Ian Mackenzie's, so he dialled it—one o'clock in the morning—'God damn you, Ian, where have you been?'

'Donald, you woke me up,' came wearily from the other end. 'Go back to bed—I'm tired.'

'Where have you been, you son of a bitch,' in an ascending Scottish roar.

'Mackenzie King's prorogued Parliament tonight—called for a dissolution. You're the House leader—and you're not there!'

The receiver went down with a bang, leaving Maisie much intrigued at the thought of a dissolving government, but there was no more from her husband. He turned from the phone, disrobed himself and was soon snoring peacefully. At Laurier House, however, after answering a sustained ringing, the butler was padding up to awaken Mackenzie King. The prime minister was padding down to the telephone. 'Chief—Chief!' came Mackenzie's anguished voice, 'why did you dissolve the House without even seeing or talking to me?'

'Mackenzie, you've been drinking again,' came the deadly tones of the schoolmaster, 'now you go to bed—we'll discuss this matter in the morning.'

'I haven't, sir—I haven't had a drop all night! Why did you dissolve the—'

There was a sharp click in his ear, and his way to the Senate was eased. The country woke next morning with its government still intact. Maisie woke too, looked in the paper for headlines and found nothing exciting. 'Donald, I don't see anything here about the dissolution of Parliament.' Her husband groaned, blinked sleepily and looked at her completely baffled. 'Dissolution?—of Parliament?—what the hell are you talking about? Who said there was?'[10]

He was as incorrigible as he was invaluable, and he was becoming the prisoner of a legend. The former Czar of price control no longer seemed to have a function. He was consulted on the affairs of the bank, on the financial problems of the country and his voice was heard abroad. But he was not the maker of decisions and there was no release in action. He had a hand in foreign exchange control as he had a hand in everything, but one of a dozen incidents had summed up his position. There had been an application for exchange, not normally authorized but made on special grounds for substantially good reasons. Gordon had seen the reasons and as usual had found a way, outside normal routine. Yet a meeting in Towers's office had raised a number of questions. Routine had its place, precedent could be important and the time of great emergencies had slipped away with the past. 'Towers turned to me,' said one of the officers present, 'and asked me what I thought. I said—if this application is approved we'd have to reverse one-two-three-four-five processes.

'Graham, without even calling on Donald, said, "If that is the meaning of the god-damned thing, this application is turned down."

'Donald didn't look up—didn't say a word.'[11]

Through his last years with the Prices Board, through Maisie's recurrent illnesses and through all the changes of the official Ottawa scene, there had been one enduring element. The weekends in the Gatineau and the noisy nights of the Five Lakes Fishing Club had provided welcome relief. On the Saturday afternoons and the Sunday mornings after, he had delighted in the piney freshness, the peace of woods and water and occasionally in some of the work. 'He never took any exercise,' one of his friends recorded, 'but he was a demon to start on projects.' An ambitiously large wood-sled which involved the hauling of timber, the sawing of many sections and the hammering of many spikes, remained as an unfinished memorial to a burst of Gordon zeal. It was also, perhaps, a warning of the fires of frustrated energy that were taxing the big frame. 'He worked on the damn thing from early morning till noon, then went into the front room, stretching out on the couch and never got up the rest of the day, just utterly exhausted. He used to get terribly tired sometimes.'[12]

A larger project involved a home for himself. The apartment dweller in Ottawa envisioned a sylvan cottage on the shore of Trout Lake, looking across at the club. He had the point for his house selected and had become enthused with the plans when difficulties began to develop. 'He wanted to build his place right out on the rocks,' Ross Tolmie records, 'but there was a path round the lake that people used to go walking on. So we sat down in solemn conclave and drew up the conditions under which members could build cottages. We called it the Treaty of Versailles and I wrote Donald a very formal letter—"Dear Mr. Gordon: We have received your application to build a cottage and we wish to inform you of the conditions"—and I listed them, 1, 2, 3, 4—about ten or twelve one of which was that the path round the lake had to be reserved. No matter what structure was built on it the right-of-way persisted. When Donald got that and compared the walk with his plans the explosion blew up the Treaty. "Why, god-damn it, that's right through the master bedroom—you could walk in on that path over me and Maisie!"'[13]

For several months he was a surly member of the club, faced with the defenders of the path who remained genially unyielding. The country home, however, had become a Gordon fixation and eventually the answer came. On August 12, 1947, 'Donald Gordon, Gentleman,' in consideration of the sum of $20,000, of which $5,000 was cash, became the owner of 'the property of Luster Lake in the Municipality of East Hull, with the buildings thereon and the whole as now presently occupied and fenced'.[14]

He was the lord of some one hundred and fifty acres of rough Gatineau real estate which he would keep for twenty years and share with a second family. In the meantime the first family shared all his enthusiasm. 'He wrestled with it quite a while before he bought it,' his son Donald recalls, 'but it was absolutely beautiful—at the end of an old gravel road—two cabins each with about four bedrooms, log-cabin type—woods and hills all around—and the jewel of a lake about half a mile across. The last two summers of high school I ran the place, acted as grounds-keeper, kept the water pumps and the generators and the mowers going. He called me his gillie, and when the jobs went well it was quite enchanting to be with him— he was a great leader, no question.' Frequently, however, the jobs did not go well. The Gordon war with machines extended to things and tools. 'When he tried to hammer a nail into an elm plank and it wouldn't go, he used to blame first the plank, then the nail and then me.'[15]

Joe Barter, at home as one of the family, had also his observations. 'When you were up there it was just like you were on Mars—there was no phone, no communication with the outside world.' The outside privy, however, as eventually remodelled by the master, did provide its amenities. 'It was a two-holer, with the one hole just massive—you'd think an ordinary person would fall through, but nobody did. If you stumbled up there in the night he had signs pointing the way, and inside, very thoughtful, a magazine stand. Almost anybody could make a long stay—financial papers, comics, everything.

'He was a great fellow for instructions, and I remember a sign by the pump. It was just an old-fashioned pump—you had to start it by hand but it used to kick sometimes and he'd give up. If this doesn't work or that doesn't work, his notice read, "fiddle with it and then if it still doesn't work curse all forms of pumps, time not to exceed twenty minutes." He had instructions for everything, including how to close the refrigerator door. In case Maisie or somebody didn't do it right he had a sign: "Take your right hand up . . .".'[16]

His directions for reaching the lake, mimeographed at the bank and handed to prospective visitors, were probably the masterpiece of all Gordon instructions:

1. Cross Inter-Provincial Bridge and turn right on Highway No. 8.
2. *Don't* take the River Road . . . but turn left at the road showing a white sign 'White Horse Race Track' (at present a bit mucky because of repairs) . . .
3. Take your mileage and keep straight up road.
4. *Landmarks* (a) At about 2.9 miles there is a jog—keep right on up; do not turn left or right but follow the jog. (b) At about 4.8 miles is the crossroads—still keep straight ahead although the road becomes a little bit rocky.

Note: In the early spring there is a short portion of the corduroy road that heaves a bit—nurse your car along slowly. (c) At about 7.4 miles a fairly sharp hill—keep on going up.

(d) *Alternative Route*: At 8.3 miles the road forks and you *take your choice*: *First*: The road straight ahead as it passes the Masson farm gets pretty bumpy. Go into low and don't let your car bounce and you'll have no trouble (some parts of this road get muddy in the Spring and once or twice I've been stuck. If you get stuck walk up to the Masson farm and get his horses.)

Second: Instead of going straight ahead take the left fork . . . there is a short, sharp hill not in very good shape, usually with rolling stones. You will have no trouble, however, if you stay in low . . . at 8.8 miles you will see a terrible-looking cottage labelled 'Chez-Moi'. (Whatever the weather, this road is hard and rocky, so you won't get stuck.)

(e) From the main road into the cottage is a short distance but since there is a fairly steep hill it is better to take it in low gear. In the early spring this part needs to be taken in a rush.

(f) Report at the log cottage on the right-hand side as you go toward the Lake. Blow your horn![17]

The document, for all its promise, did not seem to be a deterrent. The Gordon ménage at weekends was usually a full house, often with distinguished visitors. Sir Stafford Cripps could boast of having made the northward journey in company with one of the world's worst drivers. Sir Alexander Ross, then president of New Zealand's national bank, 'climbed into a real old jalopy that Donald used to keep—once you saw the roads you knew why'.[18] Safely delivered to one of the two cottages, he discovered the charm of the lake, the Gordon propensity for accordion recitals in the small hours of the morning and the fact, astonishing to a New Zealander, that his host could not swim. 'There he was in the middle of the lake, sitting in a big rubber tire with his knees up around his neck. He had the lust of life, did Donald. He was like a big, romping boy.'[19]

The big, romping boy, however, was a dangerously troubled man. By the beginning of 1949 he was forty-seven years old, at a decisive point in his lifetime. Valued at the Bank of Canada as the second man from the top, he was hardly indispensable. That fact was a daily rasp to his ego and occasionally to his uncertain temper. Yet he had a dazzling record behind him, a national reputation, a job of enough importance to satisfy most ambitions and a plague of opportunities. It was, in fact, the choice among offers open to him that provided the greatest irritant, since he could not make up his mind.

'I think,' says Joe Barter, 'he wanted to get out of Ottawa,'[20] and there was opportunity for that. Hovering over him from the middle of the year onward was an inviting prospect with the International Bank for Reconstruction and Development. The immediate firm offer was for the vice-presidency of the bank, with the likelihood of becoming president in two or three years. 'Among other things,' as he recorded himself later, this would have meant 'not only an interesting and challenging assignment, but as well a very large income with freedom from income tax in any of the countries that were members of the Bank.'[21] If he had been as willing to leave Canada as he was to leave Ottawa, he might have jumped at the offer. But with much of himself invested in the country he had made his own, he delayed, dithered and hesitated at the thought of closing the books. And beyond that, always gnawing at decision, was the thought of Maisie and the boys. Somehow, whenever he struck a reckoning, the price of all his successes and all his prestige and prospects seemed very high for them.

Donnie, brilliant as he was, had had to repeat his final year in high school and had gone on to Queen's an unhappy and disturbed boy. Michael, at thirteen, was fulfilling his early promise as a dweller in hot water. 'I was always in trouble . . . I got caught with a bottle of Scotch in my locker—I guess I was nine or ten years old . . . we used to head downstairs, all of us, and sniff the cap . . . and at Lakefield I got into a whole lot of trouble and was subsequently asked not to return . . . they found me in a hut in the woods with a twenty-two rifle, some two thousand rounds of ammunition, three bottles of Scotch, a carton of cigarettes and I don't know what else, entertaining some of the young ladies of Lakefield . . . usually I got out of trouble before father knew, but of course he would find out afterward.'[22]

Above all, and worse than the scrapes of the prodigal which time usually erased, was the condition of Maisie herself. Tired of Ottawa too, where her occupation was gone, she loved Luster Lake. In the summer of 1949, the last summer the family was to spend together, she had busied herself with the opening up of the cottages from the time the last snow left. She had the same need as Gordon for guests, gaiety and commotion, and the eternal lust for work. Yet the sinus trouble persisted and was taking its steady toll. Pain she could fight back, but she used too many pills for it and the strain was taxing her heart. She was an overtired, overanxious, secretly failing woman who was living beyond her strength. She snapped when the strength gave, and her husband snapped back at her. Involved in the old dilemma, he had only the old response. He could not help, he could not admit his helplessness and in the fog of his guilts and angers he even denied the need. He wanted the boys successful in his own terms of success. Instead, that summer, daily commuting from Ottawa over the maddening road, he came home with his problems multiplied by those of his wife and sons.

There were guests as usual at weekends, and the usual quota of stories following the guests home. The ingenious nonswimmer had improved on the spare tire. 'You should see Donald now,' a returning Torontonian reported to Byrne Hope Sanders. 'He's rigged himself up a hammock that floats in the lake—he gets into it in his bathing suit with a roof over the top to protect himself from the sun and floats in the lake with his bottle.'[23]

Uncle Jack, as an aficionado of affluence, remained attached to his brother, though less so to Maisie. The lady companion of fifteen years who accompanied his visits to the lake did not add to his welcome. 'When my father and Jack played chequers,' recalls Donnie, 'it was total war, with neither of them trusting the other or lifting his eyes from the board. When Jack wanted a drink he would just stamp his foot and the lady would come a-running with his glass of Scotch. Not mother, when father tried the performance. "There's the god-damned liquor," she said. "If you want to poison yourself, get it!" '[24]

The weekdays, however, had darker memories for the boys. Neither of them knew the trials and frictions of the office or the sufferings of the sick woman, but the result for both was misery and some long-enduring scars. 'They were battling tooth and nail,' Donnie records. 'My father was coming home every night and getting drunk and my mother was spending the entire day coming out of sleeping pills and looking at herself in the mirror, and they were both abusing each other and it was pretty awful. I tried to leave home that summer—just walked out on the whole insane situation—but he came driving after me and brought me back.'[25]

'I think,' says Michael, 'he did a lot of damage to Don, psychological damage. I tended, being substantially younger, to ease out of the situation and not have a hell of a lot to do with it.'[26]

Yet in the routine of life at the lake, in the blur of pain for the mother and the locked-in drives of the father there was no escape for anyone; the boys were witnessing a kind of culmination. In retrospect, to his son Donald, every night was the same. 'He'd drive 18–20 miles from Ottawa five nights a week. We'd eat at seven and by eight-thirty he'd be drunk—twelve ounces of Scotch before dinner and he'd drink Scotch through the meal, seldom anything else. There'd be my mother, my brother and myself, quite often a guest. The guest would frequently be ignored—acutely embarrassed. Father

would kind of pick a target for the night—sometimes my mother, or me—
less often Michael because he was quite young and got away to bed. We used
to vie with each other on how to get out of the dining room—I used to
sneak off and do the dishes.

'Whoever he picked on, it went on nonstop—the sign of it was his lower
lip would start curling out and he just looked nastier and nastier till he
finally went off to bed, or else we put him to bed.

'Yet those two, my mother and father, were close to being what I'd call
star-crossed—couldn't live well with each other or at all without each other.
I remember Saturday night fights when they almost came to blows—one
time he went at the wall with an axe, incoherent, falling-down, gibbering
drunk—yet on Sunday morning when we came across from the other
cottage they were all sweetness and light; everything seemed to be forgotten.
And it was forgotten with him—I've come to understand about this terrible
man—he had no recollection at all of some of those awful sessions. Beside
that, they didn't seem to leave a mark on him. Every week morning he was
shaved, dressed, ready and away at seven-fifteen. He would stop drinking,
he said, when he couldn't make work on time.'[27]

By the end of summer Maisie was back in Ottawa on the verge of total
collapse. The heart trouble was aggravated, in September she entered hospital and she was still there as her husband approached a decision. Both
knew that they had come to the end of a road; that there had to be drastic
change. The position with the World Bank was still open for the taking, and
it seemed now to offer much that they needed. Prestige, authority and
affluence might channel the banker's energy and give him some real direction. The excitement of new surroundings might restore Maisie's health.
She had always responded to change, as Gordon responded to challenge,
with a burst of new vigour. The cloud overhanging the offer was the thought
of leaving Canada, but against that was the prospect of release from the
Ottawa shoals. By the late days of September, preoccupied, unenthusiastic
and for once concerned as much with his wife as himself, Gordon had
decided to accept.

Meanwhile, and quite outside his purview, other wheels were turning.
For Louis St. Laurent who had been prime minister since 1948, for C. D.
Howe who had shifted to Trade and Commerce and for Lionel Chevrier,
then minister of transport, the Canadian National Railways had become a
major problem. The great, complex system, never quite recovered from the
strains of wartime traffic, was in need of massive renewal. Equipment had
been run down, personnel was aging and the era of huge deficits was

threatening to return again. Coincident with all problems was the imminent departure of the railway's present head, Robert Charles Vaughan, who had reached retirement age. Of several able railroaders in the direct line of succession none seemed, at least to their political superiors, to be the right man for the job. The eighty separate companies and the thirty-three thous- and miles of trackage that had been welded together in the network were an obsolescent maze, rigid with old methods and burdened with old debt and the fixed charges of haphazard capitalization. From Mackenzie and Mann onward in the building of the national enterprise politics had done its worst, and more than the work of railwaymen was now required to redeem it. Jack Pickersgill, who was in on some of the discussions, put their tenor succinctly: 'Mr. St. Laurent felt that the CNR had become so ingrown that it would never be any good unless it was shaken up.'[28]

Vaughan was willing and even anxious to remain, but he was not con- sidered a ruthless shaker-up. Other names were circulating and rumour ran in Ottawa, but it was on the rim of Gordon's horizon. He was not thinking of railways, he was thinking of the World Bank and preparing to take the post. 'Less than forty-eight hours before my definite acceptance, however, I was approached to succeed to the position of Chairman and President of the Canadian National Railways.'[29] The approach came, as he recorded later on, from his friend H. J. Symington, the senior director of the board. It had been maturing for some time in Ottawa and Montreal among various com- peting ambitions and much debate on the succession. Yet there had been almost total secrecy and Gordon was quite unthought-of by any but a chosen few. Norman MacMillan, who was then vice-president and general counsel for the railway, remembers only some casual questions from Symington. 'Herbie had asked me, did I know Gordon, what had I heard of him, etc., but that was all. It hadn't meant anything to me.'[30]

The questions and answers were now coming together and some inter- views confirmed the choice. Behind the approach from Symington was the authority of the prime minister and the support of Howe and Chevrier. The prospective world banker was being asked to run a railroad as a matter of public duty. The thorny job, moreover, was being pressed on him 'partic- ularly by Mr. St. Laurent, who asserted that my departure from Canada would not be in the public interest'.[31] Once more, as in the old days at the Prices Board, he was to be offered a mess of trouble and given a free hand.

He went to Maisie at the hospital and the issue was never in doubt. A move to Montreal meant at least escape from Ottawa, and there was challenge along with change. His $50,000 a year as chairman and president of the railway would be not much more than half of what he would get at the World Bank. Yet he would remain a Canadian in Canada with an enormous job on his hands and he would be the man at the top. Maisie was instantly electrified, almost a well woman. She would be well, she claimed, this was the cure she needed; and decision came with that.

During the first week of October the rumour came out on the evening news from Ottawa that Donald Gordon was to be the new head of the railway. It was heard with incredulity by Vaughan, the aspiring officials and all but one of the directors. MacMillan, who was not an aspirant, was surprised but moderately pleased. Yet he could not help but sympathize, as a railwayman himself, with the consternation and resentment of some of his senior colleagues. Their long years of service and fund of intricate knowledge seemed to have been ignored; this former banker and onetime czar of the Prices Board was invading a new field.

Yet the big wheels ground on. On October 11 Vaughan convened a directors' meeting and immediately walked out. Symington rose in his place with a brief and gruff announcement. 'We're here to elect a president, and you all know who it is.'

There was a long moment of silence as the directors looked at each other and then one spoke up. 'Herbie, is this the way it has to be?'

'This is the way it has to be.'

'All right. In those circumstances, I move that Donald Gordon be appointed president of the Canadian National Railway Company.'[32]

By three in the afternoon the resolution was passed and inscribed on the company's books. By ten minutes past three Symington was on the telephone and in touch with C. D. Howe. The twin appointment as chairman was a matter for government action, to be confirmed by order in council. With that made, later in the afternoon, Chevrier rose in the House. R. C. Vaughan, the minister of transport announced, was retiring as chairman and president of the Canadian National Railways, effective January 1, 1950. Donald Gordon, just elected as president effective from the same date, had now been appointed chairman and the appointment ratified by cabinet.

By early November Maisie was out of hospital, frail but glowing with excitement and facing a round of engagements. In December the uprooted Gordons moved to the Chateau Laurier and the boys came for the holidays, joining their parents there. To Michael, as he looks back, the change in the family's prospects seemed to have renewed his father and mother. 'It was a wiping clean of the slate—they saw a new life for each other on the horizon.'[33]

First, however, for the incumbent chairman and president, came a visit to Montreal. It was a notably chilly affair. 'Vaughan,' MacMillan remembers, 'asked me to go to the station with him to meet Gordon. I did, and when we got in the car Vaughan sat in the front seat, leaving me with Gordon in the back. It was a grim ride to the Mount Royal Club where we had a luncheon arranged, and from there after a bit of an oratorical contest it was a grim ride back to the office. Gordon spent the rest of the day with Vaughan but there was no rapport at all. I don't think he was ever back in the building till the day he came as president.'[34]

In contrast, among the ceremonies of farewell, was the dinner at the Chateau Laurier given by Graham Towers. There, among the sixty-odd guests around the big horseshoe table, were old friends from the bank, old friends from the Prices Board and, enigmatic among them, some senior officers of the railway. Enigma seemed to depart, however, with the food, drink and speeches and, inevitably, the later song. With Gordon at his high best few men could resist him and at least for that evening most gave up the attempt. There had been presentations interspersing the speeches and the guest of honour, warmed to total benevolence, was the man to make the most of them. As the toasts came to an end and some of the guests departed, he was in full stride. Wearing his trainman's cap and his engine-driver's scarf, he was making the rounds with his silver-plated oilcan, filling glasses with Scotch.

CHAPTER 11

'The worst year of my life'

B y the last week of December 1949, the Gordon family had moved to Montreal and was established in the Windsor Hotel. Amid a cloud of publicity surrounding them the first group photographs showed a beaming, determined father, a radiantly smiling mother and handsome, excited boys. As always with all the Gordons when they settled on a course of action, they were into it head first.

For the CNR's officers a forewarning of what awaited them might have drifted down already. At the Chateau Laurier, in addition to Towers's banquet, there had been other occasions featuring the incumbent president. A night or so before he left he had passed a convivial evening in one of the rooms of the hotel with David Mansur and some of his old friends. As the Scotch flowed and song rose guests had begun to complain and finally, with much diffidence, the house detective had knocked and looked in. He had been asked by the assistant manager, he said, to request the gentlemen to lower their voices a little.

The new boss of the railway, and incidentally the hotel, had received the injunction mildly and invited the detective in. He had poured a drink for the visitor, encircled him with a great arm and started another song. The embarrassed recruit was not much help to the chorus, but Gordon was understanding. Solicitously inquiring for the assistant manager's name, he went to the telephone and called him, thanking him warmly for his interest in the proceedings overhead. There was one difficulty, however. 'Your friend you sent up is an awfully nice fellow and we all like him very much, but the problem is that what we need is a tenor and he's a baritone.'[1]

In Montreal, as the last days ran out pending accession, a program of formal festivities loomed ahead. They were in a much different scene, however, and they were to be gone through by Gordon in a steadily changing

mood. Vaughan had publicly admitted and the newspapers had reported
that the railway was threatened with a coal shortage. It fell, however, to
the luckless E. A. Bromley, vice-president of Purchasing and Stores, to inform Gordon of the effect on the last day of December. 'Nobody else had
told him—I had to—that starting January 9 we were going to have to cut
passenger service by twenty-five per cent.'[2]

The railway's coal, bought in a futures market, was normally brought in
during the summer and autumn and stored in great piles at the lakehead,
the Lake Erie ports and smaller western stockpoints. This year all piles were
down. Vaughan, balancing the cost of inventories against his own view of
the market, had maintained throughout the summer that coal prices were
high and would certainly have to fall. 'It was a guess each year,' Norman
MacMillan says, 'and this time the guess was wrong.'[3] Instead of a fall in
prices a strike of American coal miners precipitated near-disaster. Bromley,
who was faced that afternoon with one of the Gordon explosions that were
soon to become familiar, had been 'sweating blood' over the situation for
three months. He was to sweat for three months more before normal service
resumed, and his relations with the new president were off to a bad start. So
was Gordon himself. The hard-bitten banker who was taking over a railway
would be judged by his first move, whether it was forced or not. He would
be charged by many newspapers and some voices in Parliament with lopping
off a quarter of the service offered the nation's travellers because the business
did not pay.

He began with that presumption, and some rather ham-handed public
relations work did little to improve his mood. On Sunday, January 1, he
went with Maisie to a reception for the railway officers and their wives held
in the Rose Room of the Windsor Hotel. Over four hundred were expected
and fewer than three hundred came, partly, in MacMillan's view, because
the weather was bitterly cold and more because railway people, like others,
'didn't want to give up their New Year's Day'.[4] The mild fiasco had resulted
simply from bad planning, but after the warmth of Ottawa it seemed to
signal to the Gordons the attitude of Montreal.

The formalities of the same day included calls on the Roman Catholic
Archbishop and the Anglican Lord Bishop. Word came over the wires from
Kamloops, B.C., that the first baby born there in the new year had been
christened Donald Gordon Smith. That evening, much in his wartime
manner, the new president of the railway addressed the nation by radio. He
spoke, he said, as head of the largest Canadian family, the Canadian
National family, and his work would be to promote their best interests. Next
day he addressed a luncheon meeting of the St. James Club; and through

every day or evening of the six weeks that followed, interspersed by visits to railway yards and photographings at throttles in engineer's caps, there were receptions, balls, signings of golden books and a round of other occasions at which Maisie was always present. She loved the whirl and appeared to Gordon to thrive on it. On February 10, interviewed by Ethel Tiffin of the Montreal *Star*, she seemed more than ever her fresh and vigorous self— 'frank, forthright, humorous . . . a warming personality, fun to be with'.[5] About the same time she informed her husband that the only day of the month for which they had no engagement booked was February 29. There was no February 29, he informed her crisply; it was not leap year.[6]

Meanwhile, in a generally uncertain atmosphere not improved by the New Year's Day reception, Gordon was making acquaintance with the men about him. There were fourteen vice-presidents, four of them near retirement and none of whom he knew well. Vaughan, the retiring president, had divorced himself from the railway on the day he walked out. The one remaining pillar was Norman Walton, chief of operations and executive vice-president, who was himself ready for retirement but had been persuaded to stay on. Gordon liked him immediately, knew he was indispensable and had three weeks of his help. Late on the afternoon of January 20 Walton called to say that he had a very important matter to discuss and to arrange an appointment for the morning. In the Windsor Hotel at two o'clock that morning Gordon's telephone rang; Walton was dead of a heart attack.

There was no other man to whom the president was yet close and he was more than ever aware of the doubts surrounding his coming. 'He built a wall around himself very quickly,' Norman MacMillan records, 'and it was difficult to penetrate. There was no outward warmth toward any of the officers. I think he cursed the day he had taken on the job.'[7]

The job was there, however, and the vast gap left by the death of Walton had to be filled at once. Where Gordon was sure of no one and inclined to trust few he went ahead by his usual brusque methods. On January 31 he called up all the officers who might expect Walton's place and told them he had made his decision. The new vice-president of operations was to be the 48-year-old Stanley F. Dingle who was a comparatively junior man but had served as Walton's assistant. 'If you have any objection,' he said to the men in the outside regions, 'jump on the train and come down and see me.'[8]

One man from the west was in Gordon's office next day, Dingle remembers, 'with a Who's Who in railroading that showed his career and all that sort of thing. Gordon and he had a chat and when I was called in the man jumped up and shook hands and congratulated me. After he was gone Gordon squinted at me from behind those thick glasses: "Do you know what happened?" I said I had no idea. "I told him you were the man and he could like it or lump it, and I'd know what his answer was when you walked in the door".[9]

The huge presidential office on the third floor of the Canadian National Railway building at 360 McGill Street was equipped with a panel of buzzers, one for each of the eight vice-presidents resident in Montreal, several for other officers and one for the private secretary. Except for calling the secretary, Gordon would have nothing to do with it. 'I don't like buzzers because they're bad for the morale of the buzzee.'[10]

In that view at least he was of the same mind as Maynard Metcalf, the vice-president who became his executive assistant. Metcalf disliked rigmarole, answered his own phone and saw the panel of buzzers as a waste of time. 'It looked like a great big keyboard with all the names and numbers— the boss had to put on his glasses and say, "where the hell is that so and so?" ' That changed, however, with the arrival of the new regime. 'A couple of days after Gordon came I was wondering who was getting the buzzer rings . . . about the third day my telephone rang and I answered it as I always did. It was the president and he said, "When you're free come in for a minute— I'd like to speak to you." Three years later, when I went down to the traffic department, the first ring on my telephone was Donald Gordon. "I just wanted to make sure you were still answering your own phone".'[11]

There was one exception to the rule on the morning of March 1, 1950. That day Metcalf's buzzer sounded and he went in to find a shaken president struggling into his coat. For two weeks Maisie had seemed to be tiring and displaying some old symptoms. There had been medical examinations, a day or two in hospital but she was now back at the hotel. Earlier that morning she had phoned Gordon jubilantly; the doctor had come and given her a clean bill of health: 'everything is fine now'. As Metcalf entered, however, there had been another call; Gordon was required at the Windsor.[12]

'We heard through our medical department,' Stanley Dingle recalls, 'that Mrs. Gordon was in trouble, so Norman MacMillan and I hiked over to the hotel.'[13] By then it was all over. The huge, broken man was sobbing helplessly beside Maisie's body on the bed. She had been eating some fruit and had choked on it and in the resulting spasm the weakened heart had failed.

Gordon was inconsolable, and in the Gaelic imagination all the guilts and failings of a quarter-century of marriage grew to an enormous burden. He would never quite shrug it off and he would never be the same man. 'I'm your luck,' Maisie had often said to him, and that was gone too. Around a core of emptiness there would be a fiercer need for work and for all the drink and roistering that brought relief from the work. Real as the change was, the one brother who had always disliked Maisie was not the man to sense it.

'When my mother died,' her son Donald recalls, 'Jack got on the first train—rode all night from Toronto—marched into the Windsor where my father was literally prostrate with grief and said, "Och, Donald, you're well rid of her." My father, from that day on, never spoke to my uncle Jack.'[14]

On March 4, the coldest March in the history of Montreal, the Church of St. Andrew and St. Paul was crowded with railway officials and old friends from Ottawa who heard the presiding minister give thanks 'for a gay and gracious spirit that brought fresh lustre to the common days of all who knew her'. An hour later Maisie was laid to rest in Mount Royal Cemetery.[15] Then the man alone, with his only refuge work, turned back to the railway.

From the days of Sir Henry Thornton, the first masterful genius of the government-owned railway, an annual ordeal for the president had been his appearance before the parliamentary Committee on Railways and Shipping. That test was the next ahead of Gordon. Here, in the full glare of publicity and before a group of members that included the most hawk-eyed of the opposition critics, he was to submit his report for the year, account for every mistake and justify future plans. The high formality of the proceedings was always mixed with politics, not infrequently with vendettas; and occasionally turned to farce. However severe the grilling, there was reassurance for the president in the fact that the railway's budget was not directly affected; it was submitted for cabinet approval and then tabled in the House. To Dingle, the hardened railway man with a sour view of the work done by the committee, 'it was just a waste of time . . . of course they dragged out all the dirt they could, but there were none of them there knew enough about railroading to ask the right questions. . . . An MP from Timbuctoo would wonder why he didn't have running water in the toilet of his station when the MP from the next constituency did, something like that.'[16]

Nevertheless, the examination by the people's representatives of a publicly owned enterprise which represented several billions of investment and was currently running a deficit of some $42 million was a serious and necessary affair. Scheduled to begin on March 24 in 1950, it required the assembly of an enormous amount of information, since no one knew where the members' questions would strike. As usual, Metcalf remembers, 'there was a hell of a lot of scurrying round head office'; and there was the first real taste for many impressed officers of the new president at work. Stunned by the loss of Maisie, driving himself through sixteen-hour days and drinking hard at night, he bored into the mass of the railway's problems. 'He absorbed information like a sponge,' Bromley recalls, 'and he never tried to bluff. If he didn't know, he'd ask. "Coupler?—what's a coupler?"—he'd stop a conversation a dozen times, sorting out railway jargon.'[17]

He was not receptive at first to the suggestion that other executives share in giving the report. At the Prices Board he had had much experience of parliamentary committees; he was now head of the Canadian National Railways and as the man responsible he intended to be the man giving the answers. During his first return to Ottawa he was flanked only by the vice-president in charge of his accounting department and by Stanley Dingle, his chief of operations.

Norman MacMillan, as general counsel of the railway, had usually accompanied Vaughan. To Gordon's mind, however, his quarter-century of railroading was outweighed by the fact of his profession. 'Donald decided right off that the guy who ran the law department didn't have any position before a parliamentary committee dealing with accounts. The first time he went down there he thought it was a matter of arithmetic, and he never did realize what an error that was. It got him into some real hassles.'[18]

The hassles of 1950 were mere deceptive preliminaries. There was hardly any warning of the breaking of future storms. Parliamentarians, taking note of the death of Maisie, had considerately offered to postpone the hearings and give the president more time. Gordon declined the offer; he wanted the rush of work and he was already hacking at the nub of all his problems. The CNR in 1949 had had a net operating surplus of $4 million, but interest charges of $46 million had brought the resounding deficit. It had been the same for most of the company's history. Hammered together by politics and various national necessities, the railway was staggering under a capital burden of $1,533 million of which more than half represented the cost of acquiring insolvent lines. They had been taken over and were being operated, not because they were profitable, but because they were presumed to be in the public interest. If so, in the eyes of Gordon and all his predecessors, the country should share the load. The CNR, which the public owned anyway, should be operated on a business basis with a revised capital structure that would spread the weight of the debt.

On Friday, March 24, in the big railway committee room where he had stood up nine years earlier as the appointed head of the Prices Board, he came before the committee. Three months before he had told newsmen that the only thing he knew about trains was that the berths were too short. Now, before Liberal friends, potential Conservative enemies and still more dangerous critics representing the CCF, he had to unfold the balance sheet and explain the railway's working. On the whole he carried it off. His argument for a revision of capital structure was strictly in his own field; and it was masterful and well received. There was a good deal of sympathy for him and a disposition to accept his explanations of firings and hirings, of various gaps in service and of trouble in the Fraser Canyon in British Columbia. He dealt with the Fraser landslides quite in the Gordon manner. 'Speaking as an amateur and therefore knowing all about my subject', he pointed out that it would cost some $175 million to repair an old mistake. Where the CPR had chosen to climb by heavy grades, the CNR had taken the low route round the mountain. 'The trouble is, the whole darned mountain comes down on top of us.'[19]

His farewell to the committee on March 30 was in a vein not to be repeated. 'I do not suppose members realize how much of a nervous strain it is for any witness to appear before a parliamentary committee, however hard-boiled his reputation might make him out to be . . . the manner in which you have treated me, both in regard to questions and the consideration at all times accorded me, has turned the experience into one of positive enjoyment. I enjoyed it immensely. Thank you very much.'[20]

For all that, most of his 'positive enjoyment' of the occasion must have come with the moment of release. Gordon's old friend Tom Boyles, transferred to Ottawa by the Bank of Nova Scotia, had encountered him in carpet slippers in the lobby of the Chateau Laurier. He was still wearing the slippers as he delivered his valedictory, and through most of the luncheon and dinner recesses of the session the president of the CNR had sat profanely with his feet in a pail of analgesic solution. The stress of the committee hearings, topping a grisly month, had pushed him close to his limit. 'After the first twenty-four hours,' says Norman MacMillan, 'he couldn't put on his shoes. He'd contracted athlete's foot as a sort of nervous reaction and the pain and itch of it nearly drove him mad. He really had a hell of a time.'[21]

With the sessional committee disposed of and the railway's budget approved, the next duty was a tour of the company's lines. The huge maze could not be entirely covered but even the main sections embraced Cape Breton and Newfoundland, extended west to Vancouver, reached north to Prince Rupert and south as far as Chicago. The southern, western and eastern trips began in Montreal, and former heads of the railway had made them in some state. 'There was a tradition that the president was an emperor-like figure,' says James A. McDonald, who was at that time a newcomer on a low rung of the hierarchy. 'The president travelled in what citizens call a private car —the railway calls it a business car—and a lot of other officials came along.' Since several of these had business cars as well, the entourage for the tours had been impressive. Gordon, McDonald says, 'was going to have none of this'.[22] The only car in addition to his own was that of Stanley Dingle, who as head of operations was to guide and instruct his chief.

Gordon's work was to learn and to make himself known. He was well aware that he was suspect to many of his officials. The banker running a railway had much to overcome and he worked by his own methods with much of his old panache. For all its formal name the business car was suitable for entertainment and it was seldom out of use. 'When he was on the first run through the United States,' says Paul Martin, 'I was on the train en route to the United Nations and he insisted that my wife and me join him in his car. We never got to bed that night. At every station he would make stops and U.S. railway officials would come on and pay their respects. He drank with all of them.' A last glimpse in the dawn near Poughkeepsie was of a diminutive local president squirming in Gordon's arms. 'He'd come on to pay his respects and Gordon just grabs him and holds him up and tosses him into the seat.'[23]

Early in May the western trip began, with Jim McDonald and Donnie added to the company. Spotted by Gordon in the CNR's Research and Development department, McDonald was along as speech writer, 'though he kept assuring me all the time that this wasn't really what he wanted me to do . . . he was looking for a young squirt—someone he could bounce things off—sort of an extension of his thinking while he got on to something else'.[24] Donnie, lost without his mother, was now on holiday from Queen's and was developing some first connections as a broadcaster and reporter. As a freelance with an assignment from the CBC he recorded public occasions and frequently deplored his father's conduct in private. 'Percy Alderman, the steward on his car, started off having no use for him—thought he was a sloppy, noisy drunk. . . . Percy and I commiserated with each other often. But Percy later on came to feel that my father could do no wrong; there were qualities in the man, no question.'[25]

The qualities developed as the train went west from the lakehead. A daily grind of inspections and a round of public speeches were interspersed with a roar of entertainment. Stanley Dingle in his own car was glad of a night-time refuge, but the president claimed his days. 'He got the feel of the railway, and he got it through hard work. I had to explain things to him . . . instructions were that I was to receive a copy of the train orders that the crew got and I'd hand these over to Donald. He had a lot of savvy—he caught on fast. I couldn't drink with him; I'd go to bed and he'd keep on, but every morning, six o'clock, an inspection car would pull up alongside and we'd be on it. He never missed an appointment.'[26]

It was a good year to discover the trials of railroading. On the prairies one of the coldest winters on record had brought blizzards and blocked lines. The Red River flood was a major disaster in May and special trains were still carrying relief supplies to washed-out communities. Far to the east in the Gaspé spring floods had isolated several ports and steamers had to be chartered to make connections. During a run from Jasper to Red Pass Junction Gordon viewed the mountains from the engineer's cab, and as he came down to Vancouver the Fraser River was in flood. Not so much of an amateur now, he promised reconstruction in the Fraser Canyon. 'I hasten to add that it will not be started this year or next, but it is of high importance in the future.'[27] A week later, as the western odyssey concluded and the return journey began, the president stopped at Kamloops, birthplace of the five-months-old Donald Gordon Smith, and presented an appropriate mug.

The whole trip, followed a month later by a similar tour of the Maritimes, dissolved some early hostilities. 'That was one of his great times,' his son Donald records. 'Every division, all the way across, the superintendent got on the train. Every one was against him—my father wasn't a railway man, he was a banker. But he broke out the bottle and he had done a lot of home-work—he knew the requirements of the area, the problems and everything else—and he made human contact with every one of those people. He went out grudgingly tolerated and came back a hero—he really did.'[28]

Near Red Pass Junction on the north line to Prince Rupert the young man had evidence of another of his father's qualities. The superintendent of the area was asking for a large expenditure, claiming that a section of the line was dangerously overhung by several thousand cubic feet of loose rock. Gordon had had other advice but seemed prepared to be convinced. 'He stopped the train under this overhang, got out and stood talking to the superintendent beneath it. I was scared. There were big boulders up there with a drop of seventy to a hundred feet and if they came down they would have smashed everything. But my father just stood there and when we got back on the train and the superintendent was gone I asked him why. "Well," he said, "I wanted to see how serious he was. That man wasn't paying attention to the gravel when he was talking to me—I don't think he was really worried at all." That was his style—he had a way of testing people.'[29]

To Jim McDonald, immersed in the toils of speech-writing, Gordon's delivery of a carefully prepared text was occasionally rather flat. The banker, when he was not enthused, seemed to be addressing other bankers. 'He was best at the beginning when he could ad lib—he could get the feel of an audience and warm it up in no time at all.' A reception in Saskatoon, where he had not expected to speak, provided one example. 'He complained that it was a dirty trick when they called on him to make a few remarks but he rose to the occasion by recalling—where he got it I'll never know—a newspaper account of a visit to Saskatoon by Sir Henry Thornton. "In the course of my research," he said, "I came across an event that occurred in Saskatoon when my very illustrious predecessor came out here to visit. At that time there was great excitement because the CNR was expected to build on the site where the Bank of Montreal now stands. Sir Henry himself said so and when he left there were great headlines in the paper. Now I'm unable to promise what Sir Henry did because what the headlines said that night in the Saskatoon *Star* was 'Sir Henry promises erection next spring'.[30]

The common touch was also applied in Toronto at another stage of the tour. Just ahead was one of the worst periods of labour relations the railways had ever known, and Gordon was to meet with union men as a newcomer and a banker. 'Here was this stranger who didn't know anything about the railway business,' McDonald says, 'and he had to have a speech for them. We both sat up the night before worrying through it and I tried to match Gordon about one drink for two—I later discovered that one for five was the right ratio for me. Anyway we finished the speech and he sent me off to bed. "Breakfast 6.30 in the morning."

'I made it—just—but when I tottered in with a hangover there he was at the table, fresh and full of beans. He marched into the hotel, down the length of the meeting hall and climbed up on a chair. "Donald Gordon," he introduced himself, "I'm the new president—chairman and president. I guess you've been wondering what this big son of a bitch would be like." In no time at all they were all cheering and applauding.'[31]

Yet charisma could not do everything; there was still a railway to run and there were unconvinced railroaders. 'I doubt very much,' says Norman MacMillan, 'that in the sixteen years he was here he rode two hundred miles on a locomotive. He didn't know what the hell to say when he got on— he'd hope the guy would ask him something he could talk about. There were people on the road who got the idea he was arrogant—he'd walk right by them, say nothing—to the guy bending with an oil can or the wheel knocker with a hammer. Partly, of course, it was his eyes—he couldn't see fifty feet with those spectacles and he was always in a hurry, thinking of something else. But really it was because he didn't know what the guy did when he walked along and hit the wheels with a hammer.'[32]

Somehow in the intervals between the tours Gordon had revised his own living arrangements. By early summer, with Donnie home for the holidays, he was established in a moderately luxurious suite in the Chateau Apartments and served by a Japanese houseboy. Michael, contrary to first intentions, was spending his summer in Toronto with Molly and David Mansur. The invitation from the wife of his old friend had been declined early in May; the president had room for the boy and would be quite able to cope. 'All right, Donald,' Molly Mansur had conceded, 'but don't forget to call me when you find your arrangements are no good.' The call had come, with the warm concurrence of the houseboy, after the lively fourteen-year-old had batted around the apartment for one week: 'When can I send Mickey up?'[33]

Overhanging the summer and coming to a head in August was a bitter dispute with labour. It was not to be soothed, as it had seemed to be in Toronto, by any climbing on chairs or swapping of genial abuse. Since early June, confronting the CNR and the CPR alike, were some epoch-making demands from the fifteen international unions of railway workers led by Frank Hall and the two Canadian unions of A. R. Mosher. Altogether, some 125,000 nonoperating railway workers were asking first for a sizeable increase in wages and secondly for a work week shortened from forty-eight hours to forty with no decrease in pay. The five-day, forty-hour week, already creeping across the United States, was approaching the Canadian boundary.

It was going to come, the railways were sure of that; but they wanted time to adjust and to impose change on the unions. With a huge burden of costs, there would be wide disruption in the industry. Shipping houses, banks and all the business of the country were still on a six-day week. How could the railways cope, without additions to freight charges and dislocation of traffic, if their week was cut to five? They would have to follow the country if it went to reduced hours, but they were prepared for grim resistance to the attempt to make them lead.

In that mood the endless series of meetings involving junior negotiators collapsed on August 8. Gordon and W. A. Mather, the president of the CPR, were faced with the prospect of the first national railway strike ever to be held in Canada. They did not expect it to come, and neither did the unions themselves. In the view of the *Financial Post*, commenting later, both parties, as their last ace in the hole, were looking to intervention by the federal government. What still remained, however, was to carry the private battle to the stage where that must come. On the morning of August 10, with his usual bulky briefcase, Gordon left his apartment to attend a meeting himself. It was to be on 'the presidential level' with the heads of the two railways and the heads of the embattled unions.

W. A. Mather, able but inarticulate and not a good negotiator, had been called to Western Canada by some urgent business. N. R. Crump, as heir-apparent to the CPR president, was to stand in at the meeting; and 'Buck'

Crump, for all his brilliance and pugnacity, was still a junior man. Mather was available by telephone but Gordon was on hand and predominant and he accepted the senior role. It was rather too familiar, but the familiarity was deceptive and he was not aware of the traps.

Norman MacMillan was. As a wary lawyer with a taste for the middle way, he had caught the scent of trouble early in the summer. 'I'd been here a long time and my work had brought me in contact with the unions. I usually took my holidays from mid-July to mid-August, but this year I thought the situation looked bad and I offered to stay around. Gordon said, "No—labour relations are not your business."

' "I've had a good deal to do with labour."

' "Well, you shouldn't have. I don't want you here—I want you to go on holidays".'[34]

Under that fiat MacMillan was relaxing in Muskoka on August 10. Gordon and Crump, on the presidential level, locked horns with the union men and backed off at noon. There was to be a resumption after the lunch break, but it promised nothing at all. Neither Hall nor Mosher nor W. J. Smith, Mosher's assistant and successor, were prepared for major concessions or any display of confidence. Stalemate had not quite come but Gordon fully expected it and was not prepared to wait.

According to Blair Fraser, reporting two years later, he must have lunched by the telephone with Crump dubious beside him. 'Let's get a statement out,' he had told Mather. 'Usually it's the union that makes the statement and puts management on the defensive. This time let's take the initiative ourselves.'[35]

Around six o'clock, as the second meeting broke up with a third scheduled for the evening, the result of the initiative appeared. A statement in all the newspapers, released by the press bureaux of the CNR and the CPR, charged the union leaders with rejecting a 'final offer' which represented 'the ultimate which can be expected'. The wage and forty-hour week demands, if agreed to, would cost the railways something like $123 million and result in an increase in freight rates of between 24 and 38 per cent. The railways, 'questioning definitely that the union representatives are bargaining in good faith', had kept them wrangling through a dismal afternoon over terms already rejected.[36]

As a bid for public support it was in the old way of the Prices Board, but it could hardly have been better calculated to stiffen the bristling unions. The president of the CNR, eight months in office, may have felt some inner doubts. 'He was due home,' Donnie records, 'and Fred, the Japanese house-boy who looked after us, was on his day off. I was cooking dinner and I'd decided to give him corn on the cob, which I knew he liked. He came in tired and angry and tense, poured himself a good stiff drink which he very much needed and then sat down with me.'

Donnie, for all his helpfulness, was then in some disfavour. Still budding as a correspondent and broadcaster, he had written accounts of the labour dispute and leaned a little to the left. That fact, though it was not actually the trigger, underlay the coming explosion. 'He took two bites on a cob of corn, broke his bridge, and everything just snapped. He leaped to his feet with a howl of rage that I can hear to this day and literally chased me round the table. "You're in league with them!" he yelled, and he was really ready to kill me. I've never before or since felt like a man with his name on a bullet, but I did then. I'd been twice around that table before he cooled off. And another thing—he had to go back to the meeting that evening and he had no upper plate and he lisped.'[37]

The foredoomed evening lisped to its sullen end. A strike of 125,000 railway workers, expected to paralyse the national economy, was called to begin on August 22. The president, however, had not run out of resources. His bridgework was repaired and the always potent radio was near at hand. In Muskoka, a day or so later, MacMillan's telephone rang with bad news from another of the vice-presidents.

'This labour business is absolutely sour—he's going to do a very stupid thing—get time on a national hookup and address the railway employees and their families.'

'My God—he can't do that!'

'Then get back here and stop him.'

The next day, in his Muskoka slacks and sport shirt, MacMillan was in Gordon's office. The president was not welcoming.

'What are you doing here?'

'I've been told things about this labour dispute that I don't like.'

'It's got nothing to do with you.'

'I don't like the idea of your giving this radio broadcast.'

'That's what I'm going to do.'

The presidential glare was 'as grim as death warmed over' but MacMillan stood his ground. 'I'm the General Counsel, the keeper of the company's conscience, I solemnly advise you not to make this railway address.'

'God-damn it, I will. I'm going to give the bloody talk!'[38]

With that the interview ended and MacMillan went back to Muskoka. At 7.30 on the evening of August 15 he listened over the radio to the engaging Scottish burr. Warm, intimate, persuasive and undeterred by his counsellors, the former chairman of the Prices Board was trying his luck again:

It is because I am deeply concerned with your real welfare that I speak to you this evening. I cannot but feel that if all of you were aware of the facts surrounding the present dispute you would say at once that strike action is not justified and that railway managements have tried honestly and fairly to deal with demands put forward by union leaders on your behalf. When you have these facts my confidence in the judgment and sense of responsibility of railway workers is such that I believe they will take appropriate action to bring these long drawn-out negotiations to an end and do so without the agonizing experience of a strike. Your voice in the right place is all that is required.[39]

He had stepped from railway management into the field of the union leaders and done his best to displace them. In later years, though some of them came to relent, they never came to forget and there was no forgiveness now. On the 16th, though the unions agreed to a mediator, they refused to delay the strike. On the 17th an army jeep with a captain and two sergeants rolled up over rutted gravel to the Five Lakes Fishing Club. The two sergeants went climbing off through the bush to the farthest lake. From there W. A. Mackintosh, now vice-principal of Queen's University, was hauled away from his trout-casting to the dispute in Montreal. Gordon's old friend, as an industrial inquiry commissioner, was the one remaining hope.

At 5.30 on the morning of August 22 Mackintosh gave up, citing 'an almost complete lack of confidence between the parties'.[40] The nine-day strike began to the dismay of all concerned, punctuated by demonstrations against Gordon, cries for his resignation and a series of fruitless meetings between the railway heads, the union leaders and the prime minister himself. It culminated with the recall of Parliament and ended at 9.56 p.m. on August 30 with Senate assent to the Maintenance of Railway Operation Act. Nineteen minutes after the passage of the act the unions ordered their men to return to work, and at 6.30 next morning the first train was rolling. The strike had been stopped by law, but it was to prove almost wholly successful. The arbitration that followed not only granted the workers most of their wage increases but established the five-day, 40-hour week, effective June 1, 1951. From that time, in the words of William Dodge of the Canadian Congress of Labour, 'it caught on and went through the whole country like wildfire'.[41]

The defeat for Gordon was total and the effects were long enduring. He was tough enough to take them, elastic enough to change and, again according to Dodge, 'he was successful as time went on in earning the confidence of the workers'.[42] The hard-eyed Frank Hall passed from grim hostility to a measure of cool respect and W. J. Smith was even warmer. Gordon, Smith says, 'was not opposed to more money for railroad workers but the idea of a 40-hour week violated his basic Victorian instincts. At the same time he had a humanism about him that finally enabled him to adjust to a period when labour relations were coming of age.'[43]

Pending that adjustment there was a considerably changed relationship with his general counsel. A year later, as the two men were together thresh- ing out another problem, the president offered a proposal and MacMillan dissented mildly. Gordon looked up. 'Are you saying you don't really give a damn, or are you solemnly advising me not to do that?'

'No, no—I'm not solemnly advising—it's just intuitive in this case. Why?'

'Because you solemnly advised me once and I ignored it. I'll not make that god-damned mistake again.'[44]

From one change, inevitable enough but helped along by the mistake, the railways would not recover. 'The truckers really sort of made a name for themselves during the strike,' says Maynard Metcalf. 'They were ready with everything that moved on wheels and they got a lot of traffic, some of which the railways never got back.'[45] Ten years later, with considerably more formality, the report of the Royal Commission on Transportation chaired by M. A. MacPherson endorsed the same finding:

> If there is any purpose served by putting a date on the emergence of our modern competitive transportation era, it could be said that the events of August 1950, when a nation-wide rail strike tested the capabilities of the alternative forms of transport available, gave clear evidence that a breakthrough had been made and that the railways had finally lost the monopolistic position in Canadian transportation which they had main- tained for almost a century.[46]

Meanwhile 1950, which Gordon recalled later as 'the worst year of my life', closed with an ironic flick. Michael was to be home for Christmas, the first without his mother, and the president wanted to make it as good as possible. Donnie, at Queen's, was expected to shop for presents but he was pre- occupied with exams. They would end, he wrote, on the afternoon of December 20 and he would need a day to recover. His father called peremptorily; he would need nothing of the kind. He would take the night train when it passed through Kingston on the 20th and be in Montreal in the morning.

At six o'clock on the morning of the 21st Gordon was wakened by a call from Stanley Dingle. Number 16 from Toronto via Kingston had gone off the rails at the Dorion bridge in Vaudreuil. It was going to be a near thing; the train seemed hanging by a hair, suspended on smashed trestles which the engine had ripped away. Four hundred passengers, probably including Donnie, were looking down at the cold, fast-running water of the Ottawa River.

The bridge somehow held; no passenger was hurt and the one casualty was a dining-car steward scalded by hot water. In the noon paper, however, came a glowing account of the accident: 'CNR Train Goes Through Dorion Bridge' with the byline, Donald Gordon.[47] Donnie, the incipient newshound, had been on the train as ordered and alive to his opportunities. 'The first thing I did was phone Canadian Press—I got a hundred bucks for the story.'[48]

CHAPTER 12

'Dieseling Donald'

M r. Gordon,' said E. A. Bromley, his vice-president of purchasing, 'had the happy faculty of being able to get money.'[1] During the early years of his incumbency, and to some of his hard-core colleagues, it seemed to be his principal virtue. The burly banker, whatever his ignorance of railroads, was well acquainted with Ottawa and knew his way to the vaults.

He was at home with his six directors, who had been appointed by Liberal governments. Of them all, perhaps, he leaned most heavily on Symington who was already an old friend, and he learned much, if slowly, from Wilfrid Gagnon. It would have been better if he had learned more and absorbed the lessons sooner, for that successful businessman, a wise, witty and perceptive French Canadian, might have saved him from later trouble.

Meanwhile he was forming his own impressions. On March 10, 1951, he submitted to Lionel Chevrier, the minister of transport, his report on operations for 1950. Along with it went a series of lamentations on the general condition of railways:

> The lean years have been characterized by excess capacity and financial stringency; the boom years by equipment shortages and inflated capital costs. Meanwhile freight rates have been increasingly subject to erosion by highway competition, and have proven to be inflexible at the upper levels. With heavy capital investment in highly durable equipment, sweeping changes in design are impracticable in the very short run. Industrial development in urban areas tends to surround and confine the growth of railway terminal and other operating facilities, at the same time adding to the requirements for rail service. New branch lines must almost be regarded as investment in perpetuity because of the difficulty in securing approval to make abandonments even where substitute services can be provided.[2]

As an overview it was as familiar to the CPR as it was to the Canadian National. Both railways had come out of the Second World War physically exhausted. They had struggled along through the aftermath wrestling with old conditions, and were seeing change outrace them as the country approached a boom. The Korean War was adding a flood of traffic to the grain, timber, pulpwood, oil, ore and minerals that were moving in new volume from developed natural resources. Cities were sprawling out with the growth of secondary industry, and the short-range haul between centres of manufacturing was doubling and trebling in importance. At the same time the problem of costs and freight rates was assuming a new dimension. The long-haul rates, established for bulk commodities, were a relic of times past, of the old days of monopoly when everything went by rail. With high profit on the short hauls of manufactured products, grain, timber, pulpwood and all the long-range freightage could be carried at near cost. This was no longer true, with trucks competing for the short hauls and eating away at profits, with pipelines feeding oil and threatening to feed more, with rising costs everywhere and an incessant demand for speed. Nevertheless the railways, locked in by law to the framework of old rates, were becoming more and more identified and more confined in function as the deliverers of heavy goods.

The passenger business, as another function, was also a wasting asset. The bus and the automobile, competing for local traffic, were making branch lines redundant. Suburban commuter services were operated at a dead loss. Trans-Canada Airlines, though it was a wholly owned subsidiary of the CNR, was stealing much of its traffic on the long, cross-country runs. With the acceleration of life, the new car in the garage and the building of superhighways, the Canadian traveller was turning away from railways. Yet he would not give up the branch lines, even though the trains ran empty. 'I am continually amazed,' Gordon commented acidly, 'to see how communities which constantly fail to patronize our services can marshal such eloquent arguments about our indispensability the moment abandonment is contemplated.'[3]

Facing both the railways were enormous problems of adjustment and huge capital expenditures. Antiquated and depleted rolling stock would all have to be replaced. If passenger business could be made to pay at all it would have to be done by speedier and better service. Freight traffic, always dependent on volume, would have to be moved in faster and bigger trains. The locomotive was the real answer to that, and the age of coal and steam was already passing. Oil-firing was cheaper, particularly in the oil-rich west, but even that was temporary. Everything pointed now to the new diesel engine which operated at half the cost and required a fraction of the maintenance of the steam locomotive. Yet the expense of changing to diesels, large enough in itself, was dwarfed by the other demands of increasing traffic. Longer and heavier trains would require improved roadbeds. Increased speed of movement would demand the addition of sidings where the slow train held for a through train could be shunted into 'the hole'. At terminal points where the trains were made up there would have to be miles of trackage and all the electronic equipment of huge, sprawling 'hump-yards', receiving the inward cars, assigning their destinations and parcelling them up in outward-bound components. Little by little, and all along the lines, new electronic equipment and automated procedures would have to take over from the old manual 'smoke signals'. All change, moreover, would have to keep pace with the needs of a booming country and with aggressive new competitors who were moving more of its goods. What confronted the new president, like every railway executive, was a revolution in the business of transportation.

In his own eyes, as a banker, the deficit loomed eternally as the first spectre to be laid. If he could lift the burden of debt by a revision of the capital structure, that would be something gained. But he did not hope for too much from it; there was a great deal more ahead. The agglomeration of services bundled together under the aegis of the national enterprise had come to include no less than eighty separate railway, steamship, telegraph, express, land development, grain, warehousing, forwarding and supply companies distributed across Canada and in the United States and Europe. Canadian National communications systems alone, by telegraph, telephone, radio and experimental micro-wave, extended from the Alaska boundary to the eastern tip of Newfoundland, serving not only the railway, the public and the CBC, but the stock markets, the meteorological services and hundreds of private subscribers. The vast, conglomerate muddle would have to be reduced to order; 'perhaps ten major corporate identities' became an early ambition, but it was to be a hope long deferred. First things came first as the banker became a railroader. In the report for 1950 he noted 'the progress of this country to the status of a major industrial power'. He looked up to the north where 'all across the country Canadian National lines skirt the edge of a newly recognized economic frontier'.[4] From the aluminum development at Kitimat in the mountains of British Columbia to the promise of the St. Lawrence Seaway and the plans for the Canso Causeway the challenge to transportation was as large as the frame of growth. The president intended to meet it.

He was hardly alone in that. On December 3, 1949, a month before he took office, the CNR's first big passenger-hauling diesel had pulled out of Central Station in Montreal on a test run to Winnipeg. Other and smaller diesels were already at work in freight yards or on some of the shorter runs in Eastern Canada. In Western Canada steam locomotives fuelled by oil rather than coal were presently competing with diesels though they were certain to lose out. Through the late Forties, in addition to experiments with motive power, the company had been improving roadbeds, developing or planning marshalling yards and testing automated systems. 'We had,' says Norman MacMillan, 'been pouring into the railway as much money as we could get our hooks on.'[5] The trouble was, there had never been money enough.

Gordon came in as president, determined to find the money. About a quarter of the company's freight equipment, half its passenger equipment and nearly three-quarters of its locomotive equipment was old or obsolescent in 1950. The condition was due to steel shortages and long-delayed deliveries as well as to lack of funds. Gordon blamed it, however, on quirks of the railway mind and on long years of penny-pinching applied to the national system. CNR officials, he confided to Blair Fraser, had been taught to consider it a crime to spend a nickel, even to save a dime. 'Quit trying to be president,' he told some of his executives. 'Your job is to tell me what you need to run a railway, not what you can get by with. It's my job, not yours, to decide whether we can afford it.'[6]

He was deliberately flamboyant in some cases to emphasize his point. Stanley Dingle, as chief of operations, went into one board meeting 'with my knees knocking a bit' to ask for a thousand box cars, a fifth of his actual needs. Gordon, however, had seen the original estimate and Dingle came out of the meeting with five thousand cars. 'I went down the stairs kind of smiling to myself and Gordon called me into his office. "Well, Stan, you did all right today." I said, yes, and he said, "You don't know how well. You also got a $5,000 raise".'[7]

With Bromley, though raises came, relations were somewhat different. Some 175,000 items were processed annually through the purchasing department as capital expenditures on equipment rose from $21.3 million in 1950 to $56.5 million in 1951, $82 million in 1952 and still continued to climb. Between the purchasing man, the executive heads of departments and ultimately the president himself, the possibilities of dispute were almost endless and they were quite frequently exploited. 'He used to eat the arse out of me fifty times a day,' Bromley records.[8] It seems, however, from the drift of recollections, that each man learned from the other.

'There was this telegraph equipment I was buying—a big order that the engineers were pushing on me—and I brought it in front of the board. Somebody mentioned a bid from an English company but I said it was no

good. Gordon asked why, and all I knew was that the engineers had said so
—I hadn't time to investigate for myself. "They're not buying this equipment," Gordon yells. "You are! Did you ever think of sending somebody
over there on a plane to find out?"—and he went on ripping me up for ten
minutes. But that was the greatest thing that ever happened to me. The next
time the chief engineer came to me and said, "Bromley, you've no right to
question my professional judgment", I just looked him in the eye and said—
"Balls!" From then on nothing went to the board in a hurry and nothing
ever went till I was satisfied about it in words of one syllable. Gordon backed
me up—he gave me tremendous authority and the authority was never
abused. . . .

'We were always getting flak from Ottawa about our purchases, and one
time he hauled me in to tell me that a cabinet minister, a couple of members
and a disgruntled supplier were coming up to give us hell for not buying
some of this supplier's steel castings. Gordon was sure, as usual, that it had
to be my fault.

' "Do we buy steel castings?"

' "Yes."

' "What are steel castings?"

'Well, I told him—told him all about it—how we made our own patterns,
sent them out to founders all over the country and had them made in areas
where they were most used. Told him what they were for, how much they
cost and why—all the rest of it. Then he got up for lunch. "All right –that's
enough. You be back at two."

'Two o'clock the deputation came in and Gordon said, "So you want to
know about steel castings." They said yes, and it was about all they got to say.
For the next three-quarters of an hour he expanded, embroidered and
improved on the talk I'd given him that morning and sent them off with
their mouths open and hardly a word let out. "Gentlemen, your representa-
tions will be given our most earnest consideration."

'When the door closed I said, "Mr. President, that's the finest dissertation
I've ever heard on the steel castings business." "Well," he said, "I kept
looking at you and you kept nodding your head so I just kept going".'[9]

Not scaring easily and quite as stubborn as his chief, Bromley walked
familiarly on the edge of trouble. By 1952, as the number of diesels in service
grew to the neighbourhood of 400, and newspapers began to speak of
'Dieseling Donald', the bronze bells from retired steam locomotives became
valued collectors' items in the charge of Bromley. 'I grabbed them all—took
them into stores. They were two and a half feet high, weighed a couple of
hundred pounds and I put a price of $250 on them. Gave a few out to

churches but nobody else. Then one day Gordon went to a party, met the lieutenant-governor and got talking about his farm. They both agreed that it would be a fine place for a bell, and I was ordered to send one. "Nope," I said, "we don't give bells for nothing—not to an individual."

'That big lip came out and his neck got red and he started to hammer the table. "What the hell do you mean?"

' "I mean I won't do it. Those bells are government property."

'That stopped the hammering and I knew I had him. He was really the soul of honesty, you know—very ethical. "Okay," he mumbled, "you've got to get me out of it."

'So I called up the lieutenant-governor whom I knew a little myself, gave him a lecture on the sacredness of government property, and then under a pledge of secrecy offered to sell him one at half-price. He jumped at it, and I reported to Gordon. If he was grateful he didn't show it. "Bromley," he said, "you're nothing but a son of a bitch" and slammed down the phone. . . .

'But all in all, you know, he was a wonderful man to work for. He didn't like me as a person but he respected me as an officer, and it was the same the other way round. It was the same with a lot of others as they got to know him. One night I was on the train with him and he had a few under his belt. He looked up at me from behind those thick glasses. "I don't understand why you fellows didn't crucify me when I first came—you could have."

' "I know," I said, "but we soon found out that you were for the railway, and if you were for the railway we were for you".'[10]

While relations formed with his executives, and assessments changed on both sides, the president turned his attention to the railway's personnel. Here too, as an Ottawa civil servant accustomed to learned experts and wearers of many degrees, he found a good deal lacking. Railway men, for the most part, had come up through the ranks. The banker was shocked by the discovery that there was no chartered accountant in his whole head office staff. A 'chief clerk mentality' and an old apprenticeship system seemed to govern training and promotion. W. H. Hobbs, his vice-president in charge of personnel, was one of the total opposites to whom Gordon took an early liking. A cool, fastidious Englishman who had been an aide to Sir Henry Thornton, Hobbs was precise, leisurely and a seeker after perfection. He was not, however, a man for expansive change and he was in no condition to realize it. Already stricken with cancer which had attacked the roof of his mouth, he was to struggle on through the five years to his retirement in steadily increasing pain.

An invaluable man because of his relations with labour, Hobbs nevertheless required an assistant. Gordon's choice for the post was an old friend from the Prices Board, W. T. Wilson. Almost as big as his chief, and occasionally as hard-drinking, Wilson proved to be a find. For the next fifteen years, tough, shrewd, genial and invariably broad-minded, he was to edge Gordon from the nadir of 1950 toward the respect and trust of the unions. To W. J. Smith, who was not given to superlatives, 'Bill Wilson had the best understanding of human relationships of any railway officer I have known.'[11]

Another Gordon import, from the Foreign Exchange Control Board by way of the Bank of Canada, was R. H. Tarr. He was to rise to a vice-presidency and become executive assistant, but in the meantime he was a familiar near at hand. He found his boss in the new environment of the railway as 'tough, snarly and blistery' as he had been ten years earlier, and afflicted with inner doubts. 'He knew something was wrong with the whole system of management, but he didn't go much for any of the modern theories. He was a one-man band, much in the public eye, a table-pounder and all that stuff. He was a real text-book case of management by crisis— he loved them—if there wasn't a crisis he'd make one.'[1u]

There was no recognizable crisis in the matter of personnel, but there were troubles of long standing. The very fact that Gordon had been called to replace Vaughan was evidence enough of one. The 'all-round railroader', the man for the job at the top, had not been found in the company. Perhaps he never would be, perhaps he was a bird of myth, but the gap between senior and middle levels of management was one crying defect. It owed much to the depression when everything had stood still and men had aged and staled within a narrow range of jobs. Yet even with better times and the opening of new horizons the system had not improved. Men moved up in the old way of the apprentice, with little regard for merit and less for broadening out.

To Tarr, as one of the newcomers, what seemed to prevail was 'lock-step promotion. The CNR was old-fashioned, almost militaristic—you didn't question your superiors. You learned how your boss did his job so that when he got promoted or retired you'd take over. It tended to keep everything going on in the same way. There were layers of people whose main job seemed to be checking on something, and their day would be made if they could catch the person under them.'[13] Gordon himself, in sessions with friends from Ottawa, bemoaned some of his problems. 'The union and seniority thing,' says David Mansur, 'just about drove him crazy. "You know," he said, "we have a department that looks after where our freight cars are.

If the senior man there is sixty-five on Tuesday he just doesn't show up Wednesday. The next man takes his place, good, bad or indifferent, and we have to deal with him".'[14]

The army attitude was common to all railways and seniority and apprenticeship were part of its very essence. That much Gordon would have to learn. Yet dieselization was coming, automation was following, and in every phase of the business there would be a demand for new crafts, skills and procedures. It had been foreseen that a staff would have to be geared for them. 'Personnel work had begun before Gordon came,' Norman Mac-Millan says, 'but what we had done we had to throw away—it just wasn't any good. The problems were too new—we didn't have enough competence ourselves—and that was what Gordon brought. He didn't normally just react to necessity—he was ahead of change—he was certainly ahead of me.'[15]

In one specific area Gordon had moved quickly. 'One of the first things I did following my appointment,' he told the sessional committee in 1951, 'was to formalize the appointment of a committee of executive officers to make recommendations for the revision of our pension plan.'[16] He was dealing here with a problem he could see in his own terms, and he was a changed man with the unions. Strong, tough, but conciliatory, and backed up by Wilson, he brought retirement prospects out of the shades of 1930 to the verge of modern times. From a basis of $25 a month plus a problematical annuity dependent on contributions, the employee's new pension became a straight percentage of his salary multiplied by years of service. Smith, for one, came out of the final meeting with a changed view of the president, and the pension issue as a cause of friction with the unions was substantially laid away.

Staff retraining, however, remained the looming necessity, complicated as always by a maze of union rules. Diesels required operators and new crafts for maintenance, and it was a comparatively simple matter to establish shops and schools. It was not so easy to man them, or to make provision for other men who had lived their lives with steam. For boilermakers, steamfitters and men of a dozen other trades the field was narrowing in. They could not cross union craft lines without the loss of all seniority, and they could not be offered retirement without their full pension. Nor could younger men be shifted without endless series of adjustments and debate with many unions. For years ahead, as dieselization crept across the system, the problem dogging progress would remain the human factor.

There was the same component to deal with in many other fields. As freight terminals expanded to deal with congested traffic, the electronically controlled humpyard emerged from the planning stage. Communication and signalling systems, always more sophisticated and involving new technologies, were extending along the lines. Office procedures changed with the coming of IBM. Staff had to be prepared, not only to run trains, but to keep the books and payrolls with automated equipment. And beyond that, still haunting the president, was the broader question of management and the need for all-round men.

The Staff Training College was conceived as one of the answers in 1952. Established a year later in an old converted freight shed at the Bonaventure Terminal, it was soon transferred to the halls of Bishop's College. Each year, for a dozen years thereafter, fifty young executives selected from across the system were tapped for a busy summer. They worked for six weeks, some thirteen hours a day, under the direction of senior railroaders and imported lecturers from the business schools of major universities. Gordon himself was on hand, at least once each summer and frequently more than once, to inspire, exhort, be questioned, 'expose my own ignorance', and close an exuberant evening with drinks, stories and song.

Out of the staff college, though it produced no all-round experts in a period of six weeks, came new vistas and considerably improved morale. Men of every region and each department of the system, as they got to know each other, were exposed to each other's problems. They were given a general insight into modern business methods and their application to the railway. They were not only better in their jobs; they were better prepared for new jobs that might be wholly different. The thousand or more men who passed through the college were at least geared for the Sixties and alive to what might come. So was the company itself as it watched the results of the experiment, gradually built around it and absorbed the functions of the college in a department of personnel. 'I think,' says George Lach, who came as an assistant to Wilson and is now a vice-president, 'that through the late Fifties and into the early Sixties we had one of the most vigorous and active training systems you would find in any company.'[17]

That condition was still well in the future in 1952. In general, however, the president's relations with his people were set on a smoother course. For one thing, to railway men who had lived long in the doldrums, he had some good results to show. Dieselization was advancing and training was keeping pace. Freight terminal development was keeping abreast, though barely, of steadily increasing traffic. There was a new thrust and direction in the competition with trucks. The CNR itself was operating some half-dozen small truck and bus lines, acquired by outright purchase. A Highball Merchandising Service for less than carload shipments was speeding short-range hauls. Truck trailers, adapted to ride on flatcars, had arrived to herald 'piggyback' as a major innovation.

Best of all for the banker was the change in the financial picture. The Royal Commission on Transportation, reporting in 1951, had agreed generally with most of Gordon's complaints. The capital structure was antiquated and unfair; the railway was overburdened. Legislation that followed had lifted or redistributed nearly half of the old debt, with striking results in 1952. A year of heavy traffic and a new system of book-keeping had actually produced a surplus. The black bottom-line figure of $142,327 was pathetic, precarious and soon to disappear; it could not, said Gordon, 'be regarded as adequate or satisfactory'.[18] Ahead of him, as he knew, if he were to produce a modern railway, were years of heavy spending and a return to deficit positions. Nevertheless for the moment, after the red-ink millions, he had climbed to a small plateau.

In his office at 360 McGill Street, 'about the size of a small railway station', the daily rumble of major and minor explosions had become normal routine. The president and the company's officers had taken each other's measure. 'He responded to people who stood toe-to-toe with him,' Norman MacMillan says, 'and a blowup was forgotten fifteen seconds later.'[19] Occupying much of a wall, and much consulted by Gordon, was a huge map of the railway which would light up by sections at the touch of an electric button. With his eternal fondness for gadgets that seldom seemed to work, he had found one that did. He had also acquired, as personal/private secretary, the ideal man for the job.

Lloyd Morgan had come to him on December 16, 1951, a slight, shy young man who had been happy in another department. He had not wanted the transfer, he had heard a little of Gordon as a tough man to work for, and all of it was borne out. Yet through some chemistry between the two a total alliance came. Seven days each week and often seven nights Morgan lived for the railway. 'I had to—I wanted to—to keep up with Mr. Gordon. He took a pile of work home with him each night and he'd be in at nine in the morning all on fire to get going—you had to be cleared and ready. And when the time came for a trip he'd just hand over the papers and the office went along. The mail followed the business car, at each stop the local telephone was connected and I handled the letters and saw he got to his engagements.' From some engagements on the travels, though Morgan does not mention them, he got the president home. Loyal, discreet and worshipful, he was the ever-present shadow. 'When you saw Mr. Gordon you saw me.'[20]

As a widower and an apartment dweller with the boys seldom at home, Gordon had not improved on his old ways. For his drinking nights he had new boon companions and he retained many of the old. Wallace Mc-Cutcheon was now based in Toronto, Gordon in Montreal, but the two were men on the move, often to be found together. On his swings across the country the old friends of the Prices Board were lavish with entertainment and eager to be entertained. The president as a public figure and the face and voice of the railway was usually a great success. After one speech to a St. Andrew's night gathering Grattan O'Leary wrote to him and quoted a distinguished listener. The journalist who had always bemoaned Gordon's failure to enter politics was supported by Arthur Meighen.

I had never before seen Donald Gordon on his feet [Meighen had written]. After seeing and hearing him last night, watching the way he handled himself and that crowd, I am convinced more than ever that I was right when I suggested some years ago that we try to get him as the Conservative Party's leader. It seems to me that he has most of the things a democratic leader should have.[21]

Yet the democratic leader was as unpredictable as ever, and as ruthless, rude and outrageous in deflating large pretensions. In 1951, on a visit to St. John's, Newfoundland, he had toured the local radio station with its rather stuffy head. The manager had stopped portentously before the main studio's microphone. From here, he said, the Queen of England had addressed the whole of Canada; one flick of a switch and the royal voice had been carried across the country to the Pacific coast. Gordon beamed admiringly. That was marvellous; was the thing working now?

The manager beamed back. It would be, if he opened the switch again.

'Good,' said the president briskly. 'Turn it on. I've always wanted to fart over the national network of the CBC.'[22]

Progress in labour relations went on by zigs and zags but Gordon and Crump, as more experienced negotiators, were not only closer together but on better terms with the unions. Hard bargaining and acrimony were now relieved by occasional lighter moments, and out of them inevitably came a quota of Gordon stories. One such, recorded by William Dodge, concerns a meeting of the presidents with some of the union leaders. Gordon had fidgeted restlessly through a long morning discussion and about eleven o'clock had passed Crump a note. Nan Young, his cherished secretary through eight years in Ottawa, was on board the Empress of Britain at the Montreal docks and was due to sail at noon. He wanted to see her off and would have to leave at once. No he wouldn't, the note came back from Crump: 'Stick with it. We have to finish this now. Will hold ship.'

Noon came and passed, twelve-thirty struck, and at last following adjournment the CPR was in action. The protesting rival president was hustled along a corridor, into a waiting elevator and down the street to a car. Crump's car followed, the sirens of a motorcycle escort cleared the way ahead and the cavalcade went screaming down to the dockyard. The two presidents with a clutch of supporting officials marched up the gangway to be received by the ship's captain. Passengers on the crowded deck who had been fretting at the hour's delay were now much intrigued by the distinguished bustle. Nan Young, however, was not one of the watchers and the purser was sent to locate her with the help of the ship's passenger list. That done, Crump, Gordon, the captain and an accumulating retinue clumped down several gangways and approached the cabin door. It was already open. The occupant had heard them coming and was wide-eyed at the commotion. 'Donald—what's going on?'

Crump was master of ceremonies and his minions answered the question. Beaming stewards seized the lady's possessions and made off for the decks above. She herself was whisked upward after them and installed breathless and protesting in one of the first-class staterooms. Maids arrived with flowers, champagne began to flow and another hour was devoted to a farewell party.

Eventually the ship sailed but the nautical hospitality of Canadian Pacific Steamships was not yet exhausted. For two and a half days, as the ship ploughed on for England, the attentions of the ship's company and the honours of a VIP continued to flood the stateroom. On the third day, from somewhere in mid-Atlantic, the cable arrived for Gordon: 'DONALD TELL THEM TO STOP'.[23]

Luster Lake had all of its old attractions and the weekends when he could be there were good days for Gordon. He floated and dozed as usual, fished with his big toe, and when the boys came there was the flavour of old times. There was a group effort on a cold Thanksgiving weekend in October 1952, when Gordon, Donnie, Michael and visiting friends from college were routed out in the small hours of the morning to help extinguish a fire. In that work, for the Gordons, excitement brought a closeness and emergency its own reward. The president was aware, however, even at that time, that he was facing another change.

On December 2, 1952, came the formal notice of Donnie's engagement to Helen Elizabeth Currie. She was an Ottawa girl and a medical student at Queen's University, daughter of a family of fifth-generation Canadians which included a line of doctors and one of the architects who had designed the parliamentary library. On December 17 Gordon and Michael boarded the train for Kingston, and on the 21st the wedding was held in Morgan's Chapel at Queen's. It was a gracefully arranged ceremony featuring a handsome couple but once more, at another crux of his life, the old cross-graining in the father's relationship with his son came to the surface.

Donnie went to the altar aware of 'titanic objections. He was very worried about me. I don't think he ever believed until five or six years later, when I was a correspondent for the CBC earning about $65,000 a year, that I could make a living.'[24] Gordon, moreover, had persuaded himself that he did not like the girl. The medical student was developing into the woman who was to become a doctor and the strong support of a husband with some deep-lying resentments. In Michael's later analysis she was 'a tough-minded, competent professional in her own way and a no-nonsense gal—she didn't take any bullshit from father'. For Gordon as he watched the ceremony a new barrier was rising between himself and his older son, and again he could not deal with it. He never really learned. As it had been in the case of Maisie, he translated fears and guilts into a crude, fumbling resentment, and the girl responded in kind. 'He made an ass of himself,' the blunt Michael records, 'and she never understood the strongly sentimental streak in him and his immense capacity for loving.'[25]

Added to that, extraneously, was a last, unfavourable omen. In one quarter, though the president of the Canadian National Railways arrived in his special car, he was not quite fully accepted. 'My wife's mother,' says Donnie, 'did not approve of her daughter marrying the son of someone in trade.'[26]

CHAPTER 13

'Breath of spring'

The year 1953, memorable to Gordon for wholly different reasons, opened with the ticking of a minor political time-bomb. Its components, which were frail enough, had been put together in September and the first promise of an explosion came in mid-March. On the 15th John Diefenbaker rose in the House of Commons to demand of the Liberal government of Louis St. Laurent that it table correspondence relating to one, Robert Pitt, who had been manager of the CNR's Fort Garry Hotel in Winnipeg and was now demoted to a lesser hotel in Brandon. Lionel Chevrier, the minister of transport, refused, pointing out that the letters asked for dealt only with the internal affairs of the company and were not the government's concern. They had become, however, a concern of the Conservative party. Eight days later, as Gordon arrived in Ottawa for his appearance before the parliamentary Committee on Railways and Shipping, the 'Pitt Affair' was emerging as a cause célèbre.

The facts underlying the incident were not particularly obscure. In September 1952 the Liberal prime minister had been making a tour of the west which included a stay in Winnipeg, naturally at the Fort Garry, the government-owned hotel. Jack Pickersgill, who was by then secretary to the cabinet, had arrived a day ahead of him with two cabinet ministers. They were informed by an unhelpful desk clerk that there was no room at the inn. The ministers, who were unexpected and had not made reservations, went off to fend for themselves. Pickersgill, who had reserved well in advance, was two hours cooling his heels in the lobby before his chit was found. The next day, moreover, when the prime minister arrived, there was no welcoming stir, no beaming manager and Pickersgill himself had to go in search of a bellboy. To the courtly St. Laurent the cold Conservative reception was a matter beneath his notice, but the cabinet secretary was made of sterner stuff.

In Winnipeg and in the matter of hotels, he informed his old friend Gordon after his return to Ottawa, 'the CPR is putting it over you like a tent'.[1] It was all and more than was needed, and the demand for explanations was followed by prompt action. On September 22 a letter went from the president to the manager of the Fort Garry Hotel, requiring the file and particulars on the prime minister's visit. A week later, following another letter from the general manager of hotels, Robert Pitt of the Fort Garry was on his way to Brandon.

Pitt had Conservative friends, Conservative leanings himself, and he had supplied his friends with copies of the correspondence. In the parliamentary committee the friends of those friends proceeded to go after Gordon. There had been political interference; he had been ordered to remove Pitt and had complied as a meek hireling. The cabinet secretary was involved, the prime minister was involved; an arrogant Liberal government was obviously running the railway.

On the evening of March 23, when Gordon rose to reply, he was scarred and blistered from eight hours of debate. The veins in his neck began to purple a little as he read his statement. He denied that there had been any hint of cabinet interference, least of all on behalf of the prime minister. Certainly he had talked to Pickersgill but 'do you suggest that Jack Pickersgill could scare me into removing a man from a hotel? Who do you think I am?'[2]

He had investigated a situation and acted wholly on his own. He had given his word of honour to that effect. 'No witness can say what motivated my decision but myself. I made the final decision and'—he brought his big fist down with a roar that shook the rafters and was soon echoing in the newspapers—'I won't be called a liar!'[3]

Whatever the effect of the performance, it was capped the next morning. Appearing before the committee, bright, well-shaved and smiling, Gordon informed the members that he did not 'recall too clearly what was said last night because I admit I lost my temper'.[4] He could, however, report a new development. He had been on the telephone to Robert Pitt and they had spoken at some length. The new manager of the Prince Edward Hotel in Brandon was tired of his political prominence and wanted, Gordon said, 'no more discussion of the rights and wrongs of the transfer'.[5] That statement, greeted with initial scepticism, was confirmed a few hours later by a telegram from Pitt himself to a leading Conservative member, J. M. Macdonnell. A longtime friend of Gordon's, Macdonnell grinned across at him. The president of the CNR, he observed, 'appears to have been leading this committee around by the nose'.[6] From the other side of the table Chevrier chimed in, effectually closing debate. 'The balloon that the opposition members have blown up is exploded.'[7]

For the originator of the balloon there was no lasting damage. Pitt moved from Brandon to a larger hotel in Charlottetown, was then promoted to Halifax and retired in 1968 as manager of the Macdonald Hotel in Edmonton. For Gordon there were other effects. Henceforth, after the histrionics of the Pitt affair, the railway committee sessions became a magnet for all the media, with himself as principal performer. He was to be once more at some classic confrontations the man in the public eye, and he was perilously close to politics as politics began to change. All that, however, was still a while in the future as he packed his bags in Ottawa and he had other things on his mind. He had been an engaged man since January and marriage was two weeks off.

His acquaintance with Norma Hobbs, the daughter of W. H. Hobbs, his vice-president in charge of personnel, had begun two years earlier. Attending a cocktail party for some senior railway executives, Mr. and Mrs. Hobbs had invited their daughter along. She had gone without much enthusiasm, expecting elderly shoptalk, and for the most part her expectations were confirmed. The one encounter of the evening that was even mildly memorable was her greeting from the president himself. 'Well,' he had said, bearing down on her genially, 'the first breath of spring!'[8]

Norma Hobbs had graduated from St. Helen's School in Dunham, Quebec, taken a bachelor of arts degree at McGill, and entered the Wrens in 1943. Two years in the service had been followed by two more years of postgraduate work and by 1949 she was embarked on research in Scotland, directed toward Scottish literature. Here, however, the obscurities of Gaelic poets had compared to disadvantage with travel in the United Kingdom, and by the time she returned to Canada the bards had been laid away. In 1951, and on the evening Gordon met her, she was on the administrative staff at McGill, though still vaguely intending to become a master of arts. Twenty-eight years old, a trim, blue-eyed blonde, she had had her share of admirers, was not unused to flattery and possessed a little of her father's cool reserve. She was amused but not impressed when the president turned to her mother after a half hour of talk: 'Do you think she'd marry me?'[9]

That question, said the forthright Mrs. Hobbs, should be put to the lady herself. Aware of the mood of blarney and of a Scot a little in his cups, she felt she could predict the answer. Within another year, however, as invitations and attentions came showering in on her daughter, she was no longer quite so sure. The widower of fifty-one, though he was occasionally in the company of older eligible women, was a persistent visitor at the Hobbses' and more and more with Norma. It was quite obvious, too, that for all the difference in ages the girl was seriously concerned.

Gordon, she confided to her parents, was the most interesting man she had ever known. She was definitely in a quandary about him, and that was warning enough. As the Hobbses recognized a courtship they were both considerably disturbed. The mother, with her usual directness, directly opposed the marriage. She recognized the flaws among the fascinations of the suitor, and much as she enjoyed sparring with him she did not want him for a son. Between Gordon and her ailing husband the mysterious affinity remained; they liked, trusted and admired each other and enjoyed each other's company. Yet Hobbs was too well versed in some of the president's escapades to be easy in his own mind. Gordon, he told his wife, was 'the best brain in Canada between eight o'clock in the morning and eight o'clock in the evening, but between eight o'clock in the evening and eight o'clock in the morning he can be the biggest damn fool'.[10] He would, however, impose nothing on his daughter but a share of his own doubts. 'This man,' he said to her, 'is really too old and too tough for you, but you have to make up your own mind. And you have to make it up quickly. You can't carry him along and let him think you're going to marry him and then just break it off.'[11] If he hoped for a breaking-off when her mind was made up he was destined to be disappointed. On January 12, 1953, the society columns of the newspapers carried the announcement of the engagement of Norma Hobbs to Donald Gordon, with the marriage set for the spring.

Meanwhile, on the other horn of the dilemma was the president's own ménage. He was lonely, he had turned fifty and he had made mistakes with his sons. The breath of spring that promised to redeem his autumn carried its own dangers. He had fears of the change himself; he had, as he always would have, a deep concern for Norma and he ached with need for the boys. He wanted a wife again but he was looking for more from marriage; somehow in the process he hoped to restore a home.

It was late for that in the case of the elder son, but at least he did what he could. 'I went through the extraordinary experience,' says Donald, 'of having my father ask my permission to be married.'[12] Already engaged himself, he was at home in Montreal through the summer of 1952 and observed the change from the summer of the year before. 'There was suddenly more courting than mourning.'[13] Four possible ladies seemed at first to be involved and 'I was taken to each of their places.'[14] It was soon apparent, however, that the Hobbs home was the favoured place for the father and the son was acquiescent. The acerbic young man was uneasy with Mrs. Hobbs, as she was with him, but he found Bill Hobbs 'a gentleman and a gentle man . . . a really remarkable human being'.[15] In Norma, who was only four years older than himself, he saw or sees in retrospect 'a bright youngster really enormously impressed with my father and with his magnetism, his dynamic class, his irreverence for all those icons of Westmount, McGill, Montreal and all the rest of it . . . she didn't know how he drank, she thought it was too much but didn't take it seriously . . . so they suited each other beautifully in that instant of time.'[16] Donnie had gone to his own marriage with the announcement of his father's engagement only a month away, and if the fact complicated emotions it had induced surface accord.

Michael, who was also at home through part of the summer and autumn, was the easier of the two to deal with. For one thing, among the cluster of passing ladies, he had taken a fancy to Norma. 'She certainly didn't set her cap for father in any way, but I'd met her three or four times and thought her a tremendous person.'[17] When the hour of decision came he was ready with a quick answer. 'Father sat me down and said he was thinking of marrying again and how about it? I said, fine, sure—he needed a wife. Then he said, well, you've met so-and-so and so-and-so and so on—who do you think would be appropriate? I said, Norma Hobbs—and that was interesting because she was the one he hadn't mentioned. I think he did it that way deliberately and that he'd made up his own mind long before. Anyway, I found out later that he proposed to her within twenty-four hours of talking to me.'[18]

On April 11 the wedding took place in Melville Presbyterian Church, Westmount, with the Reverend Charles Cochrane officiating. Michael was one of the ushers, though his brother was not present. It was a pretty, candle-lit ceremony in the late afternoon, with gladioli and ferns banked in the church and more of the same for the reception in the Ritz Carlton's blue room. Through several weeks preceding there had been a round of social engagements and the groom had borne up well. He had had his share of tremors, peaking the night before, and Wallace McCutcheon had sat with him till on in the early hours. All that was over as the bride came down the aisle. McCutcheon was best man, there were other old friends from Ottawa seated among the guests, and perhaps among crowding memories a few of the pangs of parting. But beginnings counted more for the burly giant in his tailcoat and the radiant girl beside him. The champagne flowed for the toasts, the wedding cake was cut, the last photographs were taken and they were off for the south of France.

They arrived at their hotel in Beaulieu-sur-mer to find an invitation awaiting them from Lord Beaverbrook, who had a villa nearby. 'I don't want to dine with that old so-and-so,' said Gordon. 'I had trouble with him during the war.' 'Well, I *do* want to dine with him,' said Norma, and the will of the bride prevailed. Thereafter, as she recalls it, 'he had us to dinner practically every night and often for lunch and swimming—we really spent our honeymoon with Lord Beaverbrook'. Whatever their wartime difficulties, the peer's interest in Gordon was as great as it had ever been and he and the railway president struck it off at once. Beaverbrook marvelled and chuckled as others had done before him at Gordon's style in the water. 'Never,' he told Norma, 'have I seen a man so out of his natural element.' The dinners were always gay, enlivened by other guests and warmed with excellent wine. On one occasion, however, the always-mischievous Beaverbrook attached conditions to his drink. With an Oxford don at the table who had rather more thirst than voice, he stipulated that each guest would have to sing for his champagne. The don, until he managed to achieve a squeak resembling a tune, had a rather arid time of it but 'Donnie had a lovely voice' and was more than adequately rewarded. He was in fine and glowing form as the time came for departure.

With their host and the other guests seeing them off, the Gordons climbed into their car and the vehicle lurched forward in the best style of the Scot. It roared up the circular driveway, missed the turn to the road and went completely round the house. Cheered on by the guests and missing the turn again, it completed a second circle and disappeared on a third. By that time Beaverbrook, 'laughing till the tears came', was out in the middle of the driveway to clock the next lap. Headlamps bore down on him in a burst of gathering speed and he only escaped by a wild, flying leap. 'I had no idea,' says Norma, 'that Donnie was such a bad driver. I had a lot of things to find out.' That lesson concluded with a squealing of tires and brakes and a final successful try for the gate to the open road. Beaverbrook picked himself out of his rose bushes, his scattered guests reassembled and Norma's alarmed treble floated back on the night: 'Donnie—Donnie—*concentrate*!'[19]

It was not the last of the adventures. On a day's trip across the border to San Remo the Gordons surrendered their passports as required by the Italian customs, parked their rented car and went off to explore the town. At the day's end, however, they discovered that they had forgotten their parking place, the location of the customs office and even the make of the car. They were without visas, without passports, lost in a strange town and the president's response was frenetic. Helplessly unilingual, he jittered beside Norma while she asked for directions in French and then in her sketchy Italian of a couple who appeared to be German. The couple, however, confessed that they had only English; could they reply in that tongue? 'Yes—yes,' said Gordon, lost in the lingual swirl, 'my wife will translate!'[20]

Even the day of departure from Beaulieu-sur-mer produced its quota of frenzy. The president of the Canadian National, intending to leave for Paris by the crack Blue Train, managed somehow to embark his wife and himself on an earlier local. The train moved out with the Gordon luggage piled on the station platform, and there was a wild yell from the owner as he caught a glimpse of his belongings. Lurching down the aisle, bellowing for the train to stop, he created a panic of passengers that endured to the next station. It was ended there by a hastily summoned official who discovered the giant Englishman breathing maledictions against foreign inefficiency which neither his wife nor a helpful little French girl was quite prepared to translate. For Norma, then as later, international travel in the company of Donald Gordon was a lively and confused affair.

The month spent on the continent was followed by a stay in London, briefly prolonged by one item of business. The British Transport Commission, looking for a new chairman, had decided to approach Gordon. In late May, when he sailed home with his bride on board the *Mauretania*, he was still considering the offer. He did not intend to accept it and declined a month later, but it added a touch of eminence to the joys of a happy man. As he got back to his office the country was doing well, the railway was following suit and a renewed warmth and richness surrounded his own life.

As July came Norma was introduced to Luster Lake. So were the two parents and all responded to its spell, each in his own way. 'Everybody had to work,' says Mrs. Hobbs, who was now 'Ma' to Gordon. 'If you weren't cooking, you had to be out sawing wood or cutting grass or something—he just never could sit still or let anybody else sit still.'[21] Only Bill Hobbs, quietly ailing, was exempted from the general rule. Norma, entranced by the lake, was less entranced by the drab cottages surrounding it and longed for some life and colour. But the exteriors suited Gordon, were obviously filmed with memories, and the paintbrush stayed inside. Even here there were only minimal changes, with some grass rugs for the floors and fresh, gay slipcovers for the chesterfields and the chairs. Yet it was hard not to be conscious of the passing of the old regime. Michael was there for a few weeks of the summer, warmly approving of his stepmother but noting the signs of change. So for a while were some of the friends from Ottawa, but most of them came less often. Wallace McCutcheon became a stranger to the lake. Donnie, the married man, did not put in an appearance; and Joe Barter, though he had no reproaches for Norma, spent his holidays elsewhere. There were no reproaches for anyone, least of all for the bride, but Luster Lake and the life there were not to be quite the same.

In early August came a familiar announcement in the newspapers: the president of the CNR would be making a tour of the west. Of all Gordon's tours it was probably the best exploited, and certainly one reason was the presence of the bride. In Bonaventure, the business car where Lloyd Morgan toiled, there was the usual round of work. There were presidential speeches, announcements of large projects in some of the major cities and booming new predictions for a boom that was under way. It was all eclipsed, however, by a whirl of social occasions. From the lakehead to the coast, with public relations experts setting the scenes ahead of them, the Gordons came to a round of 'family parties'. The Canadian National family was to meet its master's lady. She was equal to all the whistle-stops, graceful at large receptions and photogenic and charming to eager ladies of the press. She was better than her famous husband at remembering people's names. As the tour reached Vancouver to be rounded off in triumph the public relations experts were rejoicing over a coup. For his own part the president knew, as they turned back to a week of rest at Jasper, that he had found a supporting wife.

The eastern leg of the tour followed the western and preserved the festive air. Even a misadventure which was the cause of some red faces attested the springtime mood. The president did not report it but Walter Gordon did, over a year later. In the summer of 1954 the old friend and equally distinguished namesake was travelling down to the Maritimes. He found himself on Dominion Day boarding the crowded Dayliner that ran from Matapedia and without the prospect of a seat. He was, however, as the head of a large accounting firm and a future minister of finance, a man of some resource. The conductor sat at a table occupying a double section at one end of the car, obviously harried by his passengers and in trouble balancing his receipts. Gordon watched him struggling and made the offer of a deal.

'I'm a book-keeper: you give me a seat and I'll balance your tickets.'

The conductor pushed over, Gordon settled in and eventually produced the columns of matching figures. The admiring conductor asked his name and was told.

'Gordon? You any relation to the guy that runs the railway?'

'No, but I know him.'

There was a nod, a brooding silence and then a resentful grunt. 'Came down this way on his honeymoon last summer and made this same trip out of Matapedia on the Dayliner. We don't go very fast, sometimes we even stop in the middle of a field, and this day we did. Do you know what happened? That old man gets out in the field with his wife and starts to pick her a daisy chain. I don't know anything about it, think he's still aboard, so when we're ready we start up. He and that girl have to charge out to the road, hitch a ride to the station at Matapedia and then convince the guy there that he's president of the CNR. Oh no—the station agent knows better —the president's on board the train. Well, they get that settled, wire ahead to stop us at the next station and he lands in by car. If he was mad he didn't show it—maybe he didn't dare to—but I'm the guy that'll never live it down. It was me that left the president, and the president's wife too, standing in an empty field.'

There was a final sigh and a summing-up which Walter Gordon, over the shouted protests of a red-faced Donald Gordon, repeated with much zest at a dinner in Montreal. 'Imagine that old guy—supposed to be running a railway—and he's picking daisy chains!'[22]

In spite of such diversions, or even perhaps because of them, the railway was doing well. By December 26 Gordon was able to predict total earnings in excess of the record figures of 1952 and a probable small surplus. Across the breadth of the country the great, sprawling system was alive with renewal and growth and plagued by accompanying problems. The transport trucking business was growing on the west coast, to loud complaints from some of the private carriers. On November 9 in northern Manitoba Gordon had driven the last spike for a new 155-mile branch line from Sherridon to Lynn Lake, opening a huge territory rich in copper and nickel. In the same month, launched by Norma Gordon, the big *William Carson* came down the slipway, an icebreaker, passenger carrier and freight ferry designed to improve the service between mainland Canada and Newfoundland. Apart from transport needs was the growing national appetite for electronic communication. The CNR, with the CPR, the CBC and other government agencies, was expanding by thousands of miles the telephone, teletype, telex and television networks of the country. In 1953, with the advent of facsimile transmission, the company shared another advance in a wide and profitable field. Of all advances, however, the most spectacular was reserved for Montreal and it was built on an old base.

Gordon was to record later that on January 1, 1950, the holiday interregnum before his first day in office, he had walked along Dorchester Street which then served as a bridge and looked down on Montreal's 'big hole'. It had been famous for twenty years, though it was not quite what it had been in the middle Thirties. At that time, to a newspaper correspondent standing where Gordon stood, 'the area just south of the exit of the Mount Royal tunnel looked as if it had been devastated by the San Domingo cyclone . . . for an extent more than four blocks square buildings have been levelled to the ground and the earth has been gashed as if by the teeth of great glaciers'.[23] By 1950 the long, squat bulk of Central Station had filled part of the hole south of Dorchester. The tall Aviation Building rose on its eastern edge, to be completed that year. The rest, however, was cratered desolation, bespeaking a tumbled dream.

The Mount Royal tunnel, the work of Mackenzie and Mann of the Canadian Northern, had been opened for traffic in October 1917. It was a product of large plans and discreet real estate dealing which had produced title to some 5,000 acres of farmlands on the north side of the mountain and thirty or so acres of invaluable city property in the heart of Montreal. In Mackenzie and Mann's vista the farms beyond the mountain were to become the 'model city' of Mount Royal. For the railway terminal and the development they foresaw about it they had acquired ownership of some five blocks in the central area of the city, bounded on the north and south by Cathcart and Lagauchetière and on the east and west by University and Mansfield.

The completion of the tunnel, however, and the arrival of the first train had been followed all too quickly by the collapse of Mackenzie and Mann, the bankruptcies of the Canadian Northern and the Grand Trunk and the series of amalgamations that produced the nationalized railway. Sir Henry Thornton, taking over the enterprise in 1922, had inherited a dormant plan which he set about to revive. Over a period of seven years and with the help of some eighty-two engineers, architects and designers, he formulated his project and even produced a model. There was to be no piecemeal building. The development of the whole block of inner city property was to be within the frame of a master plan. Central to it all and bestriding the tunnel's exit would be the head office, the passenger terminal and the freight terminal of the railway, all housed in one massive skyscraper. Around that, and always conforming to the plan, would be streets, boulevards and buildings laid out by private developers on the most valuable land in Canada.

In 1930 Parliament approved the plan and the railway's excavation teams proceeded to knock down buildings and dig the enormous hole. They had not reckoned, however, with Camillien Houde, the mayor of Montreal, who disliked Thornton's plans and considered his model ugly. A rousing civic outcry was enhanced by the woes of the depression and Parliament's mind changed. The work was stopped, the construction crews were called off and only the hole remained.

In 1938, mainly as a makework project for the unemployed of the city, it was decided to build a station. When that was completed in 1943 it was far different from Thornton's gaudy original. Built by practical railwaymen who were hard up for funds, it was set in part of the hole, long, squat and low, and barely rose to the Dorchester Street level. But it proved to be superbly functional and built even in adversity with an eye to better times. Thornton's plans were remembered, provision was made for expansion and somewhere deep in the vaults of the railway's archives Thornton's model was kept. There was that, there was the rest of the hole and there was the Aviation Building as one private development when Gordon came to the bridge.

He was looking down on an eyesore which represented some twenty-four acres of unproductive real estate and a huge potential revenue. The city was in the doldrums with the great scar in its middle and the various departments of the railway with its head office on McGill Street were scattered about in twenty-two locations. In the air over that hole, if it could be studded with steel and concrete and tall aluminum towers, there could be transformation for the city and a new accession of affluence for the harried CNR. Thornton's old vision, haunting the new president, began to revive again.

The basis of Gordon's thinking was the same as that of his predecessor. The railway's own facilities, which would not produce revenue, should be a small part of the development. The greatest share of the property must attract private builders, drawn to the new location, confident in Montreal and prepared to risk millions. There was, however, an essential first proviso. 'I have to show my confidence in that real estate,' said Gordon, 'before I can get anybody else to do it.'[24]

Along about 1952, says Norman MacMillan, 'Donald and I started to talk about the value of the hole. We got out Thornton's old model, dusted it off, set it up in a 'model room' in Central Station and began to play with it.'[25] The Aviation Building had materialized as a world centre for the industry through the efforts of C. D. Howe and Herbert Symington. Trans-Canada Airlines was thinking of a new headquarters and wanted it in Montreal. There were other nibbles and prospects all indicating interest and pointing to large building. Above all, with reviving times for business and a flow of annual conventions, there was need for a new hotel. A hotel, however, was a traffic builder and an actual asset for the railway. When a new model emerged, 'flossied up a bit', the hotel was a flagship project and as a proof of Gordon's confidence it was to be built by the CNR.

'Yesterday,' wrote John Maffre in the Montreal *Star* on October 29, 1953, 'Donald Gordon, president of the Canadian National Railways, bestrode Dorchester Street like a colossus, standing waist-deep in 28-storey buildings while he built in half an hour a modern business and hotel centre whose 24 acres were double the size of New York's fabulous Rockefeller Center.'[26] The model envisaged a main entry to the area by a wide, tree-lined boulevard running from Sherbrooke southward along a transformed

McGill College Street and opening at its northward end on an imposing view of the mountain. Between Cathcart and Lagauchetière on the actual railway property there was to be an underground street, 'unique anywhere in the world with facilities for automobile, train, airplane and pedestrian traffic', while plans for the terminal area included a large open plaza extending from Cathcart to Dorchester and from Mansfield Street on the west to McGill College Street on the east. The CNR itself was planning a headquarters building adjacent to Central Station but that would probably be delayed for three years. During those years, assuming the approval of the budget in 1954, the new hotel would be built. Planned for a thousand rooms, capable of housing 4,000 guests and catering to 2,500 at convention functions, it represented an investment of $20 million. 'I would decline to place an estimate on the cost of the entire terminal project,' Gordon said, 'the figures would sound too spectacular.' What he could predict, however, was 'other buildings, shopping centres, theatres, high-class stores and business quarters constructed by private interests. I expect negotiations can be completed soon and work started after we build our hotel.'[27]

With that October announcement there had been a new spring-like quickening in Montreal itself. The press showing, however, had been lacking one detail. 'When we were talking about a name for the hotel,' says Norman MacMillan, 'we wanted one that would have some significance to Montreal and attract tourists to a French-Canadian metropolis. We tossed "Champlain" around, somebody mentioned "Maisonneuve" and we consulted a University of Montreal professor who came up with "Bonaventure". That one we liked; it suggested voyageurs and coureurs de bois and that was fine, but then somehow we got worrying that it also hinted of chancy risks and gambling. In any case it didn't seem too important and we hadn't made up our minds.'[28] The new hotel, when it was first unveiled to the reporters, was a project without a name.

CHAPTER 14

Making Money

The president rebuilding a railway and determined to show a profit had entered along with marriage on the rainbow years of his term. The pot of gold was elusive and the company's fortunes, judged by the bottom line, still oscillated wildly. The predicted small surplus for 1953 was less than a quarter of a million. It was followed in 1954 by the 'crushing disappointment' of a $28.7 million deficit. Yet in 1955, as freight rates were increased and the country's boom took off, the black figures returned. A surplus of $10.7 million in that year rose in 1956 to $26.1 million, the largest and last surplus of the whole Gordon regime. Results changed with a nerve-racking responsiveness to the flow of national traffic, yet it was possible to hope in a good year that the upward trend had come. The company had broken even in 1952 and since then, in spite of the one large dip, it had averaged out to an annual net revenue of $1.7 million.

Gordon had pruned the rambling corporate structure from the eighty companies he began with to a total of forty-five. He had set in motion a host of technical advances. He was at home, if sometimes stormily, with all his senior executives and he had an eye for new men. 'Never in its history,' he said in 1956, 'has the railway been so involved in change and adjustment. In virtually every phase of its activity the Canadian National is conducting analytical studies or carrying out tests and research, trying new methods and striving to keep in touch with developing technology.'[1] His own method, he was once quoted as saying, was to decide to do the impossible and then hire others to carry out his orders. Following that prescription, he had made some notable recruits. In Robert A. Bandeen, an economist of twenty-six with a formidable scholastic background, and in Pierre Taschereau, a many-faceted lawyer and student of transport problems, he had a future president and chief executive officer and a future chairman of the board. Ralph Vaughan of Halifax, stolen from C. D. Howe, was on the road to a vice-presidency and a role as shrewd adviser. So was Omond Solandt, distinguished in many technologies, who had been attracted for a few years to the field of railway research.

With Star Fairweather, the erratic genius and autocrat at the head of Research and Development, Gordon had a working truce; they disliked, admired and sparked the best from each other with the clash of new ideas. To Metcalf, Bromley and the others who did not socialize with the president the bibulous night-time Gordon was the stuff of office stories. What they saw was a well-honed mind at work, constantly under pressure. 'When we had something on,' Metcalf says, 'we'd just take lunch at his desk—chicken sandwich, piece of apple pie, coffee, brought up by his chauffeur—I never remember an occasion when we had a drink.'[2] On the other hand, relieving some of the pressure and enlivening office conferences, was an old Gordon potential. 'He really had a devilish sense of mischief,' remembers Ainslie Kerr who was then a junior listener. 'In many ways he was like a small boy. In the middle of a very serious situation, sitting there with his solemn look and his thick glasses, you'd suddenly know he'd seen a ridiculous side or been struck by something funny. There'd be the trace of a curl at the corner of his mouth, a glint in his eye and then a minute later the crack would come. You could see him working them up—and he loved getting them out.'[3]

As Norman MacMillan was drawn closer to the president the small-boy aspect was one of his trials and delights. MacMillan knew railroading as Gordon never would, and was turned to when his master seethed with plans. 'He gave me a thousand laughs—he'd get himself all cranked up to do something and then he'd try it on me—I was the dog.' In many cases, as a watchdog and one with legal knowledge, he could skirt the edges of pitfalls. 'Gordon carried the ball and if he got into trouble we pulled him to hell out. That Pitt affair, for instance—he was so mad that first night he wanted to read his statement on the floor of the House of Commons. "You try it," I said, "and they'll impeach you."

' "What's that?"

' "Well, they march you out of the committee room and up to the bar of the House. You'll be on the floor, brother—in charge of the Sergeant-at-Arms."

'He blinked. "What are you trying to tell me?"

' "I'm telling you to shut up".'

There were other occasions in the office where a lion-tamer was called for. 'He raised hell—yelled and whooped and marched around with his face all screwed up—some of the guys didn't know whether to tell him to go to hell or kick him in the teeth—but nobody ever did either. Someone would pass me the word that he was in high gear and when I came in he'd usually calm down.'

As Gordon responded to MacMillan in the daily rubbing-along, he revealed some of his quirks. 'He didn't like planes,' MacMillan recalls. 'Even in his business car the walls seemed to close in on him. He had a kind of extended chesterfield built on one end so he could lie there and see the lights and country outside through the window. Then there was the night he got stuck in the office elevator. It was about six-thirty and I was still at my desk when the night watchman came running in. The elevator was stopped about a foot above the ground floor and there was a hell of a row coming from inside it. I dashed down and I recognized Gordon's voice. He was in there with Red, his chauffeur, and he was screaming, almost hysterical.

'I yelled in, told him to calm down and pry at the place where the doors met with a key or a knife or something. I knew his trouble was the darkness, so I struck my cigarette lighter when the door opened a crack and asked if he could see the flame. He said he could. Then I got the watchman to bring a metal waste basket, fill it with newspapers and set it on the tile floor in front of the elevator where it couldn't start a fire. I lit the papers to give him some real light and we talked for half an hour till the elevator men came. But by God he was limp when they got him out.'[4]

The Gael who feared darkness and was inclined to believe in spirits had a complement in the cool lawyer who liked to keep out of trouble. The one was the great planner but the other could measure risks and reduce the quota of mistakes. By 1955 the two were not only intimates but a smoothly working team; and by 1956, as executive vice-president, MacMillan was tacitly confirmed in the direct line of succession.

The CNR itself was becoming a better railway, modernized in equipment and much improved in morale. The dieselization program, with its first phase completed, was to be extended to cover the system in a matter of five years. Automation and electronic signalling procedures were advancing at the same pace; and telecommunications, particularly with the new telex, were one of the steady earners. Freight generated profits and Gordon was concerned with moving it by every form of transport. By 1956 he had transformed the railway's rolling stock through the purchase of nearly 24,000 freight cars, including double-deck automobile transporters, new piggy-back carriers and many other specialties. Supporting this development were the new marshalling yards from one coast to the other. In Montreal in 1956 work began at last on the Côte-de-Liesse humpyard. It was to be one of the largest in North America, making up trains by computer and closed-circuit television, and its prospects fascinated Gordon to the exclusion of much else. 'I was poking away at him all the time about a headquarters building,' says MacMillan, 'but he always countered with his plans for Côte-de-Liesse. Finally he said, "Listen, we'll start the humpyard this spring and your office building next spring—okay?" And I said, okay—that was the deal.'⁵

In the case of passenger business, though MacMillan and Dingle were mildly optimistic, Gordon dragged his feet. New equipment was added on some of the main lines and old cars were modernized. A long series of experiments began with budget meals in diners, cafeteria cars, 'incentive fares' and various forms of excursions. Tourist and convention promotions produced some added traffic, but nothing convinced the president that he was onto a good thing. He was not enthusiastic about ingenious minor gimmicks, such as smaller plates in diners which made the steaks look larger. He looked at the figures on all passenger business and bemoaned the stubborn loss. Where it was worst of all, in urban commuter services, he was often inclined to rant. 'I feel,' he said prophetically, 'that metropolitan areas are going to have to solve their own problems in the long run.'⁶ In the one field, moreover, that offered a hope of profit he let himself be outpaced by the CPR.

In 1954 the gleaming new stainless steel cars of 'The Canadian', the competing transcontinental, made their appearance. By March 1955 Gordon was sniffing at its domed scenic cars and piously telling the parliamentary committee that it was 'better to spend money on modernizing equipment in general'.⁷ A month later the CNR's Super-Continental took to the Montreal–Toronto–Pacific Coast run, but though it was a handsome new train it was not quite an answer. The Super-Continental, operating in conjunction with the Ocean Limited and the Nova Scotian, cut sixteen hours off the old time between Halifax and Vancouver, but it came in an hour and a half behind The Canadian. Gordon haughtily refused to engage in a 'speed war' with the Canadian Pacific, but railway men thought otherwise. By 1956, though the Super-Continental had shaved its time by a matter of forty minutes, there was still some stinging comment. The CNR, said *Canadian Transportation,* 'looks like a bunch of amateurs when it comes to going after passenger business . . . please, please, Mr. Gordon, can't we show Mr. Crump our tail lamps just once?'⁸

That aim was to be achieved by the clipping of an additional hour and fifteen minutes from the schedule, but it would wait for another year. Meanwhile, over the course of three years, a dispute with Lionel Chevrier who was now engaged in building the St. Lawrence seaway had simmered down to a conclusion. Hardly welcomed by the rail carriers, the great new waterway was not only threatening traffic; it was also imposing changes. Between Cornwall and Cardinal a forty-mile section of the CNR's main line would have to be shifted to make way for flooding, while stations, yards and round-houses were to be torn down and rebuilt. Facing this, Gordon's reaction was firm. 'We start off in the frame of mind,' he said, 'that we are quite satisfied with the facilities we already have.'[9] If the seaway wanted changes it could expect to pay the shot; and he applied this more particularly to its plans for Montreal. Here the CNR trains crossed the St. Lawrence by the Victoria Bridge, which was venerable, costly and historic but impeded navigation. 'They're going to cut my track and cut my bridge,' he said to Norman MacMillan, 'and I don't mind them doing it but I'm going to be paid.'[10]

The projected work, however, became more complex than he expected. Over a hundred trains a day crossed the bridge and it was estimated that about a hundred ships a day would be passing up and down the St. Lawrence. 'What we need,' said one engineer, 'is a bridge with a lift span that raises and lowers itself sixty feet in five seconds, allowing ships to steam under-neath at fifty knots.'[11] The assorted impossibilities called for another plan, and what it came to involve eventually was a ship canal and lock paralleling the St. Lawrence. Over this were two vertical lift spans, one at either end. When a ship entered the lock a first span was lifted, severing the line of rail. At the same time, however, a long section of trackage—in railway parlance a 'shoofly'—swung out from the bridge itself to connect with the second span and allow trains to cross. The reverse process, when the ship left the lock, diverted trains to the first span and kept traffic moving. It was a large and ingenious plan which Gordon came to admire, but it was well in a cloudy future at his first meeting with Chevrier.

'It soon became clear,' the head of the Seaway Authority has recalled, 'that this was going to be anything but an informal talk. Gordon was flanked by Star Fairweather and Norman MacMillan. The atmosphere in the office was formal, almost chilly. After some discussion unmarked by any spirit of compromise I was forced to point out that the rights of navigation took priority over those of rail traffic.'[12]

The response was a first sample, soon to become familiar, of the presi-dential roar. 'I'll be damned if anybody is going to tell me that a canal has got priority over a railway!'[13] From that, concludes Chevrier, 'the discussion quickly reached a point where both of us obdurately refused to concede any-thing.'[14] In the long run, however, as Gordon came to realize, the cards were stacked against him. George Marler, the new minister of transport, who was cast in the role of arbiter, pointed out the facts: the rights of navigation were superior to those of rail. MacMillan as the railway lawyer, less suave than usual, tried to tell Chevrier that 'your god-damned ditch' ran a hundred yards inland and was not a part of the seaway.[15] St. Laurent joined in, mildly amused by the contenders, to emphasize the legal principle and rebuke the hard language.

By this time, driven to concede the paramount rights of the seaway, Gordon was concerned with costs, of which he intended to pay none. Chevrier had other ideas. 'I was still adamant that such expensive additions were not all the seaway's responsibility. . . . Gordon was getting one-third of a new bridge and we should not be asked to pay for this.' As the months passed plans for the work took shape and there were various announcements of agreement between the Seaway Authority and the railway on the changes to Victoria Bridge. 'Perhaps unfortunately,' says Chevrier, 'we did not say *what* agreement we had come to.'[16] Ultimately the transport minister had to decide that. At a meeting in Montreal from which Gordon chose to be absent, perhaps for the sake of peace, Marler delivered his verdict. 'You two guys,' he said to Chevrier and MacMillan, 'have got to quit fighting. Lionel, you build your canal; Norman, you build your bridge. You'll each keep your costs and later on we'll arbitrate them.'[17] On March 22, 1956, with that summary conclusion to the two years of battle, formal agreement was signed and the engineers and the bulldozers were allowed to go to work.

Labour relations for the president had settled down to the status of a normal problem. In 1954, as the railways faced the unions under the threat of another strike there were no flaring statements. The immoveable body and the irresistible force simply waited for the inevitable. Legislation was threatened, arbitration conceded and on August 19 the Vancouver *Province* announced in optimistic headlines, 'Railway Strikes Ended Perhaps for All Time'.[18] St. Laurent praised the unions for 'patriotic labour statesmanship' and voiced the conviction that for practical purposes the railway strike 'just can't be used'.[19] Whatever the truth of that, there were sizeable gains in wages and by 1956 a new health and welfare plan had been installed in the CNR through the joint work of a union-management committee. In the annual report Gordon could point to two-year agreements with all the major unions and there were no pending disputes.

One thing Gordon had recognized was the restlessness and insecurity brought on by change and adjustment. He had tried to cope with that through a broad range of instruction courses, all arranged in cooperation with the unions. By 1956 the company had over two thousand men who had gone through the first phase of diesel training and were moving on to the next. Operations, maintenance, office management, data processing, computer work and freight, passenger and accounting work were the subject of

other courses. They were removing some of the fears that went with automation and some of the benefits of progress were being shared by the staff.

W. J. Smith, as one of the old-time union men, had a good word for the
work. 'All the old procedures went out the window. There were new machines and procedures to do the jobs, and the unions worked out the retraining plans with management. You could walk into the old Turcot yard
offices and see grey-haired men who had spent their lives with a pencil
making up train manuals and consists sitting at those machines and the
car-checkers sitting at TV screens checking the trains as they came into the
yards. It was amazing how many were able to adapt so late in life. It was a
trying period in some ways and we did have our failures, but basically morale
improved. It was a more pleasant working day.'[20]

On June 1, 1954, construction began on the still unnamed hotel and by the
end of 1955, along with the announcement of his first substantial surplus,
Gordon could point to 'the steel skeleton of the structure clearly visible on
the Montreal skyline'.[21] He was less alert to problems surrounding the
structure though there had been some early warnings. The large plans were
encountering large objections which he simply brushed aside.

The hotel, as he saw it, was to be one of the finest in the world and if it
was to be a profitable investment for the railway it would lean heavily on
convention business attracted from the United States. With this thought in
mind he had been highly receptive to overtures from Conrad Hilton of the
famous Hilton chain. That lank, mild-spoken genius who had started out
from a filling-station in New Mexico and built an empire from nothing
appealed instantly to Gordon and returned the feeling in kind. His proposition was the usual Hilton arrangement, improved for a special case. The
company, with its world-wide experience of hotels and facilities for attracting business, would take over the management and return a percentage of
profits. Where the usual return, however, was twenty-five per cent, the
Canadian National would receive a full third.

There was also an impressive codicil. The terms offered Gordon improved
so much on the chain's usual arrangements that they were to be kept confidential; otherwise there would be complaints from other Hilton hotels.
Despite some reluctance on the part of his board and some doubts raised by
MacMillan Gordon decided to accept. 'He worried the thing to death for a
couple of days—that was one of his techniques—and then made up his
mind: "I'm for it."

' "That's all right," I said, "I'm still agin it."

' "Why?"

' "Well, it's not a bad idea but it's not a good one either. We've got hotels of our own—good ones. To some extent it's a reflection on us if we turn to an American chain to operate this one".'[22]

MacMillan, however, was obviously impressed by Hilton and merely sitting on the fence. Gordon took the plunge. It was announced on November 16, 1954, that the CNR had concluded a five-year agreement with Hilton which would become operational when the hotel was ready for occupancy, probably in 1957. Following that came the rumble of the first storm.

'Canada's Dignity Hurt by CNR Hotel Plans,' announced a headline in the Kitchener *Record* on January 13, 1955.[23] Protests by the Hotel Association of Canada had reached the House of Commons and appeared on the order paper. The president was assailed by reporters on one of his trips to Ottawa and gave them a brusque reply: 'I don't know what you're talking about. I don't know of any protest made by hotel associations and I don't know what business it is of theirs, either.'[24] By March he and members of the parliamentary committee were engaged in familiar roles. Not only American management but the cooperative deal with Hilton was attracting political suspicion. Gordon, however, not only refused to change; he refused to open the books. The choice of the hotel's management and the terms on which it was arranged were both business decisions, within his power to make. The deal with Hilton was highly advantageous, but he would not reveal the particulars. Why not? Because if he revealed how good it was Hilton would be in trouble with all his other hotels. The CNR would be in trouble if it became a business sieve, making its affairs public. 'You seem,' he said to one of his persistent naggers, 'to have started a new regime in respect of how to treat the president of the CNR . . . no other executive that I know of in the country would stand for it or put up with it for a minute.' On that note and at that point the ruling of a friendly chairman closed off discussion.[25]

The seeds of a larger discussion were sprouting at the same time. In the offices and boardrooms of the company the desultory search for a name had been brought to an abrupt conclusion. On November 3, 1954, just two weeks before the Hilton arrangement was made, it was announced that the new hotel would be called The Queen Elizabeth. 'We are now authorized,' said Gordon, 'to announce that with the personal permission of Her Majesty, the largest and most modern hotel in the Commonwealth will bear the most illustrious name in the Commonwealth.'[26]

To a loyal Scot and his wife, in the coronation aura, it was in every way fitting. Gordon was personally delighted and the letters filtering up to him through his channels of communication seemed to bear him out. There had been hundreds of suggestions, he said, covering 'a wide range of historical and geographical names. But by far the largest number of both French and English citizens writing me wished the name to be identified in some form with the Crown.'[27] Yet, for all that, he had hardly imposed the choice.

In MacMillan's terse summary, 'Bang out of the blue we discovered that the Queen had consented to the hotel being named after her. Someone had approached the governor general or one of the people on his staff, just asking them to inquire what the procedure was in London if we wanted to obtain permission. The next thing we knew, we had it. The prime minister approved —thought it was very nice that the Queen had agreed—and people in his office with people from the University of Montreal worked out the French version of the name, 'Le Reine Elizabeth'. It was all on a high level—right at the very top—Donald and I were totally out of our water. He was the one who was condemned for it, but the poor bugger had nothing to do with it.'[28]

Somehow, along a chain that led from the railway's public relations department to the Secretary of State's office and on up from there, a casual inquiry had become transformed to a request and the request graciously granted. It might have been as graciously withdrawn if diplomacy had seen the necessity, but no diplomat and no official did. In the House of Commons a French-Canadian member got a motion as far as the order paper, asking that the name Queen Elizabeth be changed to Chateau Maisonneuve or some other name reflecting the French character of the city. The St-Jean-Baptiste Society circulated a petition which was said to carry two hundred and fifty thousand names by the time it reached the president, but nobody bothered to count. *Maclean's Magazine* came in on another tack, lecturing Gordon for allowing the Queen's name to become a subject of controversy; while the sharp-tongued Judith Robinson, writing in the Toronto *Telegram*, suggested the adding of fuel. 'It might be an idea if the Grand Orange Lodge of British America were to take over where the Société-St-Jean-Baptiste left off and suggest to Mr. Gordon that it is not seemly thus to impose on Royal courtesy only in order to make the name of Canada's monarch a catchy trademark for a U.S. chain hotel subsidiary.'[29] Yet in Quebec's own legislature, dominated by Maurice Duplessis, a motion to rename the hotel Chateau Maisonneuve was defeated 57–17 in a straight party vote. To the president of the CNR a minor question was settled and he had larger affairs in hand.

In Montreal, as the new hotel was rising on the city's skyline, another figure loomed on Gordon's horizon. William Zeckendorf of New York, who had joined the small firm of Webb and Knapp in the middle Thirties, had made it the greatest speculative developer of real estate in North America.

He had changed the fish markets and slums that bordered the East River into a home for the United Nations, and his wide streets and skyscrapers had rejuvenated the decaying cores of other cities. Smooth, jovial and rotund, with all the qualities of a high-living promoter, he was used to enormous risk-taking, dealt and talked in millions and was usually better than his word. In 1955, with his attention turned to the north, he appeared in Gordon's office.

'He and his party had come in by their private plane,' says Lloyd Morgan, 'and they looked like Arctic explorers—bush clothes, heavy beards—all the rest of it.'[30] The dramatic entry was quite in the style of Zeckendorf, but its purpose was to see the 'great, angry-looking open cut where railroad tracks ran out of a 3-mile tunnel under Mount Royal'. At the end of that gaunt prospect was the newly rising hotel, and the intended signal of confidence had at last found a receiver. 'I thought I was going to have to sell him,' Zeckendorf quotes Gordon as saying, 'but after a walk around the place he was selling me.'[31]

Within another month Gordon was in New York, much impressed as he was intended to be by the spectacular office of the promoter, the constant flow of calls and the staff of two hundred and fifty architects, planners and builders, all hard at work. He was more impressed, however, by Zeckendorf's proposition. The great gap of twenty-two idle acres in the heart of Montreal scandalized the American and challenged him. He saw in it the potential for a new centre of gravity and a fresh start for the city. What he wanted to do was develop the whole area, starting with a 4-acre section which Webb and Knapp would lease and on which they would complete a building within a period of five years. The tall, cruciform tower of Place Ville-Marie was not yet in being or even quite envisaged but its embryo had been conceived. As proof of that a plan and model for the building and the whole surrounding development would be prepared at a cost of some $250,000 which Webb and Knapp would absorb.

Gordon blinked. 'Without obligation?'

'With no obligation at all.'

The president shrugged and agreed; he knew a gambler when he saw one and he recognized a fellow actor. He was also well on the way to acquiring a boon companion who gave him deserved respect. 'He was the only man I know who could outdrink me,' Zeckendorf recorded later. 'When he was a third through I had had it.'[32] For his part, Gordon was to ascribe his good relations with Zeckendorf to the fact that 'we're both the biggest hams in North America'.[33] All this was still at an early stage but he was convinced of one thing: he had found the man who would fill the rest of the hole.

By the spring of 1956 the preliminary plans and model had arrived in Montreal. They dwarfed the plans of the past in the glow of a new prospectus, dazzling as the work itself:

> In the heart of Montreal lies a row of three great blocks which ought to belong to the living centre of the city. Yet they are nearly untouched by the busy life around them . . . the plan proposes to transform these three blocks into a city within a city. It calls for a complex of modern buildings related to each other within their own spacious setting, and at the same time organically wed to the rest of Montreal.
>
> When completed this city in microcosm will bear the proud name of Ville Marie, a name given . . . in 1642 to the first European settlement on the island. . . .
>
> The most striking element of the Ville Marie plan is the metal and glass tower—a cruciform skyscraper 550 feet in height with forty floors of office space. . . . This structure, the tallest and largest in Canada, is designed to house major corporations, four of which will be provided with their own separate ground floor lobbies. Each office floor contains an area of 38,000 square feet. The cross shape gives the building elegance of proportion and also permits natural light to flood through the working area.
>
> At the foot of the tower stretches a spacious Plaza . . . only pedestrians will move on Place Ville Marie, which is reached from St. Catherine Street by a tree-lined Mall extending the line of McGill College Avenue. Along the Mall the way leads gently upward, overpassing Cathcart Street and the sunken promenade, onto the broad free space of Place Ville Marie. Here is the monumental focal point of the city. On one side stands the cruciform tower, and in the distance rises the mighty outline of Mount Royal.[34]

Nor was this all. 'Place Ville Marie is only the upper deck of a many-platformed scheme which ties the development into the activities of the surrounding city.'[35] Directly beneath the Place would be the great Concourse, a glittering, sheltered netherworld of shops, theatres and restaurants, service centres and walkways leading to the buildings above. And with all that two more blocks remained:

> The two southerly blocks are planned to contain additional elements which will make them the transportation centre of the city as well as the convention and trade-display hub of Eastern Canada . . . the Central

Station of the Canadian National Railways, two office buildings and The Queen Elizabeth are supplemented by a large structure fronting on Laugauchetière Street.[36]

The large structure was to become MacMillan's headquarters building. To Zeckendorf's great regret the boulevard running to Sherbrooke Street and opening on a view of the mountain would be somehow lost by the way. There would be other changes in the plan and in the streets round the development, creating assorted troubles. One of the required changes, the knocking-down of the St. James Club, would make Gordon anathema to some of his old friends. The great, cruciform building towering up in the model would have a million and a half square feet of office space, not one of which was bespoken. Money loomed for Zeckendorf as a multi-millioned problem, and the plan was not approved. There would be six months of study by the railway's engineers and five more by the government before that came about. But Montreal was humming with the very thought of the plans, and it had become the Montreal of Jean Drapeau. Gordon's luck was holding; he was again the man for the times.

At the centre of all planning was The Queen Elizabeth Hotel. On the outside it was beginning to near completion, and on the inside it was a hive of assorted experts concerned with fittings and décor. The fitting-out of his flagship was a relentless theme with Gordon and he worried every detail. The colour of bathroom basins, the tableware and the drapes were subjects of long discussions which he continued at home with Norma. 'He'd sit with me in the study asking my advice about things—none of which he took, of course.'[37] The twenty-one storeys and 1,216 guest rooms were planned first and foremost with the convention delegate in mind. The Grand Salon was to provide accommodation for two thousand people at dinner or three thousand at meetings. Escalators were to climb from the main lobby to a Convention Floor equipped with its own kitchens, bar, meeting rooms and foyer. Sliding moveable partitions would divide the space of the floor into large and smaller conference rooms in which as many as a dozen medium-sized conventions could be held at the same time. Hilton's world-wide network was to draw the delegates in and they were to lack nothing in comfort or facilities for a good time.

The choice of manager was all-important to Gordon, and though he admired the efficiency of the Hilton chain, he was not to be overawed. The first candidate proposed by Conrad Hilton was quick to discover that. Arriving in Montreal for a meeting with CNR executives, he proved to be as brash as the dollar sign and as loud as the stars and stripes. Starting out with the proposal that the stodgy, monarchical name, Queen Elizabeth, should be changed to Hilton Elizabeth, he outlined his other conceptions to a wall of stony faces. When he had finished Gordon rose and delivered himself of a story that was prelude to a brusque farewell.

He was somehow reminded, he said, of a lusty young man from a small town in the west who had paid a visit to New York. Having heard much talk of the city's professional ladies, he had brought along an address. It was something like 54 East 32nd Street, but the young man in his excitement had managed to reverse the figures. When his taxi driver put him down it was in front of a large brownstone edifice at something like 32 East 54th Street. He climbed the inviting steps, pushed the doorbell and when the door opened favoured a startled dowager with a brisk slap on the behind. 'Okay, lady—where's the girls?' There was a loud scream, a burly butler materialized and the visitor picked himself up after a hard landing on the street. 'Lady,' he said as his vocal powers returned, 'you people in New York may be pretty smart, but I can tell you one thing. You've still got a lot to learn about how to run a whorehouse.'[38]

After this fiasco a chastened Conrad Hilton came up with another man. Donald Mumford, who had transformed the aging Statler into one of the best hotels in Detroit, was invited to accept the challenge of The Queen Elizabeth. During his first week with Gordon the only thing he was sure of was that Gordon liked his wife. 'Mrs. Mumford,' the president said, concluding an early meeting, 'I've got no comment about your husband. All I'm prepared to say at the moment is that we're pleased you're here.'[39]

From that ambiguous beginning relations began to ripen. Mumford was a good hotel man, Gordon knew what he wanted, and in the eyes of both The Queen Elizabeth was unique. It was at a centre of cosmopolitanism where two cultures met and the very fact of that meeting, the atmosphere it created, would have world-wide appeal. There would be no hotel dining rooms, there would be a dozen separate restaurants, each distinguished for its English or French Canadianism. The guest in The Queen Elizabeth would be served by a bilingual staff, choose from a bilingual menu, read bilingual signs. He would eat and drink and sleep as well as he could anywhere in the world, and he would sense at the same time that he was in the Paris of North America.

It was a large ambition for a Scot and a hotel man from Detroit, and it was based on their own assumptions. The hotel in French Canada was hardly French Canadian but it was not intended to be; it was a hotel for all the world. That, in the president's eyes, was all that had to be thought of. 'He came into an English milieu in Montreal,' says Norma Gordon, 'and he didn't learn from the English what the problems were—he didn't even know there *was* a problem.'⁴⁰ Within his own frame of reference he was satisfied with his plans and he was soon satisfied with Mumford. 'Some of my laddies,' he said, 'will try to tell you how to run your job. If they do I want you to tell them to kiss your ass. Do I make myself clear, Mumford?— if you're in trouble come to me.'⁴¹

With his investment promising well, the president was settled firmly on his good intentions. The hotel was going to be a moneymaker, a boon to Montreal, and it would reflect the character of the city. What more could anyone want? There were many answers to the question, and they were far older than Gordon, but one came from *Le Devoir*. 'We have not spoken of a Canadian republic for a long time,' wrote André Laurendeau. 'However, Mr. Donald Gordon imposes the subject on us. He arranges to clamp on our heads the QUEEN ELIZABETH symbol of the Crown. Thus the name of a hotel, given by a civil servant in despite of the popular will, poses symbolic-ally the problem of the regime.'⁴²

As he rounded out his seventh year in office the president's railway seemed to be well on track. So did his own life. If Norma Gordon had ever intended to change him she had not had much success. He was still the heavy drinker and he could still be the public rowdy, disrupting sedate occasions. There were the bad evenings when Norma left humiliated or was helped to help him home and there were brisk exchanges with his mother-in-law who remained a potent force. 'And yet,' said one observant pessimist from Ottawa, 'I always felt that marriage got on rather better than I'd expected.'⁴³

'I was often mad enough to kill him,' says Mrs. Hobbs. 'He was the total egoist, the most completely selfish man I've ever known—and yet when the chips were down he was always extremely generous.'⁴⁴ Known as 'Donnie' or 'Pussy' in the Hobbs family where there was a taste for such diminutives, he had a persistent need for good relations with 'Ma'. He was a seeker of invitations to Sunday dinner with his in-laws, and he arrived often as a repentant sinner 'on the wagon' who was only drinking gin. At home at any time he was usually moderate with liquor; the public over-consumption seemed to be a sort of priming. 'A case of nerves,' diagnosed Mrs. Hobbs. 'I think it was shyness,' Norma Gordon says. 'Also he drank too fast—I think he didn't realize how much he was drinking. They'd give him another drink without his even asking for it—but of course if they didn't give him one he'd ask.'⁴⁵

Of one fact overriding all the failings both women were sure; he had a deep concern for his wife. The Gordon stories continued to enliven boardrooms and shock Westmount drawing-rooms, but they were not told within the hearing of Norma Gordon. He gave respect for respect, there was under-lying tenderness and as he began to approach his sixties there was another preoccupation. For all his big job and his fifty thousand a year, he was in no position to leave his wife secure.

That thought had come with a jarring shock as he considered the matter of his pension. It was zero, and would be zero until 1962. He had given only 'perfunctory consideration' to his transfer rights when he came from the Bank of Canada and they were now lost in a tangle of regulations. He was debarred from adding to his income by accepting lucrative directorships on the boards of private companies, and so far as pay was concerned the directing head of the world's largest railway was still in the minor leagues. His salary was about a fourth of that paid to the presidents of smaller American railways and it was half that of the president of the CPR or the heads of Canadian banks. In 1955, as he neared the end of the second of his three-year appointments, all that had to be thought of by a man who was getting on.

He took his problems to Ottawa for a discussion with St. Laurent, who proved as always an understanding friend. There was no doubt that the government wanted Gordon, and not much doubt that the president wanted to remain. But there were private offers elsewhere, and they were assuming a final tone; in three more years Gordon would be fifty-seven, with the time for changes gone. He was standing at a kind of watershed as he faced his reappointment and he wanted to have the ground surveyed. The pension tangle was fairly easily resolved with the help of Norman MacMillan. There could be no private directorships; the rules stood on that. For the rest, St. Laurent, as another man who was growing poor in office, was prepared to do what he could.

On March 7 Gordon reported to Symington, his oldest friend on the board. He had had a very good talk with the prime minister, who had agreed that salary should be made commensurate with responsibilities and that some increase was in order. 'I think,' he went on with a faintly peremptory note, 'I would be happier to stay with the CNR at least until I get the organization farther advanced and some clean-up of the many projects now in hand—so does my wife. But I also know this is probably the last occasion on which I will have much choice—so I want to get the matter settled.'[46] It was settled at the reappointment with the green light from Ottawa and some complaint from some of the country's newspapers. At a salary of $75,000 a year, the highest-paid public servant in Canada, the president went on with his projects.

On April 30, 1956, it was announced that the Donald Gordons had purchased a house on Edgehill Road, looking down toward the St. Lawrence River from the heights of Westmount. On May 9, before they had moved to its spacious, sunny rooms, Campbell Gordon was born, the son of Donald and Norma. Concurrent with the baby's baptism, which was to take place in the Melville Presbyterian Church where Gordon and Norma had been married, the father developed an interest in the claims of formal religion. The Reverend Charles Cochrane, who was a salty man himself, was drawn in to support them.

'He boxed me in between Norman Vincent Peale and Billy Graham by asking me at fifteen-minute intervals what I thought about each of them. Well, neither of them is my dish of tea, and I couldn't do anything but say so. Then we began to discuss, in a way that was unique in my experience, the implications of the Christian faith and I remember him telling me that he was not really good enough to be a member of the Christian church. I said, "Well, what do you think that makes me?—I don't consider myself a particularly good man." We went on from there, and the interesting thing is that I was making the claims and he was quoting the scripture to back them up. It was a fascinating thing, that magnificently retentive memory of his. It wasn't exactly display, but then again it was—and I still didn't know when I left him whether he was going to join the church or not.'[47]

He did join the church on the day of his son's baptism, but the pre-announcement was made in his own way. As the story came back to Cochrane, 'he walked in on a group of his cronies at the St. James Club and said, "On Sunday morning I'm going to do something that none of you sons of bitches can do—I'm going to carry my little son down the aisle and have him baptised".'[48]

At about the same time news of his first family was coming by peremptory telephone calls or transatlantic mail. Michael was in trouble as usual and this time at Bishop's, where 'my problem was liquor. . . . I didn't get thrown out, though, because I was a damn good football player . . . the question was whether to throw out Gordon or blow the football season.'[49] Disruptive, disapproved of and now becoming balkily independent, Michael had discovered 'justice' as it applied to football players and was acquiring arts of survival.

In 1955 Donnie had taken a Master of Arts degree in political economy at the University of Toronto. Following that, and a year with the *Financial Post*, he had disappeared abruptly in the direction of Oklahoma. Returning in September 1956 after six months of travel as the advance agent for a circus, he and Helen were now established in London. Much persuaded and well funded, he was enrolled at the London School of Economics in quest, as his father hoped, of a Ph.D. Pending that, however, came word of another event. On January 25, 1957, Donald John Gordon, born to Helen and Donnie, entered the world. The president of the CNR, a proud father in May, had also become a grandfather pursuing a new ambition. He had hopes, he told his friends, of becoming the first man in Canada to receive the old age pension and the baby bonus at the same time.

CHAPTER 15

Canadian National

On June 21, 1957, the government of John Diefenbaker was installed in Ottawa. In September George Hees, the new minister of transport, announced that Gordon's term as president of the CNR would be extended for three more years. The massive political upset was not displacing the senior public servant, but it had changed the atmosphere round him. A host of his old friends were gone in the great sweep and for the first time in his career, except for a brief eight months in the waning days of Bennett, he was under a Conservative regime.

He was also into a period of heavy capital expenditures, generally declining traffic and disproportionate returns. Committed to modernization, the railway forged ahead. By 1960 dieselization was completed and the last steam locomotive retired from service. In the company's offices and marshalling yards, and along thousands of miles of its lines, automation, the computer and electronic signalling procedures were making up trains and moving them with new speed and precision. Trucks, trailers and freight cars were now mobilized at specially designed railheads, combining old competitors in profitable local shipments. On long hauls and short hauls improved equipment and efficiency reduced unit costs. Communications, branch building, general service to the country and even passenger service all reflected a decade of large expansion. In the ten years between 1950 and 1960 there had been capital expenditures of some $1.7 billion. They had produced, Gordon claimed, an annual saving of some $100 million in the cost of operations. Yet the results ground out by the automated book-keepers were locked in a stubborn trend. In 1957 the surplus of the previous year became a deficit of $29.5 million. Three years later, at a red-ink figure of $67.5 million, it plunged to a historic nadir.

The declines reflected as usual the general state of the economy, which was into a mild recession. Added to that were the burden of fixed charges, the increasing cost of labour, a variety of government restrictions and the always-disputed freight rates. There was some hope for change in the MacPherson royal commission, which by 1960 had produced thirty volumes of testimony on the state of transportation. There would be more hope when the country turned the corner, and by the end of 1960 the turn seemed to be in sight. Meanwhile, however, the profit-seeking president was occasionally hard to live with, and not the least so during his annual bouts in Ottawa with the parliamentary committee.

Haunting these sessions, moreover, was the still-unexorcised question of the name of the new hotel. In March 1957, during the last committee meeting under the regime of St. Laurent, it was raised by the Conservative member, Léon Balcer of Quebec. By that time the railway's theologians had provided a careful answer. The Queen Elizabeth had been selected as a name, said Gordon, because of 'a belief that it, of all names, would symbolize the unity between the two language groups in our country; that the Crown was the symbol of that unity and therefore the name of the Queen was most appropriate. . . . I can say definitely my considered opinion is that the great majority of the reasonable people of the province of Quebec find the name quite acceptable.'[1]

That considered opinion, though the committee received it mildly, struck sparks in Montreal. A week later, on March 27, Gordon looked down from the window of his fifth-floor office to see some five hundred high school and university students blocking McGill Street traffic. Stamping, singing, shouting and generally in high good humour, they paraded a straw-filled effigy of the president of the CNR and hung it from a corner lamp-post while grinning policemen watched. Signs bobbed under the figure with various hostile slogans: 'A New Name or Gordon's Hide'—'A French Name for Montreal's New Hotel'. Within another hour, however, the effigy was down from the lamp-post with most of the straw stamped out of it and pick-up trucks were clearing away the rubble. The chants had become an echo and McGill Street was again its peaceful self. As he drove home that evening to the heights of Edgehill Road the president could dismiss the incident as 'just a student lark'.[2]

It was not so easy to dismiss some other issues that rose with the new regime. By 1958, presenting his annual report to a Conservative-dominated committee, Gordon was faced with a notable new man. Douglas Fisher was not a Conservative member; he was the CCF giant-killer who had defeated C. D. Howe. A big man himself, almost as big as Gordon, he had been, as he liked to say, associated with the railway from birth. His mother was a pensioner of the company, he had friends among railway workers, and he had become a friend of the leftward-leaning Donnie in their years together at Queen's. More importantly than all that, he extended his sphere of interest from his own constituency of Port Arthur to the whole of northern Ontario. It was a region built by railways and the steam locomotive, served by many divisional points that had become railway towns and were now threatened by the advance of dieselization. 'Run-throughs'—the by-passing of division points by long-range diesel engines that did not require their service—had become a northern nightmare. What was to become of the towns that had grown with the CNR, and the hundreds of railway workers who faced change or uprooting? It was a legitimate concern for a friend of railway labour and a member of the CCF, and Fisher at first was mild. 'I don't think he was that unfair,' says Ainslie Kerr. 'I think he was asking reasonable questions and doing his job—as long as he kept his cool.'[3]

Cool, however, on both sides, was a hard thing to keep. In 1958, during the first skirmish on run-throughs, Gordon was merely firm. Dieselization was progress and progress pointed to profits; it would certainly have to be maintained. There would be broad changes but there would also be broad retraining plans and measures for relocation; workers would not suffer. In 1959, as Conservatives joined the heckling, Fisher widened his ground. After a long battle with the unions superfluous railway firemen had disappeared from diesels. Run-throughs were amalgamating divisions and certainly displacing men. Centralized traffic control, like progress in automation, was also costing jobs. Quite true, said the president, but new jobs would be found. There had been no suffering on the part of the diesel firemen; they had either been eliminated by attrition or pensioned off for life. Of course there had been much displacement, much uncomfortable adjustment, but he had been hired to run a railway. Could anyone there do better?

From that impasse discussion broke up as usual in barrages of scattered shot. Passenger service and schedules and the meals on company diners were old, familiar targets and they received their share of abuse. A grievance of small towns, the condition of local stations, was poignantly recalled by Fisher. In the station at Long Lac, he said, 'The rest room was so cold you could see your breath. The smell left much to be desired.' Desired in what way, was Gordon's silken reply. 'What kind of smell would you like?'[4]

Another session ended with the deficit duly deplored and much of the proceedings magnified by radio and the daily press. The committee had once again 'gone several rounds with a bear'—Gordon had 'dominated' the committee and 'browbeaten' its members. Certainly he had been definite enough in one of his parting shots: 'If you come to the conclusion that we are not an efficient management, for God's sake fire the lot of us!'[5]

In the face of all that, Fisher was still mild. On May 15, 1959, he wrote to the Sudbury *Star* pointing out that reports of Gordon's 'tongue-lashing' of members of parliament were very considerably exaggerated. 'I asked Mr. Gordon more questions than any other MP for obvious reasons (there are more CNR divisional points, mileage and employees in Port Arthur constituency than in any other in Canada). Finally, as the committee was about to close, I asked him for suggestions on how to improve and speed the annual scrutiny. He made several constructive suggestions that won general approval.'[6]

By 1960, however, with deficits plaguing the system, dieselization completed and many of his own constituents in the throes of discontent, Fisher had shed his gloves. So had the willing Gordon, who was more than ready for the fight. 'How *can* we keep our noses out of your business?' asked the parliamentarian in committee. 'My answer to that,' said the glowering railway president, 'is that you just must.'[7]

A long battle had been joined, centring on an old problem. 'Like most free enterprise types,' says Fisher, 'Gordon hated to admit that a large corporation should have social goals. Whether he liked it or not, when you're a government railway you get stuck with obligations to communities, obligations that arise out of the political process and out of bastards like me. Gordon never really wanted to talk about that or face it.'[8]

What he did face was the question Fisher avoided. The first of his obligations was to provide an efficient railway, and what was the test of that? Gordon's answer was the measuring-stick of profit; Fisher's answer was service, yet he wanted a profit too. He was among those who were pointing to the red-ink budgets and saying Gordon must go. The president seemed, in fact, to be half gone already. The bland George Hees was not discussing renewal of the three-year appointment. The Toronto *Star* was noting this and drawing obvious conclusions. 'Is Gordon,' it asked in November 1960, 'out of Top CN Post?'[9]

He was not out; and though he was far from comfortably in, the railway still absorbed him. In 1950 he had come to an organization of eighty separate companies, three major districts and tangled lines of authority that all stemmed from the top. He had reduced the number of companies to a total of thirty-seven but the regions still remained; most of them too big, all with their own complexities and all depending ultimately on the decrees of head office. The grip of final authority remained in the president's hands, and he liked the feel of that. But there was too much of it and it was too loose; it denied responsibility and the motivation that came with it to the regional heads beneath him. He had forced himself to the conclusion, by 1958, that there had to be a large change.

The result was another call on Walter Gordon, the business consultant friend and the head of Clarkson Gordon. 'He asked me to reorganize the CNR,' says Walter Gordon, 'and I hesitated a bit. We don't work too well together. Donald had no feel for organization at all—he couldn't delegate. I told him right at the beginning, "You can't run the railway with every damn decision coming to you".'[10] That, said the other Gordon, was the admitted fact that prompted the invitation and the study went ahead. Geoffrey Clarkson, the firm's junior partner, spent well over a year on it with a large section of his staff, and eventually produced a plan.

When it reached the president's desk it was voluminous, complicated and radical enough to bring on an explosive meeting. 'It tentatively proposed to split the chairman's and the president's jobs,' says Robert Tarr, 'and give more authority to the executive vice-president. Walter Gordon and Geoff Clarkson came down to make the proposals and Gordon was very snarly about diminishing his authority. He was going to have none of that.'[11] Walter Gordon, commenting on the same meeting, carries the description further. 'He had a big hangover that morning and he was in no mood to be advised. He held forth himself on how the CNR should be organized—talked and shouted for two hours and I couldn't get a word in edgewise. So I just got up in the middle of his speech and went back to Toronto.'[12]

That afternoon, however, Tarr's telephone rang, and the president was on the line. 'I guess I didn't behave very well this morning.' 'No, you didn't.' 'Come on up—let's go over it again.'[13] The going-over took place, the night train left for Toronto, and at nine o'clock next morning the door opened in Walter Gordon's office and the president walked briskly in. 'Okay—you were entitled to get mad. Now what do we do?'[14]

The result announced in the annual report for 1960 was 'designed to mould the System into an instrument better able to adjust and respond to both the prevailing business climate and the shifts and new challenges of a highly competitive transportation market. . . . Responsibility and authority is being decentralized to the regional and area management levels on a geographic, as distinct from a departmental, basis . . . with five regions sub-divided into eighteen management areas or "business units", thus reducing the total number of administrative units below System Headquarters from forty-four to twenty-three.'[15]

The changes sounded formidable and they were met with varying re-actions. 'He ended up with areas instead of divisions,' says Stanley Dingle, 'and a lot of the boys on the areas never did know exactly what their job was . . . my impression is that it was all done too abruptly.'[16] It was a 'vertical' division of the organization, says Norman MacMillan—'top, Donald—me, half an inch below—and the whole company split between the two of us at this point—me looking after operations, Donald the financial affairs, policy, etc.'[17] Robert Bandeen, who was still well down in the chart, saw another effect: 'From the early Sixties Gordon changed his role and was really acting like the head of a holding company and trying to put people in place to run the operations—as basically he should have done.'[18]

Whatever diminishment Gordon felt he came to accept with grace. 'He switched right round,' says Robert Tarr, 'and I sometimes thought after that he didn't exercise enough push and authority. He was so anxious that he wouldn't appear not to be living up to the spirit of the new arrangement that he leaned over backward to keep hands off.'[19]

With modernization, reorganization and a push for passenger business featuring such novelties as CNR credit cards and 'Go Now—Pay Later' plans, came the urge for a new look. Gordon himself did not particularly feel it, but to some of the young men under him the new vitality of the railway was obscured by a fusty image. In the public relations department W. R. Wright and Charles Harris who succeeded him had mounted a cam-paign for change, spent a considerable amount of money and developed a plan that ultimately reached the president by way of the lower levels. 'Oh yeah,' he said one day when Harris nervously referred to it, 'I've been mean-ing to ask you—what's all this god-damned business about a new symbol? Stan Dingle's all upset—wants to know what you're doing to his boxcars and rolling stock.'[20]

Already out in the west, on an experimental basis, were a few of Dingle's boxcars wearing the 'wiggly worm'. A sinuous CN, it dispensed with the R for Railways and displaced the maple leaf which had been worn for forty years. It was the bald and fluid product of advanced modern design, and it produced wails from more traditionalists than Dingle. But it was simple, clean, it certainly suggested newness and it was inexpensive to apply. That much was about all that had yet developed as a philosophy behind the symbol, but Harris pressed his case. 'Okay,' said the president, agreeing to a demonstration, 'but you better make it good.'[21]

It was as good as Harris could make it with the help of slides, sound effects, a special script and a narrator. Gordon, MacMillan and Dingle sat in a darkened room while locomotives, passenger cars, boxcars, graphics, manuals, signs and every other facet of the company's public image passed across the screen, wearing the new emblem. The narrator's voice was persuasive and the cumulative effect good. MacMillan and Dingle gradually came round and finally Gordon himself, with reservations. He would go so far, he said, as to repeat the demonstration for the whole management committee and accept a group decision. 'I'm not going to say anything—just let you present it.'

At the larger show reception was at first mixed. There were uneasy rustles, the occasional mutter of complaint and a voice rose in the darkness, 'Is this what we want? I'm no expert on design, but—.' A growl interrupted the critic as the president broke his silence. 'If you haven't got anything to contribute, shut up!' That, says Harris, 'did it'.[22] The new symbol was in and by the time it came to be announced it had acquired its deeper meaning. 'Spelling out the letters "CN" in clean-flowing lines,' said the annual report for 1960, 'the trademark symbolizes the movement of men, materials and messages across the country.'[23] It had also another virtue which the president discovered later. 'Do you know why we're no longer the CNR but the CN?' he asked a member of the parliamentary committee in June 1961. 'CN is bilingual; CNR is not.'[24]

By the beginning of 1958 the plan for Place Ville-Marie was approved and Zeckendorf's new company, Webb and Knapp, Canada, was ready to go to work. First and all-important was the great cruciform building; and Io Ming Pei, the Chinese architect who was Zeckendorf's principal man, had finalized his design. He was to have Henry Cobb, one of his American colleagues, as chief assistant on the ground. Vincent Ponte, another noted American whose field was city planning, was engaged in coordination with the city of Montreal, while associated with all the work was the Canadian firm of architects, Affleck, Desbarats, Dimakopoulos, Lebensold, Michaud and Sise. Zeckendorf himself, however, was a haunt in Gordon's office, bruised by many rebuffs. The mortgage money required to commence building would only come with leases from prospective tenants, and there were no tenants to be had.

'We had a lease and a wonderful plan,' Zeckendorf recalled later, 'we had a great hole in the ground ready for filling, we even had a name for the project. But when we went looking for tenants every major company in Canada turned us down . . . we were in trouble from the beginning because we were strangers and foreigners.'[25] The plan threatened the 'stuffy stability' of St. James Street where banks and major companies had been based for years, and it was not helped in the eyes of the business barons by the

demolition of the St. James Club which lay in the path of change. In James
Muir, the president of the Royal Bank with which Zeckendorf had formed
connections, he had one combative supporter. Gordon stood committed with
the prestige of the CNR. Neither prestige nor high finance, however, seemed
able to procure tenants or solve the problem of funds. By mid-April, as the
time came for the opening of the Queen Elizabeth, the plan was standing
still.

Nevertheless, from Monday, April 14 to Wednesday, April 16, special
trains and planes brought celebrities from across the continent and poured
them into the hotel. Representatives of the federal and provincial governments, of the city of Montreal and of high society and the world of entertainment were all present and performing at a series of dazzling functions.
Conrad Hilton was there and the Hilton influence apparent in the air-
conditioned rooms, the individual temperature control, the new dial telephones, the general air of sleek efficiency and comfort and the sixty pages
of press kit that called attention to it all. More pervasive still, from the
hooked tapestry in the lobby with its scenes of Montreal to the *ancien
régime* uniforms designed for the bilingual staff, was the sense of atmosphere
and place. Whatever Wilfrid Gagnon, as a French-Canadian director, had
thought of the hotel's name, he had worked with Gordon, Mumford and a
select committee of artists to set character and décor. 'We met in frequent
consultations,' he said, 'suggested historical names for the suites and public
rooms, brought forth themes and suggested treatments of them . . . the
language was to be universal but the accent that of Quebec.'[26]

On April 14, after the stir of arrivals and reception, guests ascended to
the lofty elegance of Le Panorama for cocktails and a buffet supper. On the
15th the Beaver Club and Le Café welcomed them to breakfast, while for
those who were not up to it a swift and sumptuous room service put on a
sparkling display. Le Grand Salon received gentlemen at a luncheon sponsored by the Montreal Board of Trade and Le Chambre de Commerce, and
for ladies there was lunch and a fashion show in the salles Duluth and
Mackenzie. That evening a lively Canadian Carnival filled Le Grand Salon,
and on Dorchester Boulevard at high noon next day the Union Jack, the
red ensign of Canada, the fleur-de-lys of Quebec and the house flags of the
CNR and the Hilton chain rose with appropriate ceremony to the playing
of the national anthem and the roll of military drums. At the charity ball in
the evening, crowning the three days, bagpipes led the guests to the head
table. The master of the *Queen Elizabeth*, from somewhere in mid-Atlantic,
transmitted congratulations that were read by Norma Gordon. After that,
as French chanteuses were followed by Spanish dancers and the music of

Guy Lombardo by that of Denny Vaughan, all that remained was revelry.

Lloyd Morgan, the indispensable secretary and recorder of all engagements, had begun that day early. As Gordon's guide through all the intricacies of protocol, he had kept the president's agenda for each step of the events. For the third day he had completed his list in the small hours of the morning, sent it to Edgehill Road and followed it there himself at eight o'clock. He found his chief, however, considerably frazzled by much preceding ceremony and suffering from a hard night.

'He was sitting at the breakfast table in his dressing gown, hung over, in a foul humour and bitching about everything. Where the hell was his agenda? I told him it was sitting on his study desk since eight o'clock, just as he'd ordered. We went into the study but he didn't even look at it—he was in no condition to look—he just kept bellowing that nobody could do anything right—he had to do everything himself—and where the hell was a pencil and what was the matter with me?

'Well, I'd worked most of the night and a lot of nights before, and all at once I'd had it. I picked up that agenda, slammed it down in front of him and began to yell myself. "Look at it, will you?—if you'll just take a look at that sheet every bloody thing's there. You do this—you do that—you're here at this time—there at that time—every step you take, right through the day!" He looked up at me, blinked and gave one of his grunts. That's done it, I thought—I'm for the chop now.

'But he started to study the paper while I walked round behind him waiting for the axe to fall. Then—after a bloody long five minutes—he jumped up, chipper and bright again. "Okay, Lloyd—let's get going." And that wasn't the end of it. In the middle of the afternoon, just as he was leaving the office to get ready for the charity ball, he dropped a card on my desk. "I want you at that dinner tonight—you and your wife".'

For the Morgans it was a traumatic honour. Their home was out in the suburbs, they had four hours to get ready and Mrs. Morgan was stunned at the invitation. From a first flat refusal she was brought round through a series of urgent phone calls to start for Montreal in a friend's car. Another friend was employed at Classy Formal Wear, and Mrs. Morgan was to meet her husband at the shop. Red, Gordon's chauffeur, as a chief of staff at headquarters, arranged for a police escort through the downtown evening traffic and Morgan made the rendezvous just as the doors were closing. By seven o'clock the couple had their outfits, at eight they joined the notables entering Le Grand Salon and at the high middle of the evening they were greeted out on the dance floor by the beaming president himself. 'Everything okay, Lloyd?' 'Everything okay, Mr. Gordon.'[27]

With the hotel launched, prospects speedily brightened for Place Ville-Marie. Zeckendorf himself recalls the turn of events in the record of a conversation that was characteristic of many between himself and James Muir. That 'fierce and egotistical man who in another age would have been chieftain of a fighting clan'[28] was as profanely concerned as Gordon with the dormant state of the project. He was, however, critical of the planned building, resented the Chinese architect whose name he could not pronounce, and in spite of hints from Gordon had ignored an obvious solution. Zeckendorf tried again:

'Jim, we're not getting anywhere.'

'Why the hell should you get anywhere. That god-damned Chinaman's stopping you.'

'No, you're stopping us.'

'*I'm* stopping you?'

Yes, Zeckendorf insisted. There was a general gang-up of Muir's competitors on St. James Street and he had one way to beat them—move the headquarters of the Royal Bank to Place Ville-Marie. The cruciform tower would become the Royal Bank Building—'You'll be king of the hill—the business will come to you.'

'You're out of your mind. We have the biggest bank in Canada in the biggest building in Canada.'

'I'll buy it from you.'

'You've got no money to buy it, you (triple-expletive) Jew!'

'Think it over.'[29]

Five weeks later Muir, one of whose closest friends and most influential advisers was Lazarus Phillips, the leader of Montreal's Jewish community, had completed the thinking-over. He was prepared to renounce St. James Street for Place Ville-Marie and the Royal Bank would house itself in the western section of the building. With that news, as it filtered through the business world, the ice-block suddenly gave. The prospect of having the entire building sheathed in aluminum brought in the Aluminum Company of Canada; Montreal Trust followed and Trans-Canada Airlines put in for the fourth section. With those major tenants the smaller fry would follow, but there was one remaining rub. Muir was adamantly insisting on a major structural change.

W. Earle McLaughlin, who was to become Muir's successor, had a part in negotiations that were 'no honeyed love feast'. In the cruciform building, as planned, the banks of high-rise elevators were to ascend from the ground floor. Muir contended that they would take up too much space and would not leave room for the large ground-floor banking office he saw as a first essential. It seemed for weeks, as that problem emerged, that the whole deal was off. Then, says McLaughlin, 'at one of the early-morning meetings in smoke-filled rooms somebody—nobody quite knows who—suggested that we lift the whole building, set it on four quadrants and start the elevators a floor above the ground.'[30] With that massive change, involving a few more millions, a street level area of considerable grace and beauty provided the space required.

In May 1959 Muir approved the plans and by December, with the principal leases signed, building was under way. Of a host of new difficulties one loomed up as major, and the solution was differently viewed by different parties. 'Our own architects,' says McLaughlin, 'had only built banks but they could see one thing. With that cruciform construction the wind would get to the building and make it twist and sway; it might actually fall down. The whole construction formula had to be redesigned.'[31] Norman MacMillan concurs. 'The wind tunnel studies indicated that there had to be a vast amount of money poured into what is a great cube of concrete buried in the ground to the west of University Street, really a kind of anchor.'[32] Against the sway and twist factors huge steel girders, some of them weighing as much as a ton per foot, had to be sunk in the concrete and run through the lower structure. All this, to Zeckendorf and his own architects, was rampant Canadian conservatism and quite unnecessary change. The expense and the six months work required for redesign was 'a five million dollar misunderstanding' which 'hit us like a torpedo in the bow'.[33]

Gordon sat at the centre of it all sparring with his friend, Muir, while both sparred with Zeckendorf. To the two Scots in their almost daily telephone calls Zeckendorf became 'the beast'. Yet, everlastingly in trouble, he was adept at pulling out of it, and as the building climbed on its quadrants money began to flow. The large leases began to beget small ones, and each allotment of floor space produced its trickle of funds. 'Don't worry about tenants,' the promoter told McLaughlin. 'Tenants are like mice—they just come out of the walls—we'll get them.' As usual, he was as good as his word. 'At first,' says McLaughlin, 'when we got a lead on a tenant we'd pick up the phone and say, we hear you're interested—we'd love to have you. In a little while, however, we were getting the phone calls to see if we could get someone in.'[34]

The building was filling up as the steelwork climbed, the rest of the development was on schedule and it was changing Montreal. That much, in spite of the dismal balance sheets, could be credited to the CNR. By the end of 1960, as Gordon looked at the stir of work around him, he had cause to water his worries with a fair dash of content.

The working life of the president was as wide as the range of the railway and kept him much on the move. He had his old gregarious fondness for lively social occasions and was not averse to combining them with some of his public duties. In the garb of Simon McTavish at the annual revels of the Beaver Club, he was a loud reminder of the fur trade and not the least of the advertisements promoting the new hotel. Each June, when the Shakespeare festival brought its thousands to Stratford, Bonaventure was parked on a railway siding and Mr. and Mrs. Gordon were among the distinguished guests. He was called on from the west coast to Newfoundland to enhance the openings of branches and the launching of other projects, and with all that he still found time for Queen's.

Always a potent figure in the university's fund-raising, he was now a member of the Board of Trustees. 'He would delay what I would think would be important business to go to those meetings,' says Dr. J. B. Stirling who was then chancellor;[35] and for once in this atmosphere he was not the dominant Scot. Dr. J. A. Corry, who became principal in 1961, found in Gordon a careful, quiet listener who remained something of an enigma. 'I could never predict what he would think about any question—he wasn't always on the right, he was just as likely to be on the left. He took it for granted that in a changing world certain kinds of change were inevitable and he was always prepared to support moderate reform. In university terms, he was left of centre.'[36]

He was also left of centre in his taste for entertainment and in Leonard Brockington, lawyer, journalist, nationally sought-out orator, rector of Queen's and fellow-member of the board, he discovered a kindred spirit. For both men, after the day's meeting, the mildly convivial university reception left a good deal to be desired. There was Bell's Scotch in the hospitable Bonaventure lying on a Kingston siding and there were all the world and its problems awaiting a night's discussion. That they duly received, with frequent literary side trips. The minds clashed and the egos showed genially in competitive quotations from the scriptures, from Shakespeare and Gilbert and Sullivan and of course from Robbie Burns. Padre Marshall Laverty, the university's chaplain, was listener and referee. Detailed as aide to Brockington who was badly crippled with arthritis, he helped him down at the end of one of the sessions from the rear steps of the car. The dawn glimmered in the east and the host loomed above, weaving a little like his guest. 'Ah Gordon, Gordon,' Brockington intoned reproachfully, 'you're just the kind of man my mother warned me against.'[37]

In 1958 brother Jack died, and for all the long estrangement there was a sense of loss in that. From his first days in Ottawa Gordon had seen little of the rest of the Toronto family, and still less after his move to Montreal. 'The Gordons,' said his niece, Margaret Garbig, 'didn't really know how to congratulate Donald and be proud of him when he got his appointment with the CNR. They were all so damn determined that there would be no way Donald would think they were asking favours. Gordons wouldn't be condescended to.'[38]

With his nephew James, who was doing well as a lawyer, Gordon had kept in touch, and there had been occasional liquorous reunions during brief stops in Toronto. Now, however, the president wanted more. 'Among the many New Year's resolutions which I will probably break,' he wrote to his sister Maggie on January 5, 1959, 'is to see something of the Gordon family this year.'[39] As he neared the sixty bench-mark he was feeling concern for his roots, and he remembered a bible and an album which Maggie might well have kept. Perhaps, too, she could write down some of her memories, identify forgotten relatives and help him 'sketch out the beginnings of a family tree'.

Maggie was appreciative of the letter and eager for the get-together but only moderately helpful. 'I think the best place to meet would be at Jamie's.' She and her husband, she said, 'lead a very quiet life. The only income we have is his old-age pension of $55. per month. We live in a basement apartment of Isobel's home—we are quite comfortable.' As to recollections and relationships she was prepared and eager to talk but could write nothing down. 'I am a very poor letter writer. . . . Annie has the family album but she says she does not know anybody in it, and I have the Bible. I remember the day our father bought it. Our mother said there were things we were sairer needing.'[40]

The receipt of that letter brought a telephone call to James. 'I'd like to see my family—will you do something about it?' The lawyer agreed, braced himself and the assembly of the clan began, with occasional complications. 'They were a noisy group,' says Michael, 'who enjoyed their Scotch whiskey and singing and loved to argue about anything—politics, art, religion—a big, brawling, opinionated and very loving family', which nevertheless had certain inhibitions. One aunt was very nearly excluded for reasons that remained private until privately divulged by another: 'Well, when she drinks she farts.'[41]

There were, however, no excluded Gordons when the night of the reunion came. The president and his wife, fresh from Bonaventure, gathered with the clan at James's house and cocktails broke the ice. It was a party in full flow when it arrived at James's golf club, which the prudent lawyer had selected for the main brunt of the affair. As in the case of an earlier Gordon at another Toronto golf club, the event was long remembered. 'Boy,' says James in retrospect, 'they really had a wing-ding. I can see Donald yet singing "The Road to Mandalay". The management came in a few times and just looked and shook their heads and walked away. Nearly cost me my membership but somehow I lived it down.'[42]

The president's wife, encountering the formidable family, stood up to the strain well. 'Norma, of course, would shudder when she thinks of that re-union,' Michael speculates,[43] but if that is true she allowed nothing to show. 'We enjoyed your visit *very* much,' Maggie wrote to her brother after it was all over. 'I guess I don't have to tell you that you married a *real* lady. She didn't make us feel our humble circumstances at all.'[44]

In the same year there was a return to the older home. Actually it was a second coming. Leaving for London in July and going on to a tour of the Western Isles, Gordon retraced with Norma, and in much grander circumstances, a journey he had made with Maisie twenty years before. That journey he had lovingly recorded at a St. Andrew's Night gathering:

> Going to England in 1938, and being on an expense account, I managed to take a brief side trip to Scotland with my wife. We journeyed up to Aberdeen and then took a bus to the little village of Old Meldrum which nestles in the hills at the back o' Benachie. We drove through the well-remembered countryside as the sun made its morning struggle through the mist, and as I saw the burns still running where I left them, the dew-wet heather purpling on the hillside as we edged up into the highlands through the glens of the Dee and the Don, my heart choked in my throat.[45]

There was all that to be repeated, but not in a lowly bus. This was the real return for the lad who had 'done well'. In Aberdeen he was 'The Watchmaker's Son Who Earns £25,000 per Year'.[46] In Old Meldrum he added a page to legend as he travelled familiar Cowgate Street beaming in a Rolls Royce and broached the champagne he had brought with him for a first impromptu reception. Formal welcomes followed, forgotten friends emerged, 'Mrs. Gordon's movie camera whirled all day' and the Town Council were the Gordons' hosts that evening at a memorable civic dinner. Hospitality, moreover, was still persistent in the morning. 'My waiter,' Gordon informed the always-clustering reporters, 'insisted that I should breakfast on herrings fried in oatmeal. Delicious. But my wife could not look a herring in the face that early.'[47] Scotland was still Scotland and hard on the less robust, but a grand place to come back to as one of its taller sons.

At home in Canada the three-year-old Campbell was mastering the art of speech, and a French-Canadian nanny had taught him in her own tongue. 'When I was first able to communicate with father we couldn't understand a word each other said.'[48] That amused the president and provided grist for his mill when he was accused of anti-Frenchness. The shadow over the family was the condition of Bill Hobbs who was now retired from the railway and succumbing slowly and painfully to advancing cancer of the mouth. Dreading and hating sickness, oppressed by the sombre certainties that haunted the Hobbs apartment and making talk with a man whose speech was barely intelligible, Gordon was nevertheless a constant visitor. He arrived with books and policy papers, read out company reports and took the invalid along with him, in spite of embarrassed protest, on trips in the private car. For his own part, there were painful periods with Norma following some of his lapses and occasional lively dust-ups with the still outspoken 'Ma'. Overshadowing all, however, in the minds of both women, was the rough-hewn Scottish tenderness he showed to the stricken father.

Michael, the determined prodigal, was weaving his way to redemption by his own circuitous route. 'In my third year at the University of New Brunswick I retired from football. I was the cause of the establishing of the Student Discipline League—suspended for an entire term, prohibited from going to classes and banned from campus. But I was allowed to use the library and I knew I was really under the gun, so I'd go there every day and read. I got permission to write the exams, came out with very good marks, started my fourth year by selling pots and pans during the holidays—made about $16,000 and then went to law school. The summer of that year I met the lady who eventually became my wife.'[49]

On August 13, 1960, Michael Gordon and Anne Elizabeth McAllan were married in St. Andrew's Kirk, Saint John, New Brunswick, with the father of the groom approving. 'He liked my wife immediately' and that portended much. The second son, who was doing well in law school, seemed back in the paternal fold.

With the first son the father was still defeated. He had confessed as much, in November 1957, to one of the gossip columnists of the Winnipeg *Free Press*:

Mr. Donald Gordon, a visitor to Winnipeg this week, was telling us how the newspaper bug had bit a member of his family. His son—also Donald—after a spell as a reporter was finally persuaded to go back to school and the last his father heard from him was attending the London School of Economics. Mr. Gordon senior picked up a Montreal paper the other morning and began to read a story from Palestine. Suddenly the byline caught his eye. He was amazed to note that the writer was none other than Donald Gordon, junior.[50]

By 1959, still officially a student of economics and often writing for newspapers and syndicates, Donnie was also serving as a European correspondent of the BBC. Burdened with the thought of the thesis he was never going to complete, he was also driven by the conviction that 'the newspaper and broadcasting business was one of the very few where I could achieve anything on my own . . . the son of a very famous or very notorious person can do only so many things.' He had all his father's energy but nothing he hoped to do with it could win his father's approval, and the strain of ambitions and strictures was slowly wearing him down. 'I started jumping off cliffs in Cornwall—came in one day like something out of a Goon show, literally trailing seaweed, at which point my wife said, "Let's have a little chat".'[51] The result of the little chat was to be 'two years of very intensive psychotherapy in London' and Donnie was embarked on this course when Gordon and Norma arrived en route to Scotland. There had been no confidences exchanged, no easing of any of the old strains and Gordon had rebuked the student who was not completing his degree. From this son the father parted as usual, baffled, aching, resentful and more than a little blind.

By the end of 1960 the president was fifty-nine. In spite of the perennial deficits, the increased efficiency of the railway wearing the new symbol did much to justify his work. So did the new hotel and so did the rising structure on Place Ville-Marie. But he was not at home as he had been in this changing Montreal, and certainly not in Ottawa where the question of his reappointment was still studiously avoided. It did not matter much, except as a question of ego, that he was a man unsure of his job; there were always jobs to be had. The trouble was that in some ways he was less sure of himself. It was hard to measure success and hard to account for failure; in life, work and even family relationships there seemed to be a mixture of both.

CHAPTER 16

'Gordon must go'

I n mid-March of 1961 the first volume of the report of the MacPherson Royal Commission on Transportation arrived in Montreal. It was destined to become for the railways a symbol of rationalization and an augury of better times, but it would be six years in working its way through Parliament toward actual legislation and its first reception in the offices of the Canadian National was not particularly promising. Every page of its thirty volumes of testimony had been avidly read by Gordon, to the amazed discomfort of his staff. Through a long year, says Robert Bandeen, who was still low in the hierarchy but close enough to the president to share part of the ordeal, 'he'd be down here each morning steaming about something on page 35 or some place—we thought somebody must be reading it for him or marking sections, but it wasn't so—he'd read it all.' At the same time he had been notably pessimistic. 'He'd got the idea that it was an insignificant commission. He had a theory that royal commissions came along about every five years and only every second one was important—the other was a sort of filler.'[1] That conviction was changed speedily and dramatically by the first volume of the report.

Two copies, the only two 'that our man up there could get', arrived from Ottawa late one afternoon, hot off the duplicating machines. Gordon went home with one and Bandeen picked up the other since his boss, Omond Solandt, was going out that evening and would not have time to read it. By the next morning two opinions had been formed. Bandeen, with Ian Sinclair who was rising in the CPR, had had much earlier discussion with some of the writers of the report. In his view they had done a first-class job; the railways' integration in a new pattern of transport had been clearly and fairly outlined. The president, however, with a hard ten years behind him and not expecting much, had been bristlingly prepared for trouble. He had skimmed off out of context and with many markings in pencil and exclamation points a variety of mild comments on 'institutional rigidity', on services which the railways 'were not always able or willing to meet', on defects in existing rate structures and on the fact that 'the motor car, the motor bus and the airplane have replaced the railway as the favoured means of travel for the majority of Canadians'. Standing out for him starkly on page 8 of the report was a reminder of his first fiasco. It was following the nation-wide rail strike of August 1950, said the commissioners, 'that the railways had finally lost the monopolistic position in Canadian transportation which they had maintained for almost a century'. That morning when Bandeen got to his desk a note was glaring up at him: 'Meeting at 9.30—Crisis—We have to discuss this Thing.'[2]

There had been the same or similar summonses for each of the senior officers and they gathered uncomfortably in the boardroom. 'They all sat sort of in protocol,' Bandeen recalls. 'Gordon was at the head of the table, I ended up of course at the foot, and we were the only two in the room who'd read the report.' The president's mood was delineated in a half-hour oration. 'He was fit to be tied—I've never seen him so mad—he felt the report undermined the railway industry, undermined his position, undermined the CN and was a disaster. We had to get out a press release—he loved issuing press releases—and condemn the whole thing. First, though, he was going to go round the table and get everybody's opinion. So they said what they'd do or wouldn't do, based on his version which was the only one they had, and finally he came to me. "Now let's have your thoughts".'

With some twenty pairs of eyes swivelling in his direction the young man gulped and swallowed. 'Well, I read the report—I think it's pretty good. I think it helps us immensely—it's right down the line—exactly what we should have. And'—as the familiar purple tinged the president's ears—'before we issue a press release we should take another look.'

There was a long, uncanny silence instead of the expected roar. 'You could see the look of consternation on everyone's face—they all thought I'd get thrown out the window bodily.' Instead of that the president got to his feet. 'All right, I'll read it again—but you better be right.' At nine o'clock next morning he was on the phone to Bandeen. 'Come up here. You *are* right—I want a favourable press release and you can help me write it.'

'As a matter of fact,' said Bandeen, 'I already have one written.' There was a laugh on the other end—'Get it up here.'

'And,' Bandeen concludes, 'we changed the release a bit and sent it out. That was the measure of Gordon. I, a young guy, had confronted him by accident at a meeting with his senior staff and he could turn round before all of them and admit I was right. He was an amazing individual in that respect—a great man.'[3]

He was also a judge of men, and he had found one he wanted. A year or so later, says Dr. J. B. Stirling, 'we were looking for a Dean for the Business School at Queen's and Robert A. Bandeen was our prime candidate for the job. I tackled Donald for permission to approach him and he said, yes, certainly—I could go right round then and see him in his office if I liked. "Only, John,"—and he gave me that bland Scots glare—"I'll make it god-damned hard for you to get him".'[4]

The MacPherson report, from the first hour of his conversion, became an article of faith with Gordon. The more he studied its two succeeding volumes, the more he became convinced. Its many drastic proposals and their underlying purpose were actually a broad summation of his own targets. Old tariffs and rate structures were to be brought in line with costs. Passenger services and obsolescent branch lines, where they were operated as a public service, were to be 'compensated from public funds'. Rail, road, water, air and pipelines were all to be assigned their places in a general scheme of transport. The report recognized the arrival of an 'era of competitive coexistence' but it still conceded to the railways their position as 'the backbone of the transportation system in Canada'.[5] A man could hope from that clearing-away of cobwebs for a little less of the tangle of regulation, a relief from fixed charges and eventually a return to profit. Gordon was not to see it as president of the CNR, but it was one gleam on the horizon in the midst of thickening storms.

An unpromising year had begun with the government's announcement that it intended to provide a better regional representation by expanding the CN board of directors from seven to twelve members. There had been no mention of the reappointment of Gordon and no subsequent action. Instead, amid the stony silence of the prime minister and his cabinet, a vocal faction in Parliament was out for the president's head. So far as it had a leader, it was led by Douglas Fisher and there were all of the old complaints. The deficit stood up starkly, innumerable flaws in the services could be found and pointed out and above all there was the character of Gordon himself.

He had demanded huge resources, spent them as he saw fit, and it was not denied that he had produced a modern railway. But his big diesels and his humpyards and his automated procedures had closed down division points, shifted and altered jobs, created doubts and worries among men exposed to change. In Gordon's eyes he had widened opportunities and actually increased security through a maze of union contracts, but they were confidential arrangements in the files of head office. They could not possibly be explained to the average man on the ground, he had invited members of Parliament to keep their noses out of them, and to the big man from Port Arthur there was challenge enough in that. 'From what I hear in my constituency', Fisher was inclined to believe that not only the president of the railway but the union heads themselves had lost touch with their workers. 'The employees are complaining very much about the situation. They have lost faith in the present management. Morale is shot and all you have to do is look at the changes in the employment structure and the number of jobs that are disappearing. All you have to do is visit some of the divisional points to see just how serious things are.'[6]

There were few statistics of job loss or displacement and not much else in support of other claims. 'Fisher,' says Jim McDonald who was by then a vice-president, 'seemed at that period to have become disillusioned about public figures—convinced they had feet of clay and determined to point a flashlight at them. . . . I never could figure out what he was trying to do.'[7] That, however, was clear enough to members of the House of Commons. Fisher got up before them on February 27 to bring his thoughts to a point:

> Mr. Gordon is a very blunt, outspoken, forthright man . . . he wants Canadian National Railways to be treated as a private enterprise organization with a balance sheet and all its efficiencies. I do not think that is what Canadian National Railways should be but if that is what Mr. Gordon thinks it is . . . then on that basis I think Mr. Gordon must go. He has had his decade in charge of Canadian National Railways and it seems to me that all he has accomplished every year is a bigger and bigger spending program and in most cases a bigger and bigger deficit. I know that the morale of the railway employees has nosedived and there seem to be no future prospects for efficiency or for any kind of balanced budget on the Canadian National Railways as long as we have Mr. Gordon.[8]

The dispensable man of February was no safer in June. The cabinet watched and waited, the scattered sniping in Parliament had become a barrage in the press, and gossip extending rumour had broadened to Luster Lake. The president's log cabins were pictured as a sybarite's mansion maintained by the CNR. His canoe and leaky rowboat had acquired the status of a yacht, for which the company bought the fuel. Even his private laundry was done at public expense. 'Burly, bellicose Donald Gordon,' wrote Gerald Waring on the eve of the opening session of the parliamentary committee, 'seems teetering on the brink of being fired from his $75,000 a-year job.'[9] Gordon came to the meeting surrounded by that aura, and much of the six-day fracas confirmed the reporter's view. Flanked by vice-presidents, with Norma sitting in the gallery and with Ralph Vaughan beside him as custodian of the chief's temper, he was at times apart from a battle that seemed to break up in rambling skirmishes round him. Liberals wrestled with Conservatives and Créditistes with former CCF, now New Democratic Party, members, but it was still Fisher and Gordon, glowering as the main adversaries, who took the final falls.

The deficits, the run-throughs, the freight, passenger and express services and even the company's news agents came in for sharp attack. The trucking service, on which Fisher had acquired a statement removed from company files, provided a high moment. 'It was really a funny scene,' Fisher recalls. 'We were standing nose to nose wrestling over this piece of paper—this "stolen document" as he insisted on calling it—and it looked like he was going to take a punch at me. Mrs. Gordon was sitting over there at the side of this big railway committee room with her little handkerchief and sort of tears in her eyes.' She certainly was not, a steely Norma recalls, she was merely powdering her nose. She had no cause, however, to differ with any of the rest of Fisher's version: 'Here was this great banker and corporate mind being chivvied and harried by this lunkhead MP, this shrill mugwump bastard from up in the bush.'[10] Ralph Vaughan, with his pencil raised in a familiar signal of warning, tugged at Gordon's elbow, trying to part the antagonists, while Jim McDonald on the sidelines prepared himself for the worst. 'I remember watching the flush starting at the back of his neck, deep purple and his ears were purple—I was just waiting for the mercury to get to the top of the thermometer.'[11] It did not get there—quite. The chairman retrieved the document which was promptly tabled and forgotten and that incident passed.

It had set the mood and the stage, however, for Fisher's central issue, the company's labour relations and low company morale. On the Sabbath between the sessions, following a rancorous Saturday, Gordon produced a statement which he handed over to Norma. He respected her criticism and in Norman MacMillan's view, 'she helped him; no doubt about that'. In this case, aware of her husband's mood, she spoke as her father's daughter. 'There are a couple of things wrong with it but just don't give it at all—don't make any statement.'[12] That advice, on this occasion, after his hours of work, the president would not accept. He started Monday morning grimly ready for Fisher and a little irked with his wife.

It was well after the lunch break before he had a chance to suggest to the committee that it might be appropriate for him to make a statement, but he had lost none of his warmth. Times were hard, he said, the railway industry was 'no longer top dog in transportation' and much change was necessary. Each man affected by change was likely to say, 'Well, it looks all right, but what's going to happen to me?' He was also, very often, likely to assume the worst.

> Now, Mr. Chairman, there is the general situation with regard to labour disputes, and here is a matter which I think should be cleared up for the benefit of the committee. The fact that we have had major disputes over the years, which came pretty close to strikes, has raised the impression that management is continually fighting with labour. That is not so. Our relations by and large are good . . . since 1950 the Canadian National Railways have negotiated 275 agreements. The number of these that were settled through direct negotiations was 214 . . . there were 67 which were taken to conciliation boards, and of the 67 which were taken to conciliation boards 51 were settled in favour of the company's position.

He went on, gathering heat. 'I want to say that in my opinion there has been a stream of irresponsible, uninformed, hostile and malicious statements made in the House of Commons and naturally carried on radio and television, all seeking to disparage Canadian National management . . . it is sufficient for my purpose to select a few of them: that I am "arrogant" and "haughty" in my dealings with this committee and in the conduct of my work; that I have been "inhuman"in my treatment of CNR employees; that I am "hated" by them, that I am "enemy number one of national unity".'

Then he produced his carefully assembled bombshells. The first was a statement by W. J. Smith, issued a week earlier. His union, said Smith, 'representing one-third of the CNR employees',

> takes a great deal of pride in the knowledge that the CNR is an efficient and vigorous enterprise serving the nation well, and compares equally with the best of railways on the North American continent. The criticisms of Mr. Donald Gordon as an individual to our knowledge are not warranted.

Dated two days later from the head of another union, the Brotherhood of Maintenance of Way Workers, was a personal letter to Gordon:

During the past several weeks you have been subjected to a sustained and vicious attack by certain members of parliament and by certain members of the press . . . as you know, we have on many occasions questioned some of the decisions you have made and some of the results of policies adopted under your direction and we reserve the right to do so in future . . . however, we have never questioned your integrity and honesty of purpose . . . statements made in the House as to your lack of status with the employees are grossly exaggerated.

Following that, with the help of friendship and telex and a nice sense of timing, a paper was passed to Gordon by his chief of personnel. He glanced at it and held it up. 'Mr. Wilson has just handed me another document which seems to be a statement made by Mr. Frank Hall at Winnipeg today. This I have not seen and I shall just quote what I have in front of me, since I have no other means of knowing what is in it.' He read and beamed as he did so, for the toughest of his old adversaries had come through in style:

I have nothing whatsoever against Donald Gordon. . . . The CNR president is a hard man to deal with but actually he is paid to be tough. As far as I am concerned Mr. Gordon tries to get along with organized labour. If any railway employees are disgruntled it is not because of Donald Gordon.[13]

'Frank Hall,' said Fisher seventeen years later, 'cut my throat a number of times', and this was one of the occasions.[14] It did not prove that there were no unhappy railway men but the high inquest and even the chief inquisitor had begun to lose direction. When they turned on Luster Lake and the presidential perquisites they only provided a springboard from which the president sprang.

Had he been provided with naphtha gasoline? He had, he said. As he passed through Ottawa on his way up to the lake he was in the habit of picking up a 5-gallon can for his Coleman lamp. He got it from railway stores and paid the bill for it there. 'In the case of laundry, I have a monthly account at the Chateau Laurier. I go in there for all kinds of things and when I come down from the camp in the evening I might have some dirty shirts. I leave them and pay for them in the regular way. In the case of labour I had a fire at Luster Lake and in the process of getting it fixed up the superintendent used some Canadian National Railways employees and sent me a bill. I was very grateful, Mr. Fisher, for having my attention called to it, because when I went into it I found I paid four times as much by using CNR employees as I would if I had got someone from Ottawa. Now I am getting cheaper labour, I assure you.'

He went on zestfully, picking the items of the charges down to their small bones, and closed with a final comment. 'I would like to point out in my own interests and in the interest of my wife's housekeeping that the sum of $10. for a year's laundry does not represent the degree of cleanliness at Luster Lake. It merely means that I had some odd socks and shirts.'[15] One of the committee members squirmed uncomfortably. 'I am not too happy with this line of questioning. I think it is very penny ante.' The chair was inclined to concur, with only Fisher dissenting, and further discussion died. Luster Lake, as material for a public scandal, was down the public drain.

A day later the committee ended its sessions. The president had won on points in the press, the radio and Parliament and he was welcomed back by his own. When he walked in to the old McGill Street building on his return to Montreal the whole head office staff crowded the lobby and raised a resounding cheer. The always-punctual Gordon, much moved by the reception, could only summon a glower and respond with a small, weak joke. 'Just because I'm on time for work for once is no cause for a celebration.'[16]

Fisher was unconvinced and unrepentant. Criticized by the Saskatoon *Star-Phoenix* for shabbiness and irresponsibility, he had a question to put. 'When a member of parliament is convinced that a head of a government agency has lost his effectiveness, what is he to do about it? Apparently you believe that Donald Gordon has done a great job. I believe he has been an all-time bust. Am I to keep quiet?'[17] He was far from quieted yet and there was too much silence elsewhere in the realms of high decision. The year-long wait on the question of reappointment went on and on and on.

In July, amid public uproar, James Coyne resigned as governor of the Bank of Canada and was succeeded by Louis Rasminsky. Gordon in his own position was well aware of the resentments and could share the mood of his friends. Coyne, unshakeable and unchangeable in his views on bank policy, had fought the government to a standstill and finally stalked out. Rasminsky, dubious but dutiful, was hardly glad to be in. 'Your heart-warming telegram gave me courage when I was feeling at a low ebb,' he wrote Gordon. 'I hope you will let me know when you are next in Ottawa, so we can rack our brains and find something to laugh about.'[18]

To all three of these men, who had made their way under friendly Liberal regimes, the cabinet of John Diefenbaker presented a blank wall. The Chief himself, in retrospect, is friendly enough to Gordon. 'I recall there was a delay in the appointment but it wasn't because of him. I had a very high

13. Donald Gordon with Leon Henderson, U.S. price controller, in 1942.

14. Gordon being piped from the mayor's office in the Detroit city hall.

15. An inspection of CN telecommunications equipment by Gordon and CN directors.

16. Gordon with the Hon. C. D. Howe at the opening of the Canso Causeway in 1955.

17. Gordon and William Zeckendorf inspecting a model of Place Ville-Marie.

18. Gordon with train crew on an inspection trip at Joffre in 1959.

19. (*left*) Gordon at the controls of the first train from Chibougamau to St. Felicien in 1959.

20. Gordon being cheered by CN headquarters staff on his return from a parliamentary appearance in Ottawa, 1961.

21. Gordon being interviewed.

22. Gordon addressing the annual dinner of the Beaver Club in Montreal.

23. Gordon polishing the brass rail at press club bar.

24. 'The Roundup' by Jack Boothe, *Globe and Mail*, July 7, 1945.

25. 'CN President Not Ready to Retire.'

26. 'Still on the Rails' by Ed McNally, *Montreal Star*, June 23, 1961.

27. 'I told you life begins at 65 . . .' by Rusins, *Ottawa Citizen*.

regard for Gordon. He could be overbearing and offensive if he wanted to be, but personally I felt that he commanded the loyalty of employees in a way that no other person could.' Did he trust Gordon, he was asked sixteen years later. 'Absolutely. Bet your life.'[19]

It was not, however, the current view of his attitude. Within and without the cabinet, and certainly within the railway, the prime minister's hostility was widely regarded as a fact. 'If the son of a bitch hasn't got the guts to fire me, I'm not going to help him,' is one of the few outbreaks recalled of Gordon himself.[20] 'He put up with that delay in reappointment with a lot more patience than I would have expected,' records Jim McDonald, 'but there must have been times when he felt like resorting to physical violence. He'd be called up to Ottawa—kept all day without the slightest indication or apology—no word from the inner sanctum—the great man never communicated what he intended to do or whether Gordon should stay on to the next day or what.'[21]

By late September, however, though there was still no action in cabinet, something seemed to be congealing. At Luster Lake, on Sunday the 24th, there was a honk from Gordon's jeep which was parked outside the cabin. It signalled a call by the new luxury of a radio telephone transmitter he had installed on the nearest hilltop. Léon Balcer, then minister of transport, was anxious to see the president; could he be in Ottawa Monday morning? He could; and by Monday evening, installed in the Chateau Laurier, he was dictating a memorandum recording a hard day:

> Balcer informed me, at considerable length, that his list of proposed directors had been under discussion with his cabinet colleagues with the result that no agreement had yet been reached on his proposals. Indeed, practically every name he suggested had been challenged and other suggestions substituted. However, he assured me that in respect of myself there was agreement on my reappointment as a Director and as Chairman, although he could make no firm announcement to this effect until he had the Prime Minister's authority to do so. That, he indicated, would not be forthcoming until the entire Board had been selected and the Act (Bill C-94) proclaimed. He confessed that the whole matter was in a state of high confusion.[22]

By the 26th, as he fumed in his Chateau suite, rumours came to the president of further dissension in cabinet. Balcer telephoned to say that the prime minister would call Gordon personally. That did not happen but at 9.45 next morning Balcer phoned again: the prime minister had forbidden any announcement. The hapless minister of transport 'expressed consider-able personal chagrin, but in a voice of hopeless resignation'. Through the 28th, with Gordon immured in the Chateau, Ralph Vaughan, as an observer, haunted the House of Commons. There was nothing to report by noon and nothing in the afternoon, except that Diefenbaker had left for British Columbia. It was ten o'clock in the evening when Balcer rose in the House and twenty minutes later when the call from Vaughan came. Gordon had been reappointed with his new slate of directors.

He had been reappointed, however, from the expiry of his previous ap-pointment; in effect for two years, instead of the usual three. When that dawned on the president from his morning reading of Hansard he took off with a head of steam to confront the minister of transport:

> Mr. Balcer was obviously shaken by my forthright approach and hastened to assure me he had done everything he could . . . he had protested in the presence of his cabinet colleagues . . . but the Prime Minister had brushed this aside with language something as follows: 'To hell with that, Gordon would not be reappointed if I could help it.' . . . Mr. Balcer then proceeded to tell me that the Prime Minister was in a frenzy about not having been able to get his own way and had said repeatedly that only the support of labour, particularly Frank Hall, added to the wide-spread representations from businessmen, had made my reappointment necessary . . . the interview closed with Mr. Balcer asking me to stay with the job in the interests of the CNR and the country and he also thanked me for the 'splendid cooperation' I had given him personally.[23]

A call later in the day, somewhat sourly recorded, was from the genial George Hees who was now advanced in the cabinet as minister of trade and commerce:

> He telephoned to extend me very fulsome congratulations and hoped that I was feeling happy about the way everything had turned out. I replied that I would feel much better but for the last-minute expression of vindictiveness shown by the dating of the legislation and my own appointment.

To that Hees had answers and private views of his chief, which were accepted with some reserve. 'I made note of the following statements by Mr. Hees in the course of his lengthy monologue.'

It was the unanimous wish of himself and his cabinet colleagues that I stay on.

I was held in the 'highest esteem' by the cabinet.

He was 'confident that no matter how it was done this time it will never happen again . . . you would be amazed by the feeling in cabinet favourable to yourself. It was not always that way but it certainly is now and everyone admires the way you have handled things.'

In answer to my question about the Prime Minister's personal hostility he said, 'It doesn't really mean anything. I know him better than anybody. He prides himself on being the friend of the little guy. Any little jerk who writes him a letter about having lost his job will say— it's not my fault, it's Donald Gordon's. So the Prime Minister builds up his impressions from a few score letters from malcontents and forgets that there are a hundred or a hundred and fifty thousand others who are happy.'

Mr. Hees ended by saying he would like to advise me to get out more— visit the yards and shops and see the little guys. 'Wherever you go you leave a good impression . . .'[24]

The president was in once more with his new board of directors, but it was hard to be reassured. Neither the two-year renewal nor the confidences breathed from the cabinet room had the ring of old times.

In June 1961 Gordon opened the headquarters building long sought by MacMillan. He paid suitable tribute to the executive vice-president and also recalled the Sunday in 1950 when Dorchester Street was a bridgeway and he had looked north from it over a great, gaping hole. He now looked out from a seventeenth-floor office as the head of what he had claimed to be one of the best-equipped railways in the world, and rising out of the hole, five storeys deep in the ground, towering along the skyline, with its steel, glass and aluminum as a glittering symbol of the future, was Place Ville-Marie. On September 13, 1962, when La Place was formally opened in magnificent autumn weather, the flags, the bands, the speeches and the reception by the general public seemed adequate compensation for the scars of a dozen years. It was, said Gordon, 'the greatest satisfaction of his twelve business years in the city'.[25] To Pierre Berton, writing in the Toronto *Star*, 'There is no longer any sense talking about the "race" between Montreal and Toronto. For the moment the race is over; Montreal has won. Place Ville-Marie has put it a decade ahead of us.'[26]

The day had seemed to be a symbol of generally mellowing times. The deficit remained intractable but there was a slight downward trend. There were the usual disputes with unions but they were leaving fewer scars. The president seemed to be restored and rehabilitated and returning to his old self. On 'Transportation and Commercial Travellers' Day' at the Canadian National Exhibition he had been taken apart by experts for the slow rural passenger trains, the eternal smelly washrooms and the stops at icy stations in the small hours of the morning. The story of the conductor and the lady who wanted to stop the train had returned as a hardy annual: 'Lady, you shouldn't have got on this train when you were pregnant'—'When I got on this train I *wasn't* pregnant.' Gordon had received it genially and replied in the same vein. Commercial travellers, he said, had fabricated almost as many stories about railway services as they had about the farmer's daughter. 'Nevertheless, the pleasure of your company and your patronage outweigh any small harm done to our reputation for comfortable and efficient service. Much the same thing, I understand, applies to the farmer's daughter.'[27]

One factor, however, contributing to the peace of the year, had been the delayed sitting of the parliamentary committee. In 1962 it did not come in June but in the bleak middle of November, and it put an end to tranquillity. In 1961 Fisher had briefly referred to a question raised in the House: 'and that is the question as to the fact that there are 17 vice-presidents in the CNR and not one seems to be a French Canadian or French-speaking'. It was not, however, a question that was close to Fisher's heart, and Gordon had fended it off. Selections and promotions, he said, were based on merit without discrimination for or against any racial group. 'As a matter of fact I came within an hour of getting a very competent French Canadian senior executive last year. He was very, very suitable. Unfortunately he received an offer that nipped him away from me just about an hour before he decided to accept.'[28]

With that experience behind him, Gordon was hardly prepared for Gilles Grégoire. The Créditiste was part of a wave that had not been even a ripple in Gordon's days with the Bank of Canada and the Prices Board. It still seemed to the president that French Canadians in the railway had been given their due place, and that properly a small one which most of them seemed to accept. 'The rate of change of view,' says Jim McDonald in retrospect, 'was beginning to accelerate at a pace that just left English-speaking people behind.'[29] It had left the president behind and it was well ahead of Fisher, but the parliamentarian had seen Grégoire at work. 'I marvel,' he says, 'at what he got going and what he set in train. Historians will give him a lot more credit or blame for crystallizing this separatist thing.

No clubby bon entente for him between French and English members. He wasn't having any gentility—he raised hell about everything—from the menus in the cafeteria through to the rules of order which weren't available in French every day. He hammered at it—he converted Liberals into bilingualists—he set up a whole atmosphere and Gordon just walked into it.'[30]

One brief exchange was sufficient to ignite the fire. On November 19 Grégoire casually reverted to the now-familiar question. 'I note [the CNR has] one president, seventeen vice-presidents and ten directors and none of them is French Canadian.'

Gordon had statistics in front of him which could have disproved the statement, but he also had his convictions and he chose his own ground. How did Grégoire know there were no French Canadians on the list?

'Then which ones are?'

'I want to find out from you who is a French Canadian.'

The little man persisted on his own adamant line. 'Could you name for me the ones who are?'

'I do not know how to define a French Canadian. But I will say these are all Canadians, every one of them.'

Grégoire referred to his list. 'They are not the names of French-speaking Canadians.'

Gordon pointed to J.-Louis Lévesque, prominent enough in the financial world and now a member of the board. 'There are several members who can speak French,' he added, 'if that is what you want to know.'

It was not. What Grégoire wanted was the measure of French Canadianism in the Canadian National Railways and with that the president rounded on him, flat, honest and hard:

Let me say quite clearly that the promotion policy of the Canadian National Railways has always been based upon promotion by merit. Any man who by reason of experience, knowledge, judgment, education or for any other reason is considered by management to be the best person for a job will receive the promotion—and we do not care whether he is black, white, red or French.[31]

If there was an abrupt chill in some parts of the room he did not seem to notice it. Even Scotsmen, he added, sometimes received promotion in the CNR. The throw-away line, however, did not relieve the impact; the fatal gaffe had been made. Late that afternoon in a room in the Chateau Laurier Charles Harris, the director of public relations, looked at the face of Marc

Meunier, his assistant, and 'knew we had a tiger by the tail'.[32] In the dining room that evening Norman MacMillan, not particularly disturbed, was sitting with Pierre Taschereau who had not attended the session. 'Donald came in with Norma for dinner and on the way out he sat with us, told about the afternoon and repeated what he had said.' When he had left MacMillan looked over, surprised by his companion's silence. 'This,' said Taschereau gravely, 'is very, very bad.'[33]

La Presse next day was as cool and fair as it could be. Deliberately ignoring one remark, it reported only that Mr. Gordon had said he 'did not care' about ethnic origins. He had also said that 'through the recruiting done these last two or three years at Laval and Montreal universities, French-speaking Canadians will be able, ten or twelve years from now, to become vice-presidents at the CN'. It was cold comfort, however, amid the new demands and blank frustrations of the time. 'Let us sum up the debate by saying that a French Canadian will never be a vice-president of the CNR unless he is more qualified than all the other English-speaking candidates. It will not be enough for him to be merely their equal.'[34] By the 26th Gérard Pelletier, the editor, had widened out the discussion:

> Among the majority of English-speaking Canadians lip-service is paid to the great achievement of Confederation. But any practical step to favour French culture is opposed as inconvenient and a nuisance to government efficiency. If you doubt the veracity of this statement just go back to the flat refusal given by Mr. Diefenbaker a few months ago when a Royal inquiry on bilingualism was suggested.[35]

That same night words passed over to deeds. For the second time and again with waving placards—'A Bas le Colonialisme'—'Débout Québec'—'$75,000 Pour Un Tel Cochon'—Gordon was hanged in effigy in front of the Queen Elizabeth. On the 29th there was another hanging in Quebec, on December 1 a third at Trois-Rivières and on December 5 three hundred students from the University of Ottawa picketed Parliament Hill, marched to the War Memorial and consigned his effigy to flames. In the meantime, spurred by wild distortions of what Gordon had said and undeterred by his own flat denials, Parliament, the press and politicians talked. In the House an all-party resolution demanded that the CNR do more to promote French. Fisher, who had once told an audience at Laval University that French-Canadian culture consisted of little more than Maurice Richard and Lili St. Cyr, now informed a meeting of the NDP in Montreal that Gordon's 'boo-boo' in the committee represented 'another example of his arrogance and brutality of expression'. He had discovered that 'You've got to be most courtly when speaking to French Canadians . . . I think indirectly because of their supersensitivity and the fact that the chip is on their shoulders.'[36] Quebec trade unionism was beginning to enter the fray, the new Rassemblement pour l'Indépendance Nationale was seizing its opportunity and the uncourtly president of the railway was the cause and centre of the storm.

It broke over him with full force on December 11, 1962, his sixty-first birthday. About mid-afternoon five chartered buses, a flotilla of automobiles and a truck carrying a pig-faced Gordon effigy disgorged some thousand students on the plaza at Ville-Marie. Most of them were from the University of Montreal, identified by blue lapel cards and were part of a demonstration that included a deputation. The leaders were to see Gordon while the mass waited on the plaza, making their views clear. But the headquarters building was locked, with railway police in the lobby, and the president was ensconced in his eyrie seventeen floors above. By the time the four chosen spokesmen were inside the thousand outside were restless and hordes of unwelcomed newcomers were trebling the size of the crowd.

All that, however, was a distant rumble below as the four went up in the elevator, entered the outer office and were greeted by Lloyd Morgan. They identified themselves as Bernard Landry, president of the students' association of the University of Montreal; Guy Trottier, administrative secretary; Pierre Marois, chairman of the education committee, and Louis Duval, secretary. They were clean-shaven, well turned-out and formidably self-possessed. Shown in to the president, they made it clear that they intended to speak in French and he was prepared for that. Lionel Coté, the railway's general counsel, was on hand to act as interpreter.

'He wasn't needed for long, though,' Norma Gordon records. 'Since the students were all bilingual they soon got bored with the translating and started to speak in English. They got on beautifully with Donnie. What they had against him was what they *thought* he was like, not what he really was.'[37] The idealized version of the meeting was less and more than the truth. At six o'clock when the press was allowed in, much ice had been broken but a steely film remained. The big man was at his genial public best, only a little ruffled. He had supplied the deputation with copies of his testimony before the parliamentary committee because he had been very widely misquoted. Now, he assured the reporters, 'I think most of the misunderstanding has been cleared away.'

Bernard Landry was a little more reserved. 'Our protest is based on facts, not on interpretation of Mr. Gordon's statements. But now we believe there is hope—we are satisfied that discrimination has never been the policy of the railway.'

Where bilingual people were required, Gordon put in, he would see that the railway had them and Landry noted the exceptions. 'For instance, the ticket seller at Vancouver doesn't have to be bilingual.' At that remark 'Mr. Gordon smiled approval' and moved to increase the warmth: 'I haven't had the privilege of learning French because my parents were much too poor to afford to give me this type of education . . . but I can sing Robbie Burns' "Scots Wha Hae".'[38]

There was no invitation to do so, no producing of bottles or breaking out in song, as there had been at so many of his meetings in the long and simpler past. The gap remained between the cultures and the generations as the students filed out. Gordon had had no way of knowing that in Bernard Landry and Pierre Marois he was confronting two future cabinet ministers in the still unthought-of government of the Parti Québécois. In the streets below, however, where the thousand demonstrators had multiplied to three thousand, the portents for a decade were beginning to become clear. The Queen Elizabeth and walls and buildings near it were wearing ominous signs, pasted there by intruding separatist organizers: '1837: Rébellion—1962: Révolution'. At the hotel's doors, where a mob with a toilet bowl containing a picture of Gordon was trying to force an entrance, a hundred city policemen had begun to swing their clubs. Commuters on the station concourse were blocked away from their trains. Swaying back from the hotel, the main mass of students, intruders and bystanders, blocking indignant motorists, waving their sticks and placards and mixing rubbers and overshoes with a cloud of flying snowballs, drifted across Dorchester to the plaza of Ville-Marie. The red ensign was hauled down from the flagpole and ripped into lengths of ribbon. Then with the ribbons round it, pig-faced, bulging and blazing, the effigy of Donald Gordon was hoisted to replace the flag. Somewhere off on the sidelines a woman in a stopped car turned to accost a policeman: 'What's this all about?' 'Lady, it's kind of hard to explain.'[39] Among the throng around the flagpole in the full light of the blaze a youngster stopped his chanting to inquire of the nearest friend, 'Who is this Gordon anyway?'[40]

At that moment, according to one report, he was a man on the verge of tears. 'I did everything I could—and then they attack me like this.'[41] On his sixty-first birthday, in his seventeenth-floor office, he was caught in a dilemma far bigger than he was and hardly of his making. Yet if he was small compared to the problem he was not a small man, and there were other big men too. He had talked with Jean Marchand and consulted Gérard Pelletier, and the next day in *La Presse* the result of the work appeared.

It was an interview arranged by Pelletier, conducted with cool reserve and checked minutely in its English and French versions. There was to be no mistake in translation, no distortion of views; what Pelletier and Gordon were looking for was an actual opening of minds. Some of that, with whatever it meant for the future, the two men obtained.

In all the comment on the matter of discrimination, Pelletier asked, what was it that had impressed Gordon most?

'The remarks of Mr. Jean Marchand, Chairman of the Confederation of National Trade Unions. He has stated that "discrimination exists not at the moment when a man is named to an important office, but further back, when the system begins to groom its potential executives." This is criticism that I would be willing to explore with Mr. Marchand.'

Did Gordon, asked Pelletier, favour such a private investigation in order to avoid the public investigation so often asked for and refused?

'Not in the least. On the contrary, I believe that the best solution would be to create a royal commission that would be given the task of examining the whole matter of Canada as a bilingual country.'

'So you believe in the biethnical character of Canada?'

'It is a fact.'

'Your testimony before the railway committee gave the impression that you did not recognize this fact.'

'But I also did not recognize, on reading newspaper accounts, the testimony that I had given. I was even quoted as saying "I shall never employ French Canadians any more." Those are words that I have never said.'

'I am neither referring to newspaper accounts nor to televised comment,' said Pelletier, 'but to the official transcript of your testimony. In answer to a member of parliament who was questioning you, you said: "I do not know how to define a French Canadian. But I will say this: these (the vice-presidents of CN) are all Canadians." And further on you stated: "There are several members of the board of directors who can speak French, if that is what you want to know." To any French-Canadian listener, these two sentences amount to denying the very existence of French Canada and of the bicultural character of Canada.'

Pelletier was more than fair, totally ignoring the most inflammatory gaffe. But he had scored a hard, direct hit and there was only a lame reply.

'Do you know the atmosphere in which these committee sessions are held?

A question is thrown at you suddenly. You do not expect it and you are required to answer immediately. If I have produced the impression that I think there are no French Canadians, I certainly did not mean it.'

From that point, however, the president held his ground. 'I am opposed to two ideas, namely, that of appointing French Canadians without regard for competence . . . and the idea of creating a system of quotas.'

Pelletier wholly agreed. But 'do you admit that care for the recruiting and promoting of able men must be accompanied with care for a fair representation of French Canadians?'

'Not only do I admit it, but it is applied at the CN. I could tell you of many instances: our training courses, grants for extension studies . . .'

Yet the results were still poor, as Gordon admitted, pointing to the old reasons. French Canadians had not always been interested in technical and management callings; many of those who were had been drawn away from the railway to fields of industry and commerce. The railway industry was international by nature and required the use of English at its higher management levels. Mobility of personnel was essential to the railway system and French Canadians did not like to move.

'Lastly . . . there is no denying that men in positions of authority like to be surrounded by the people they know best, who speak the same language, share the same culture. Does this factor play an important part? Does it give rise to discrimination?'

He had no answers but he had been asking himself the questions and he had left a few for Pelletier. For this time the two men had what they wanted and prepared to close the talk.

'You do not intend to resign?' Pelletier asked.

'Do you think that such a move on my part would solve the problem we have just discussed?'

'No . . . the objective is not to overthrow you, but to get an investigation and efficient action.'

'For my part,' said the big man, rising grimly, 'I do not like to resign at the moment when I am attacked.'[42]

By the next day, as the board of directors met to consider the status of French Canadians in the railway, *La Presse* was renewing its demand for a royal commission on the status of the two cultures. Douglas Fisher supported it and on the 18th Pearson rose to demand it in the finest speech he had made as leader of the opposition. Even Diefenbaker wavered from his old and rigid stand. There would be no commission on bilingualism, but he promised a conference early in the new year to consider 'a national flag and other national symbols'.[43]

The storm built round the president was gradually shifting centre, but he was still bruised from the effects. He was rather dourly convivial with his old friend, Jack Clyne, who had been head of the Maritime Commission in Prices Board days and returned to British Columbia to become chairman of MacMillan, Bloedel. Clyne, he knew, had been mooted twelve years earlier for his own place with the railway, and the thought struck home now. 'Bottoms up,' he said, lifting the familiar glass, 'and when you look at me through the bottom say, "There, but for the grace of God, go I".'[44]

Yet he was still the resilient Scotsman, there were forgiving French Canadians, and it came to Christmas Eve. He arrived, highly illuminated, on the TV screens of the French provincial network as the heart and centre of a 'Christmas Entertainment'. An annual satiric revue, it had the genial Jacques Normandin, a bubbling group of performers and this time an all-too-willing Gordon attempting sallies in French. The result was screaming merriment, a multilingual disaster and a prolonged and painful evening for a wife who had gone to bed. Gordon reached home with the entire company around him and the entertainment continued into the small hours of the morning.

To Norma Gordon, the man who could never pronounce a French name without having it spelled out for him in phonetics—'Thériault—Tay-ree-oh' —had insulted a noble language and 'just looked like an owl'. He was made aware of that when he came down with his hangover late on Christmas morning, but a strongly dissenting verdict was rendered the next day. 'I went into my drugstore,' Norma records incredulously, 'and the little French-Canadian woman there greeted me with a huge smile. Oh Mr. Gordon!— he had been so relaxed, so natural—I was married to a marvellous man!'[45]

The year had brought him a kind of resolution of the two problems he could neither solve nor forget. Donnie, who was now a father of two, came home to Canada as a visitor on assignment from the CBC. The strained young man, who had not completed his thesis and was still undergoing treatment, was, as he cheerfully records, 'the first mad news correspondent—at least certified'. He was nevertheless, in the news field, a valuable and successful man, earning a substantial salary and beginning to find his feet. The one lack was the old lack, a reassurance of identity and a base of understanding with the man he admired and loved.

I stopped off in Montreal and saw my father and said, 'I think you understand that I have been in psychotherapy and that certain things in my relationship with you and mother and in the relationship between you two were pretty serious. I'd like to talk to you about it.' He wouldn't hear of it—he wouldn't accept it. 'Don't you listen to those charlatans,' he said. 'You're perfectly all right—you shouldn't pay any attention to this kind of thing.' He couldn't stand the whole idea and we had our first ever absolutely blazing row.

In the usual Gordon style, it was spectacular enough to attract the notice of authority:

I packed my bag, walked out of the house, he came flying down the hill after me and while we were arguing the Westmount police appeared. We all went round to the station and they tried to persuade me to go back but I said, 'Sorry, fellows, I just can't do it.' I went down and checked into the Mount Royal.

And yet, Donnie added, fifteen years later, the explosion had settled something:

We realized that we just couldn't talk about it. It took about six months to sort that out, but from then on things went swimmingly. When we met he'd sit down and drink with me, which he'd never done before. I began to think about recording his reminiscences—we started to become, well, I hope like my son and myself.[46]

With the errant Michael, as usual, things followed a different course. He was an improved man since marriage and the father liked his wife but it was at Luster Lake, where Norma still endeavoured to cement family relationships, that the real reunion came:

The second year of our marriage I was taking my summer vacation up at Luster Lake. Father was there and we were tentatively working our way toward some sort of a relationship, but we were still pretty standoffish. This day we were out working on a raft in the middle of the lake and father dropped a wrench. He was on the raft and I was in the water and when the wrench fell in it landed on my right foot. He looked at me and I looked at him and he said, 'I'm not going to lose that god-damned wrench.' I said no, he wouldn't—I'd get it and he glared at me. 'What do you mean? The minute you lift your foot that wrench will go to the bottom.' I said, let's think—we both looked at that wrench—and finally I kicked it up, duck-dived under it and came up with the thing in my hand. He just lay on his back and howled and then we both went ashore and had a couple of beers together. It was funny— the relationship cemented right there.[47]

During that same summer the six-year-old Campbell, unconscious of any strains, was commencing an industrious life. 'He had the same restless work-urge as his father,' Mrs. Hobbs says; 'all the Gordons had it.'[48] One of his self-set tasks was a large transfer of frogs which he moved from their native swamps to a more convenient pool. The result was a loss of mates and a breaking-up of families that filled nights in the Gatineau with a weird cacophony of sound. Added to that was the sound of the diesel generator that provided the camp with light, and worse still was its silence. When that came, Norma Gordon recalls, the president was instantly awake. ' "The damn thing's gone off!"—and in the middle of the night, wind, rain or hail, we'd have to get out in bedroom slippers and dressing-gowns, hunt around for a flashlight and climb the hill to the shed. That was one of the luxuries we enjoyed at Luster Lake. I wish Mr. Fisher had been there and I wish we'd dragged him out in the middle of the night to help fix the diesel.'[49]

Yet Luster Lake for Gordon retained its perennial charm. It was the place for forgetting worries, or sorting worries out. 'He never slept very well' but he slept better here, and there were echoes of old laughter and legions of marching memories on the nights he lay awake. The thoughts of Maisie were easier now, and their two boys were men. There was another boy to be thought of and perhaps time to redeem some old mistakes. Listening to the amorous bullfrogs, thinking of the sleeping youngster, he had a sense of life renewing itself, even at sixty-one.

Last Leg

During the spring of 1963 Gordon, the railway and the country were quickly disabused of any idea that 'the French Canadian question' had been settled. It had, instead, passed temporarily from the hands of the intellectuals into those of the revolutionaries. Wolfe's monument went down on the Plains of Abraham and radio stations, 'forbidden' to sign off with God Save the Queen, found bombs under their transmitters. The president's telephone rang late at night with husky, accented voices promising him death or the kidnapping of Campbell or similar treatment of Norma. He was 'the public enemy' in signs scribbled on walls; the CNR was to be 'eliminated' and 'Vive le Québec Libre' stood out in ragged paintwork on the sides of some of its boxcars. 'Those were the days of the FLQ,' says Jim McDonald, 'bombs on tracks, bombs in lockers at Central Station and hardly a week went by that we hadn't a promise of bombing in the tunnel—that was my particular nightmare.'[1] It was to lessen a little in June as police subdued the first wave of the terrorists, but in the meanwhile and abetting it was a tumultuous general election. In those mornings, when Red came round with the car to the house on Edgehill Road, he had a cosh on the seat beside him and the president drove to an office building thick with railway police. He was a shocked, angry and badly shaken man by April 22, 1963, when the Conservative government went out and Mike Pearson came in.

He was the more so because of his own intentions and the stir of work around him. Since the board meeting of December 13, 1962, he had been the driving Gordon of the high days of the Prices Board, pursuing a fixed objective. The CNR, in its employment ratios, its practices and its attitude to French Canadians, was to be turned inside out and brought right side up as an image of the dual nation. When the new government came in a committee of four directors and a swarm of internal task forces was probing the railway's routine, dissecting its promotion policies and surveying its public face. There had been high-echelon transfers of senior French Canadians, a grooming of potential candidates on lower management levels and a vast combing of statistics on employment in jobs and trades. A social research group, staffed jointly by the University of Montreal and McGill, was conducting studies in depth on aspects of discrimination, on reasons why French Canadians were not attracted to the company and on means of recruiting more. Meanwhile the president himself, true to his own methods, was well ahead of his agents in the hunt for likely men.

By May, with his friend Mike on his back in place of the departed Diefenbaker, the pressures had only mounted and the search become more intense. The Royal Commission on Bilingualism and Biculturalism loomed along the horizon, but more was required immediately and much from the CNR. J. B. Stirling, the old familiar of Queen's who was also a senior director of E. G. M. Cape Construction Company, found himself in Gordon's office. 'John,' said the president in a wheedling Scots burr, 'I've been looking at your man, Archer. I'd like to have him down here. I can offer him considerably more money than I think you're paying him, I've an opening for a vice-president—and I need a French Canadian.'

Stirling gulped, tempted to reply as Gordon had in the case of Robert Bandeen. In any case he would have to consult his president. Brigadier-General Maurice Archer was a distinguished French Canadian, prominent in Quebec society and a valuable engineer. Nevertheless, says Stirling, 'I brought John Cape down to Gordon's office and we decided that, much as it would hurt us, it was really our national duty to let a good man go. We'd need three months, we said, to look around for a replacement. But by God before we were out of the room he reached for the telephone, "Get me Mr. Pearson right away," and the door hadn't quite closed on us when we heard the joyful whoop, "Mike, I've got him!" '[2]

Such finds were rare, however, and jubilance a passing phase. The long work of the railway's groups and committees had not congealed in a report and had not been made public. It had not quieted the newspapers that yelled for Gordon's head. There was an anti-Gordon faction even in Pearson's cabinet and the president was not deceived. He was a dangerous property for government, likely to become more so, and once again potentially a man at the end of the road. His curtailed term of appointment would expire on September 30 and the storm warnings were clear enough around the question of renewal. On June 5, as one of many reminders, came a letter from Gilles Grégoire: 'As you are aware, the Sessional Committee on the National Railroad will soon be held, and for this occasion there is a whole series of questions that I want to ask. Having compiled to date 233 of these questions . . .'³

He waded through the list, assessing a swarm of problems. They were as wide and deep as history, they were far older than himself and he had not been hired to solve them. He was in his thirteenth year of office and he could claim that much he had set himself was done or almost done. The great gaps remained; the recommendations of the MacPherson report had not yet been implemented and he was still hammering as he had been doing the past three years for a second recapitalization to complete the half-way measures of 1952. If he could get these he could see the end of deficits, he would have helped equip the country with a modern transport system and he could leave with good grace. But it meant that he must hang on, perhaps for three more years, through an endless quarrel that was less and less his own. He was not running a country, he was only running a railway and doing the best he could. If it was not good enough, if he had somehow been or grown to be the wrong man in the place, it was better to know now. Better to go now, in spite of the work undone. By June 6 he was in Ottawa and sitting across from Pearson, determined to have it out.

By June 7 he was back in his own office, with his thoughts of going rejected and sure of his friend's support. He was sure of George McIlraith, the new minister of transport, and the hostile faction in the cabinet was at least going to be contained. But beyond cabinet was the country, a still-seething Quebec and the question of the reappointment of a badly battered man. On that question, however, the mood of the man himself enabled a finished diplomat to find a political straddle.

On September 10 Gordon was called to Ottawa for a heart-to-heart talk. By the 11th he was busy in his office on the draft of a long letter. By the 14th the draft, edited by the prime minister, was returning to him in form:

I recognize that flowing from my appearance at the parliamentary committee [of 1962] was much criticism, distortion, misunderstanding and some public unrest. No one regrets more than I that this occurred. . . .
I have had a fairly long and active business life in Canada, and I have never indulged in *any kind* of discriminatory staffing procedures in any business or organization under my direction. . . . I recognize full well that in these times there is a searching look at the meaning of Confederation involving a restatement of certain rights and national aspirations. Our company has performed an intimate part in the making of Canada. We are deeply conscious of this and proud of it, and our objective is to

serve not only the transportation needs of the country but to serve national unity as well; a unity which must rest on the complete and accepted partnership of all French and English speaking Canadians.[4]

Bromidic it may have been, but it was public ammunition. On October 2, with this in hand, the prime minister wrote:

Dear Mr. Gordon: Some time ago, when I discussed with you the question of the expiry of your present appointment on September 30, you indicated that while you were reluctant to bear any longer than necessary the heavy responsibilities that you have shouldered for many years, you were also concerned about the completion of certain work to reorganize and strengthen the railway.

The Government now invites you to complete the work by accepting reappointment . . .[5]

To this the president replied, accepting the heavy honour but acknowledging its implication with one significant proviso. The work he had set himself, he said, 'should be finished in about a year and a half, in which case I will, in good conscience, ask to be released from the duties which I have always done my best to perform in a way which would be of benefit to the railway and the country'.[6]

The thing had been neatly done; in the Liberal caucus and the country friends cheered the appointment while enemies cheered the proviso. The single-minded Douglas Fisher rejoiced that Gordon was to step down in a matter of eighteen months. Claude Ryan, the new hand at *Le Devoir*, was at least suspending judgment. 'Let us not dismiss him for petty politics,' he had written. 'English Canada would not forgive this.'[7] Union leaders and the English press were rallying round as usual, none of them deciding much. The real test was ahead in the parliamentary committee, which had delayed its sittings till December. Grégoire would be ready there with his endless list of questions, and they were in sum a measure of the attitudes of changing times and peoples. If Gordon failed them, then he and his national railway could write failure to all.

The committee opened its sessions on December 12, 1963, one year and a day after the hanging of the president's effigy on Place Ville-Marie. It closed the next day with the Scot from Old Meldrum a rehabilitated man. One long statement detailing a year's work was his broad answer to Grégoire, and he read it into the record. For the most part it was still a story of beginnings, but it had begun at the very roots. The groups, committees and task forces set up by the CNR were studying the case of the average French Canadian, from his first reluctance to take a job with the railway to the obstacles blocking his entrance and those ahead on his path. They were clearing away the obstacles in hiring practice and procedure, in supervision and training and in the range and scope of work. In three years, he said, major results would show, but he sketched the peaks of progression through five pages of print:

> A special examination of state-owned railways in Switzerland and Belgium, with particular reference to the use of various languages . . . a large scale French and English language instruction program has been authorized . . . a French/English dictionary of railway terminology is almost complete . . . an accelerated program to recruit graduates and undergraduates from French Canadian universities . . . an accelerated program to increase the numbers of French Canadians attending established training courses . . . the development of succession planning, the objective being a higher proportion of French Canadian officers . . . an assessment of individual departmental requirements to assure that qualified French Canadians are given opportunities for advancement . . . the objective to foster an environment in which both languages can be freely used.

Beyond that, through another page, he detailed the bilingualization of the company's passenger and freight services, its ticket offices, train schedules, properties, publications and the whole of its outward aspect. 'The general philosophy,' he said, underlying the total effort, 'was a recognition and practical acceptance of the bicultural character of Canada.' He had, moreover, as a result of the applied philosophy, some practical steps to report: 'The studies into methods of accelerating the rate of progress of capable French Canadians have resulted in a modification to senior officer career planning procedures . . . it has been possible to move promising French Canadian officers into new and more senior positions . . . since January 1, 1963, forty-five per cent of all French Canadian senior officers have been promoted, transferred or appointed to positions providing more opportunities for development.'[8]

He concluded in the afternoon and that evening, in the time usually reserved for storms in the sessional committee, peace broke out in a flood of applauding words. 'In all justice,' said a French-Canadian member, speaking in his own tongue, 'we must congratulate personally, as I am doing now, the authorities of the Canadian National Railways and in particular Mr.

Gordon for the efforts he has made . . . if Mr. Gordon wants to give his recipes to other companies I think bilingualism will progress in this country.'[9] Balcer, who was speaking now as a Conservative in opposition, was not opposed to this. 'I see that tremendous effort has been done in the CNR. I have been very much impressed by the memorandum that was presented to this committee.'[10]

It remained for Grégoire, the initiator, to put the cap on the proceedings. 'Mr. Gordon,' he said, 'I think your report this afternoon was very clear. In fact I was surprised—and I use that term in its good sense—at your report. You gave us some statistics, you gave us some figures, and best of all—and it might surprise my friend, Mr. Fisher—I think you, more than many others, have understood what bilingualism is.'[11]

Perhaps, said a sardonic Fisher who was now concerned at the cost of the bilingual program, the committee should congratulate Gordon with Grégoire proposing the motion. 'I am ready to move,' said Grégoire, 'that the report is very satisfactory.'[12] Balcer heartily seconded and in an atmosphere that was becoming jocular a member suggested that Mr. Fisher might third it. There was no response to this but the motion passed unanimously and Grégoire glinted at Gordon. 'The students in Montreal might now come to the CNR and carry you in triumph to the university.'[13]

That was not to be achieved, but there was an acceptable second-best. Eleven months later, in the auditorium of the University of Montreal, Gordon addressed a student body free with applause and cheers. 'During the last two years,' he told them, 'we have all learned a lot of things.'[14] In his late years of office, though he had barely glimpsed the emerging problems of Canada, he had pulled abreast of his time.

There was to be a hard lesson the next year at the hands of an unloved teacher. Douglas Fisher, to Gordon, was an eternal nag and nuisance, but he was a man nagged at himself by an unrelenting conviction. Bigness, power and growth were somehow being abused by corporations, by government and even by trade unions at the expense of the little man. 'Services which were bread and butter in a lot of communities have disappeared with what I call metropolitanism,'[15] and a part of metropolitanism was the thrust of transportation. It was provided by trucks and aircraft and by both the major railways, but 'the CNR in Gordon's regime was more innovative than the CPR'.[16] For all the scattering buckshot of a dozen other attacks, this was the basic issue. Gordon's big diesels, as they stretched runs between the cities, were diminishing and threatening the existence of Fisher's northern towns.

The Port Arthur MP could not prevent the change or even deny the need for it; his quarrel was with pace and method. The decrees of Montreal, even when cleared with the heads of national unions, came down too often like thunderclaps on unprepared communities. Divisional points were closed, jobs lost or transferred and lives and plans disrupted without appeal or discussion. That, in Gordon's view, was a fact of railway life, as inevitable as the union contracts that protected the men exposed. They kept their seniority, they could move to new jobs and often with some retraining they were better off than before. If there were some who were worse off, and many who feared change, management must still act. It must act as it always had done in the name of higher efficiency, when and as it saw fit. Long debate was a warning to competition and the justification of changes would lie in the accomplished fact. 'He felt,' says Fisher, 'that fears were exaggerated. If you went ahead without too many preliminaries things would be fine . . . if you talked to the union leadership at the top that was the main thing.'[17]

That view of Gordon's, or Fisher's view of the view, produced a final battle which the railway chief lost. In August 1964 the company decided on run-throughs at Wainwright, Alberta, and Nakina, Ontario; the latter point a division in Fisher's constituency between Hornepayne and Armstrong. On September 14 it broached the plan to the national heads of the unions, without much obvious complaint. The change was perfectly legal, in accord with union contracts and it assured adequate protection to most of the men concerned. Or so the railway claimed as it went to the next step, without informing the heads of the concerned locals. On September 30, in a meeting held at Nakina, they and their men were simply called together to hear the official fiat. Nakina would cease to be a division point at midnight on Sunday, October 24, and work involving some fifty railway people would be phased out over the course of the next two years. The men, however, would retain their seniority and their right to paid retraining. The work lost would be recovered in other parts of the system and the homes of those who moved would be purchased, if necessary, by the company at a fair market price. The terms were generous on paper and as seen in a head office, but they were not subject to discussion and they did not change the fact. Nakina, the railway centre with its 192 families, was to lose a quarter of its jobs.

The consternation in Nakina had its western echo in Wainwright, and both were voiced by Fisher. He was at his telling best, however, on behalf of his own people. 'Death by Dieselization,' he wrote in the Winnipeg *Tribune* on Saturday, October 2:

It sounds like a murder story. In this case it is the proposed murder by the CNR of a small village in the Ontario bush. The place is Nakina, a divisional point and home terminal for train crews on the CN's transcontinental line. On October 25 the railway management initiates changes which in two years will make Nakina a ghost town and scatter most of its population . . . without question the CN can make a good case for savings and improved efficiency through wiping out Nakina and having the train crews run through it, from Hornepayne some 235 miles to Armstrong. But . . . Nakina has recently built a new public school and a substantial new Legion Hall. Not long ago the province completed an expensive road link to it from the Trans-Canada. Down it comes a big bus-load of Nakina students to the large, expensive district high school built at Geraldton. Nakina is a going community . . .

There is a theory abroad, without proof but widely held, that the costs of technological change are more than offset by the benefits to society as a whole.

Try to prove that to the people of Nakina.[18]

The union people at Nakina, as well as those at Wainwright, were by then busy at proving something else. The long, head office view, both of management and their own leaders, had been blind to an important factor. It was the advice, consent and essentially the human dignity of the men whose lives they changed. Tied to their union contracts and hemmed in by law, the men were stubbornly asserting it in the only way they could. On October 24, when the time for the change came, there would not be an official strike, there would simply be no work; they were planning to book off sick.

The plans were tacitly accepted by local union leaders, but they were not confided to management or even to politicians. Fisher expected trouble and intended to have a hand in it, but he did not know the extent. In Montreal he had a stormy interview with Gordon which accomplished nothing at all. On October 23 he rose in the House of Commons to demand an emergency debate and was turned aside again. The real situation and the real strength of his position were revealed only when he arrived at Nakina the following night.

He had expected to find picketers and the usual threats and gestures which had been ineffective before. Instead, the buzzing office of the railway union local was the centre of an epidemic. In the Mountain Region, which included the town of Wainwright, some 1,400 men were in suddenly failing health, while Nakina in the Great Lakes Region had somehow served as an infection point for seven hundred more. Through a long night and on into the morning Fisher was at the telephone, 'busy on all fronts'. The news went to his many friends in newspapers, in television and radio and finally to the politicians. The CNR, as a transcontinental railway, was about to grind to a stop.

As the news went out on the early Sunday broadcasts it was heard at Edgehill Road, in the home of the prime minister and in the home of Jack Pickersgill, who was then minister of transport. A little later Pickersgill's telephone rang. He was still in bed recovering from a bout of flu and he was not cheered by the call. 'It was Doug Fisher and he said, "You're going to have the whole railway system tied up." He was egging those people on, but I think at the end he was a little afraid of what he was doing. It was working too well. I said, "What do you expect me to do about it? The CNR's a business corporation and we can't interfere."

' "Don't give me that nonsense."

' "It just happens to be true."

' "We want a government commission and an inquiry. You get us that and the men'll go back to work."

'Well,' Pickersgill continues, recalling that rheumy morning, 'I began thinking about it and about nine o'clock I got up and went round to see Mike. "You know," I said, "If we appoint a royal commission Donald would simply resign—we'd be interfering with the railway. But if I could get him to *ask* the government for a commission—is it okay to try?" '

Anything was okay to the harassed prime minister, who had a flag debate on his hands.

'So I went back and lay there on the bed and got Donald on the phone. It was about half-past ten, maybe a little earlier, and I told him I'd been talking to Mike. I didn't say I'd got up out of bed to go and see him; I just said, "Look, Donald, we were wondering whether it would help you to get out of this difficulty we're all in if you sent a telegram to me or the prime minister, it doesn't matter which, asking the government to appoint a royal commission."

'You could feel him winding up on the other end. "Do you mean to tell me that you've *decided* to appoint a royal commission?"

' "No, no—that's the last thing I'd think of doing. You're running the CNR and I'm running the Department of Transport—you don't tell me what to do and I don't tell you. This has got to be a spontaneous gesture on your part, and it's got to look like one. I'm at home in bed, Donald—there'll never be anything on paper about this."

' "Well"—after a long, considering silence—"I'm just going to church."

' "You'd better pray," I said, "and then think about it and call me this afternoon".'

At three o'clock the phone rang, but it was only the prime minister. Had Pickersgill heard from Gordon and, if not, should he try again? 'I said, "No, Donald is having a great struggle with his soul because he isn't entirely convinced that he's not under pressure. He's got to convince himself that *he* thought of this".' The prime minister hung up and the minister of transport waited till approximately four o'clock. 'Then the phone rang and it was Donald: "I've been thinking over that thing and I've drafted a telegram— addressed to Mike, of course. How do you think this sounds?"

'Well, it sounded fine—I could have said yes instantly, but that wouldn't have done. I mustn't make a snap decision. I pondered and mumbled a bit and said, "Read it to me once again, Donald, just to be really sure." So he read it over again and I gave a sigh of relief that I hope he took for applause —"Donald, I don't think you could put it any better".'[19]

The result of the day's doings on the upper levels of government was reported to the House of Commons on Monday afternoon. The president and the prime minister had had an exchange of telegrams. 'Mr. Gordon's telegram stated that if the Government was willing to appoint an independent and impartial person to examine the CNR's run-through proposals the company would not proceed further with its plans until a report arising from such examination would be made. The prime minister's telegram accepted Mr. Gordon's suggestion and indicated that the Government would appoint such a person to make the desired examination.'[20]

By Tuesday the railway's sick men had all recovered their health and trains were running again. A week later it was announced that the Honourable Mr. Justice Samuel Freedman of Winnipeg would be appointed a committee of one to conduct the investigation. A year later, on November 17, 1965, the Freedman report was issued and railway labour relations had passed another milestone.

What had happened at Nakina and Wainwright, Freedman found, was an illegal work stoppage winked at by union leaders. It had opposed a move by the company that was clearly within its rights under present collective agreements. But outside the agreements there were areas undefined and conditions not provided for where the company assumed discretion as management's 'residual rights'. In other words, whatever the effects of changes demanded by new conditions, if they were not set out in the contract the boss had the final say.

It was no longer good enough. At Nakina 'the decision to purchase homes so that the dislocated men would sustain no loss was an eminently decent and humane one'. But 'the company did the right thing in the wrong way . . .

union officers were not informed in advance of the company's plan or decision to purchase homes . . . to go over the heads of the accredited Brotherhood representatives and to announce its decision directly to the men at a general meeting was to impair labour-management relations . . . one witness described the company's conduct as "a dangerous adventure", and the Commission is disposed to agree.'[21]

The unions were not found blameless. 'There are responsibilities upon labour . . . perhaps chief among them is not to use its organized strength in blind and wilful resistance to technological advances. Labour must recognize the constructive role of technology in the general welfare and economic strength of the nation. Nor should it insist upon unreasonably high rewards or excessive safeguards as the price of its acceptance of change. Stubborn opposition to measures of progress can only hurt the nation, labour not least of all.'[22]

Yet management and its residual rights were also subject to change. The company's action at Wainwright and Nakina, perfectly legal as it was, had subjected men to an abrupt and unforeseen change in working conditions, 'and this without recourse. . . . Their contract was made on the basis of one set of circumstances. Now it must be performed on the basis of another set of circumstances, devised by management alone and to which they have given no consent. There is a manifest inequity here which clamours for attention and correction. . . .'[23]

'On the basis of the law as it exists today the company does have the right to institute run-throughs. Should it continue to have that right? The question here raised lies at the heart of this inquiry. The Commission is satisfied that it must be answered only in one way. The institution of run-throughs should be a matter for negotiation.'[24]

Fisher had made his point, and his work was duly acknowledged. 'Mr. Fisher, as a man dedicated to the interests of labour, has upheld the cause of the men with consistency and with vigour.' He was not the author of the strike but 'once the strike had started he did all he could to aid its development; with what success it is impossible to gauge, but probably with some.'[25] He was leaving politics by then, and it was a satisfying enough conclusion to some long and bruising years. In his own mind Fisher had reconfirmed, in relation to the stubborn Scot, an opinion he quoted later as that of another man: 'One of the fellows close to him—Ralph Vaughan—told me that Gordon, in a sense, got to the railway about five years too late in terms of disposition and flexibility.'[26]

It is just possible that by that time the president might have concurred. He was a long way from the days when, as Grattan O'Leary put it, he 'burst like some joyous firecracker on the Ottawa floor'.[27] The ingrained beliefs of

Old Meldrum had carried him through thirty years, with the Bank of Canada, the Prices Board and the Canadian National Railway. Yet they seemed now to be wearing a little thin. The plans for Nakina and Wainwright would remain shelved for a while, and the questions growing out of them, expanding to new dimensions, were summed up by Freedman: 'The run-through becomes a special phase of a more general problem; it becomes a symptom of a larger issue. That general problem and larger issue is the place of human beings in a rapidly changing technological and economic world.'[28]

On January 20, 1965, in the seventeenth month of his new term, Gordon had conducted a board meeting with some notes on a sheet of foolscap under his big hand: 'Exercise my option—enquire . . . Reappointment, note phrasing —PM to write—volunteered procedure before I had a chance to suggest— had not been possible to implement legislation on MacPherson Commission and Recapitalization—therefore asks me to continue . . . Political crisis no longer there—reference to Gregoire . . . must have understanding re legislation if continuing . . . question of succession, NJM.'[29]

As a cryptic summary of a telephone talk, it was expanded on for the directors. Gordon's half-promise in accepting reappointment had represented an option to retire in eighteen months. But it had also been conditional on the completion of work that still remained undone. The stormy Parliament of Canada had not yet touched the MacPherson report or approached recapitalization. Those questions would be dealt with if the president stayed on, and the choice was now his own. He was reestablished in French-Canadian opinion; Gilles Grégoire, in a debate a few months earlier on another public facility had suggested: 'Maybe the CBC needs a first-rate administrator like Donald Gordon.'[30] The railway head, moreover, was firm enough in the saddle to prescribe beyond his term. NJM—Norman J. MacMillan—was to be designated successor.

The board was satisfyingly unanimous and prepared to go to Ottawa to support the president's views. He declined that as quite unnecessary pressure. On February 3, after an hour and a half alone with the prime minister, he came out with all that he wanted. Pearson, he wrote that evening in his 'Strictly Personal and Confidential' file:

> proposes to write a personal letter to me referring to the previous exchange of correspondence and to the mention of the eighteen months. He would then refer to the fact that the legislation which had been in contemplation, namely that arising out of the MacPherson Commission

and our recommendations for a CNR recapitalization, had not been
enacted and therefore it was obvious that it had not been possible for me
to complete the work which I had in mind. He would try to express
himself in such a way as to invite me to continue in my position on the
assurance that his government intended to press on with the legislation
as soon as practicably possible.[31]

'Practicably possible' in political terms could be a long, long time, but
there were eighteen months ahead of him and he put his trust in Mike.
Meanwhile, as he looked at the work around him, the signs were generally
good. From 1960 onward the railway's revenues had climbed and its deficits
begun to sink. 'Heavier train loads, faster speeds and improved distribution
and utilization of freight and passenger car equipment' figured in annual
reports. Also and more significantly, by 1965 Gordon was able to write: 'No
new modernization projects of a major nature are considered to be necessary
in the immediate future.'[32] He had not reached his objectives and profits
were still elusive but he had gained a sort of plateau. The periods of heavy
spending, the automation and the humpyards and the masses of new equipment were beginning to pay off

Nor was it only the big diesels with their flaring orange noses and the long
strings and growing variety of freight cars that contributed to the new
regime. The CN symbol rippled along the highways on the sides of big
trucks. The CN presence was stronger within the country as one of the
thrusts of growth. Flowing from the Queen Elizabeth, there had been a
general modernization of all the company's hotels. Ville-Marie had its echo
in town developments, office buildings, shopping centres and plazas rising
on the company's real estate across the breadth of the country. And with all
that, passenger business, the Cinderella of the railway, was out of its drab
doldrums and showing some signs of life.

In 1960, with the transcontinentals losing ground to the airlines and
short-range traffic usurped by the automobile, Gordon had complained of
'80-seat cars rattling round the country with half a dozen passengers' who
were only served at all, and served at a dead loss, because the government
required it.[33] Passengers themselves had been complaining of dismal old
trains, surly and shabby staff, long waits for tickets from apparently reluctant
salesmen and too-expensive meals. Then, with the MacPherson report and
its far-off promise of relief, the president had shifted ground. 'If we can't
get rid of our passenger service before we all have long, white beards,' he
was credited as saying, 'then we'll do our damndest to make it pay.'[34]

He had presided, half-convinced, over several years of revival conducted with dramatic flair. Equipment had been spruced up, new equipment ordered and there had been an intensive combing of markets. By 1965, Red, White and Blue fares, keyed to the traffic volume, provided passengers with 58 standard-rate, 146 economy and 161 bargain days a year. Instead of queuing at windows they could order tickets by mail, and they could eat in cafeteria cars or smarter and cheaper diners. They were travelling in increased numbers with vastly improved service in better and better trains. They could go in groups by Rent-a-Rail at reduced charter fares; and Cargo-Rail, for the tourist's automobile, delivered it freshly washed at destination. From the station clerk to the porter all along the lines the welcome offered the traveller was enforced by stern injunctions: 'Passengers are not an interruption to our work; they *are* our work'—'Ask yourself—am I treating this person as I would like him to treat me?'[35]

The reformed Ocean Limited, with four hours shaved from its time, was actually making money. The new Panorama, as a show-train to the west, was at least exciting the public. Gordon, who had once considered the dome cars of the CPR to be merely a passing whimsy, was now providing 'Skyview' observation cars and lounges for a 529-mile trip through the Rockies scheduled wholly in daylight. There was a Hospitality Hour and a Children's Playtime Hour, with games, toys and a counsellor. The passenger was provided with newspapers, maps and hourly news bulletins, and his evenings were crowned with Bingo. 'In future,' wrote one enthusiast, returning from such a trip, CN excursions would provide 'sundecks and swimming pools, television and movies, bars and restaurants and even live fashion shows on trains that will travel at double present speeds.'[36]

Much of the impetus for change had been provided by Pierre Delagrave, one of the French Canadians who had been advanced to a vice-presidency. By 1965, though he himself had left, his verve had quickened the railway and led to a new departure. Pooled passenger service between Montreal and Toronto, jointly operated by the Canadian Pacific and the Canadian National, had been a venerable source of quarrels and a steady devourer of funds. In 1965, with due permission from the government and acquiescence from its rival, the CPR withdrew from the losing game. It had not foreseen, however, or it had discounted its rival's plans. By 1966, with the introduction of the sleek new Rapido of the Canadian National Railways, travellers were forsaking aircraft, leaving their cars at home and reserving weeks ahead for a modern trip by rail. 'A pleasant man in oxford gray takes your bag. A red-coated porter takes your coat and shows you to your wide, airplane-style seat. A steward drops by to ask at what hour you want your free dinner—

minutes later you race into the dusk at 90 miles per hour on the fastest train for this distance in North America.'[37]

Yet for all the spectacular advances and all the patches of profit, the old imperatives remained. Passenger business was a showcase for the railway but freight was the bread and butter. The fast transcontinentals sometimes waited on sidings while the through freights went past. For every paying Rapido there were a dozen losing branch lines. The cost of high-speed trains was thousands of miles of new high-speed roadbeds, and the president balked at that. Wherever his friend, technology, opened new horizons it was imposing new demands, on him as well as his men. The airplane frame and aluminum skin of the Turbo-train were still a while in the future, and he was content to leave them there. 'Do you really want this thing?' he asked Norman MacMillan.

'Yes, I want to go on with it.'

'Okay, you put her on the agenda and you talk to it and I won't say anything, pro or con. If you can sell the board, okay; if you can't, okay—is that fair?'

'Sure,' MacMillan said, and the president went on with his work.[38] He was worried about his eyes, he had problems enough in front of him and he was not so spruce in the mornings after a hard night. It was getting to be time to go.

He was now Donald Gordon, Companion of the Order of St. Michael and St. George, and since 1958 Knight of Grace of the Order of St. John of Jerusalem. A building at Queen's was named for him, he had a string of degrees from Canadian universities and every national newspaper had a thick file for his obituary. But the honours had not much changed him or altered his public image. 'He has been likened,' said Dean Woods of McGill in welcoming him to the university as an honorary Doctor of Laws, 'to a bull who carries his own china shop around with him.'[39]

His answer to that had been a quote from Ogden Nash: 'Early to rise, early to bed makes a man healthy, wealthy and dead.' He was no more given than he had ever been to following that precept. His stories were still as scabrous, he was as rough, noisy and hard to get along with as he had been in the Prices Board days, and through sixteen years with the railway he had clung to some old friends. He was true to one in particular in spite of time, distance, the demands of respective eminence and the disapproval of his wife. Wherever their paths crossed he was to be found with Wallace McCutcheon and heard too often in lubricated song, disrupting the small hours. He was a difficult companion for Norma at prestigious social gatherings and his bouts of private contrition were as short and passing as before. The public figure demanded public licence, and on some occasions considerably overstretched it.

One such, as recalled by Jim McDonald, provided a memorable experience for Ian Sinclair who had succeeded Crump as president of the CPR. 'Ian and Donald were in Ottawa on one of the periodic labour negotiations. When they finished they had a little time to spare, so they went over to the House of Commons and were ushered into one of the prominent galleries. They were sitting in front row seats, right up against the railing, and as David Lewis held forth it began to get to Gordon. Finally he leaned out over the rail, held up those great arms of his and said "Bullshit!" in a voice that carried endlessly through the House. The whole place just dissolved, and of course the Sergeant-at-Arms was detailed.' Gordon had fulfilled in part at least the prediction made by MacMillan years before. 'He was escorted out by two big, burly officials, with Ian trailing along, and no sooner did he hit the hall than a corps of reporters descended. Would he like to elaborate on that remark?

' "No. I've said enough already. Mr. Sinclair will speak for me". ' Sinclair, however, refrained and officialdom closed round Gordon. 'They escorted him right out to the very front of the parliament buildings.'[40]

Yet, for all that was still unchanged, there was much change on the way. By 1965, as he approached his middle sixties, the pump-watching, wood-chopping and pioneering austerities of the life at Luster Lake had begun to lose their charm. He was less inclined to the gruelling trip north, still less to the bouncing Pink Elephant, the wildly painted and unreliable jeep. 'He never knew how to work the god-damned gears or anything,' one of his friends noted, 'and he was restless around the place. He was absolutely delighted when Sunday night came and he got back to town.'[41] So was Norma, for whom life in the raw Gatineau with her mother and ailing father and its endless flow of visitors was becoming a bit too much. Besides that, an unwelcome spectre at the sixty-fifth milestone, the thought of retirement loomed. The time was coming when there would be no Bonaventure, the presidential car, to hook on a westbound train; they would have the drive to Ottawa as well as the drive north. They had begun to think and talk of a place in the Eastern Townships, when suddenly the place was found through the good offices of a friend. It was a lovely property at Georgeville on Lake Memphremagog, and by April 1966 a house was building. They left the plans reluctantly for a trip to the Far East, and came back early in May with all plans in suspension.

His weak eyes had been bothering Gordon since 1964, but within two days of his return the time for action came. 'I have just received word from my oculist,' he wrote to Frank Ross, 'that I have suffered a separation of the retina in my left eye.' There would be an emergency operation simply to restore the retina, and beyond that was a cataract which would have to be left for later. 'It looks as if for the next couple of years I will be fooling around with hospitals.'[42]

Even the next two weeks were a grim enough experience for a man who feared the dark. 'The operation,' says Norman MacMillan, 'just about drove him round the bend. He wouldn't let me go to see him—"Don't want you"— he was tied down with pressure bandages on his eyes and the bandages made his claustrophobia worse— it was all agonizing for him.'[43] By June 13, as he was released to convalesce, he had lost fifteen pounds, was far from reassured and had circumscribed his horizons. Luster Lake was a burden now, waiting to be unloaded, and the place where he had sung his first songs in the Gatineau was sliding off with the past. He had always kept his membership in the Five Lakes Fishing Club and returned there occasionally for one of the rousing nights. On the first day he was allowed back at the office, one of the papers waiting was a bill for his annual dues. He would not be paying them this year. 'I feel it is as good a time as any to relinquish my member-ship.'[44]

By July his mood was better, and in one last encounter with the sessional committee of parliament he seemed to be a restored man. To the newspapers yearning for fireworks he had become 'a smoothie who charms', and with his hopes built on the MacPherson report he was a bringer of good news. 'Looking fit in his first public appearance since a serious eye operation,' the president informed reporters that he could see the end of deficits. 'Barring the unforeseen, the break-even point will come in 1971, and we're not going to stop there.'[45] He was well out in his prediction but he did not know it then, and the prophet yearned to see the day of fulfilment. He could hardly hope, however, to be president when the day came. The mandatory age for retirement was sixty-five years; he had always rigorously enforced it and he would be sixty-five in December.

'He hated to leave the CNR,' says Norma Gordon, 'and he wasn't looking forward to retirement, but he intended to practise what he preached.'[46] Yet he remained susceptible to dissuasion at a suitably high level and conveyed as much to his friend, the minister of transport. 'The last few months before his sixty-fifth birthday,' says Jack Pickersgill, 'he began to drop hints to me— maybe he shouldn't retire—maybe he should stay on. I said, "Donald, you can of course go to the prime minister; he'd personally recommend you. But I will not recommend any extension of your term."

' "Why?"

' "I'll tell you why. You want to have another career—you're not satisfied to stop here and at sixty-five Donald Gordon, unlike most people, is still employable. At sixty-six you'll be marginally employable and at sixty-seven nobody will be interested—then you'd really retire."

'He thought it over for a minute and heaved up out of his chair. "Jack, I want to leave—clear out complete." And that was it.'[47]

By August another prospect had added gloom to his going. Railway workers, he had said four years earlier, were tasting the fruits of progress. With the 'beast of burden jobs' done by machines, they were 'more skilled, better paid and, with working conditions almost miraculously improved, their whole outlook on life is better'.[48] It was true within his own time-frame, a part of his own work, but the frame went on expanding. It seemed now, for all he thought he had accomplished, that he was going to leave the railway much as he had come in, at odds with demanding labour. He was even sounding another call, warning of the old bugbear he had fought in Prices Board days. 'The stage is being set,' he noted in an ominous memo, 'for another serious confrontation, the end of which is likely to spark another wave of wage increases, bringing with it increased freight rates, etc. Inflation seems inevitable.'[49]

Everything was too familiar and a little worse than before. On August 26, after ten months of threats and negotiation, a second national strike closed down the railways. By September 1 it was over and the men sent back to work by another Act of Parliament. There was to be mediation first and compulsory arbitration if mediation failed, but the mood attending any hopes of a settlement was something dangerously new. Union leaders, bitter themselves at government, were losing grip on their men; wildcat strikes and holdouts at patches across the system were threatening the rule of law.

Or so it seemed to the president as he parted with Luster Lake. The strike sat on his shoulders and old ghosts walked beside him when he came up in September to greet a prospective buyer. It was Peter Ustinov, who had married an Ottawa girl but remained a foreign actor. 'He was there for the afternoon and we gave him tea,' Norma says, 'but I had to do the talking. Donald didn't much cotton to Ustinov.'[50] Yet neither the actor nor the strike was responsible for the glowering silence. It was the last going from all that the place had meant; and once again and familiarly there was strain with the elder son. 'I feel bitter about that sale,' says Donnie, 'because I offered to match Ustinov's price and my father wouldn't agree to it—he didn't feel I could be trusted.'[51] The eccentric of press and broadcasting was now established as a professor of economics at the University of Calgary, but it had not changed the parental view of his status. With nothing reserved but 'personal belongings, keepsakes and souvenirs, couch on verandah at cottage number 1, drink cooler in cottage number 2 and hand tools for the most part stored in tool shed',[52] Luster Lake with its memories passed to other hands.

Meanwhile, amid the murk of a troubled autumn there were several glimmers of light. The railway men, though they were mutinous and still without a contract, were accepting mediation. The government, at long last, had worked its way to the MacPherson report and introduced a bill. The prospect now for the railways was of largely increased earnings and new rules for the game; and in some ways there were better prospects than that. It had been Gordon's cry for years that 'Canada is desperately in need of men who know how to live with trade unions'.[53] He had found one in the genial Bill Wilson, for the last ten years at the head of personnel, and Wilson had found him others. Gordon, Crump and Sinclair, for all their woes and shortfalls, had learned a good deal themselves. Far as management and unions were apart on terms and money, they were equally far from the mood of 1950. There was a measure of hard-eyed trust, a basic wish to agree; and in Carl Goldenberg, the lawyer and government-appointed mediator, there was a skilful linking hand.

Goldenberg was a future senator and the country's leading diplomat in the field of labour relations. He came to the work with thirty years' experience of constitutional, labour, municipal and industrial problems and he had been involved on every level, from federal-provincial disputes to the organization of Metropolitan Toronto. By November 15, the date set as his deadline, he had produced a railway contract. It shaved the claims of both sides, but to union men who look back on it as a key to new beginnings he had done a 'supreme job'. Gordon wrote of him later as 'Carl Goldenberg, for whom the impossible is only a challenge', and the president had reason to be grateful for a regal parting gift. With a three-year contract in place of the usual two, he was leaving at peace with labour.

There was not much more to be done now, or much that Gordon could do. Parliament toyed with the MacPherson report, taking its own time. 'I really would feel fulfilled if Recapitalization could be brought about,' he wrote MacMillan,[54] but he would not see it in his day; he had become resigned to that. In a drawer of his clearing desk he had three sheets of pencilled notes on foolscap under the heading, 'Invitations'. The Board of the Mercantile Bank was interested in obtaining Gordon; Arnold Hart of the Bank of Montreal was inviting him to become a director. 'Howard Webster telephoned on behalf of Max Bell, wondering "if I would condescend" to join the Globe and Mail board . . . telephone call Charles Bell, Crown Life

Assurance . . . Bill Nicks, President of the Bank of Nova Scotia, pressing hard.' Home Oil, RCA and the Hudson's Bay Company were all looking for a director; and in the case of Hudson's Bay, as the careful Scot noted, 'there is a 40% discount given all directors on purchase at stores'. Twaits of Imperial Oil, Scotty Bruce of Alcan and even Jack Pickersgill, plugging for the Board of Transport, were among the other suitors. Heading the list, however, abbreviated and enigmatic and dating back to July, was the note, 're Brinco'.[55]

He did not know much about the development at Churchill Falls except that it was very big, that the company behind it was loaded with substantial names and that it was a huge devourer of money. But the two words on his list recorded an 'invitation' and there were thoughts working in his mind. Arthur Crockett of the Bank of Nova Scotia, one of his Westmount neighbours, had had a long drive with Gordon to a conference at Montebello. 'Coming back, quite late at night, he mentioned that his term at the CN was coming to a close and I asked him—what are you going to do? Well, he started talking about water and the great pollution in the lakes and rivers and how somebody should do something about it. Whether he rambled around like that just to throw me off I don't know, but when he ended up he said, "Whatever it is, it's going to be something to do with water".'[56]

By the end of November he had had a long lobster lunch with Val Duncan, the head of Rio Algom and a power behind Brinco. Nothing was yet settled but suddenly it had become December and he was the retiring president of a railway, a man about to go. On the 11th he was sixty-five and on the 15th, answering a gaudy summons, he was standing up before his senior management people, called to a last accounting. It was at a banquet rather than a board table, and an accounting like few others. Go-go girls had saluted the president's entrance to the strains of 'Hello Donald', a gift of Public Relations as his own special song. The same irreverent department had also produced a film and down the length of the table beside each well-filled glass was a 'Hello Donald' booklet, diminutive, red and rude. As the film was shown and the presents showered down, the booklet's captions and photographs were a supplemental slander. The burly youth of the bank days stood glowering in his first suit: 'Ye lookin' fra a boot i' the arse?' The president signed a hotel register while a questioning clerk looked on: 'Mr. and Mrs. Donald SMITH?' He stood, pointer in hand, before a large map of the system, facing his board of directors: 'Now this is the local bootlegger's, and right over here is Sadie's place.' 'An' de big, bad Diefenbaker,' he explained to wide-eyed children cozily ensconced on his lap, 'went to hell, and de good Liberals lived happily ever after.' He looked out in farewell from behind the bars of a packing crate, saluting his friend, MacMillan: 'Honest, Norman, I was only kidding—I won't be back.'[57]

He had expected what he would get and prepared appropriate notes that still glint up from his files. 'Lion-tamer'—'cock-eyed rooster'—'champagne and beer'—were heads for some of the stories selected from his endless list. There was much else, gleaned from the sixteen years: 'here under summons . . . guilty as charged but plead extenuation . . . no malice or calculated design. Instead, when I saw what a bloody mess railroaders had got themselves into, conceived instant ambition to demonstrate that bad as it was I could add to the confusion. My intentions thwarted, however, by skilful officers and associates who watched carefully my orders or decisions and did exactly the opposite.'

No survey of railroading, and certainly no such gathering of intramural jubilance, could be without reference to the competitor and the president complied with that: 'My attitude toward CPR has been unfailingly helpful and based on "Alas, my Poor Brother" sentiment . . . every pioneering step ensured free lessons for CP . . . witness kindly intentions, how we rushed forward to help CP out of passenger service in the Montreal–Toronto–Ottawa triangle, the only potentially profitable market in Canada.'

There was more prepared in other veins, some of it left unsaid, but most came out on the evening. 'More seriously', a wistful note was sounded in the conclusion: 'There is an exciting future stretching ahead of the transportation industry in every aspect of it. Every mode of movement, in air, water, land and underground, is upon Cloud Nine with forecasts that stagger the imagination.'[58]

That, however, would be left for Norman MacMillan and the men who followed him. 'Bless you!' he wrote to MacMillan a few days later. 'And my warmest good wishes to you as a friend and as a valued associate of many years, as you take over on January 1st.'[59] There was a round of farewell parties, a cluster of other offers and a camping Christmas at Georgeville in the house still to be completed. Then it was about over, except for the press club dinner to be held in Montreal. As he came in for the high jinks and the gift and the ribbings he had learned to live with through his years of making copy, he was saluted with 'I've Been Working on the Railroad' and asked to sign the register. 'Donald Gordon,' he wrote, and paused and looked up, 'Can't say CN any more.' 'Donald Gordon,' the completed inscription read, '172 Edgehill Road'.[60]

CHAPTER 18

'Something to do with water'

By the beginning of March 1967, the ex-president had had all he would ever know, and more than he would ever want, of the joys of retirement. For two weeks, as the replaced man at headquarters, he had hovered in a little office on the fourth floor of the building, 'tidying things up'. A three-week holiday in Jamaica, where he hated the hotel they stayed at and drank like a thirsty bear, had been sheer hell for Norma. Following that, during a two-week stay at Georgeville, he had been waging war with the weather and with a new form of transport. The Pink Elephant, even at Luster Lake, had been a tired and aging jeep and the hills of the Eastern Townships were quite beyond its powers. Norma, who was devoted to all things English, had persuaded him to buy a Land-Rover, which as usual he could not drive, at least on a snowy road. 'Practically every time we went out there it seemed to be a howling blizzard, and we always seemed to have supplies for six months. We had to leave the Land-Rover at the top of the hill, unload all the luggage and carry it down to the house. I could see it was getting harder for him to do, but I couldn't talk him out of it.'[1] February closed, however, with a brief trip to London and a return in better mood. There had been a congenial social round, some final negotiations and 'something to do with water' had shaped up as a job.

'I have just accepted an appointment,' he wrote on March 8, 'as President and Chief Executive Officer of the British Newfoundland Corporation (BRINCO) and also Chairman of the Board of Directors of Churchill Falls (Labrador) Ltd. As you probably know, the chief objective of these companies is the development of the enormous hydro-electric energy potential of the Labrador water shed. It is imperative that decisions be made covering technical engineering matters and very large financing arrangements required, so that I shall be fully occupied in Canada and elsewhere.'[2]

He was succeeding Henry Borden whom he had known since Prices Board days and who, as a nephew of Sir Robert Borden and as president of Brazilian Traction, director of many companies and promoter of the National Energy Board, established ten years earlier, was a senior industrial statesman. Borden himself had succeeded Robert Winters, another towering figure on the industrial and political scene; and behind both men, ranging back to the first days of the project, was a cluster of dazzling names. Prime ministers and premiers, bankers and engineers, tycoons, companies and consortiums had been involved ahead of Gordon in pursuit of an old dream. Many were still involved and awaiting a consummation, the marriage of water with money to produce electric power.

The falls on the Hamilton River in the central Labrador plateau had been first seen by a white man in 1839. John McLean, an officer of the Hudson's Bay Company, had been paddling down the river 'when the roar of a mighty cataract burst upon our ears, warning us that danger was at hand'.[3] What he had seen had turned him back, and for over fifty years Patses-che-wan, 'The Narrow Place Where the Water Falls', had lain avoided by Indians as a haunt of evil spirits and unknown to explorers. In the summer of 1891, however, two groups of Americans travelling west from Lake Melville had arrived within two weeks of each other at a point on the Hamilton River fifteen hundred feet above sea level where, as one of them recorded, 'a single glance showed that we had before us one of the greatest waterfalls in the world'.[4] It remained for later surveys to determine the real potential but in 1915, thirty-two years before these were actually begun, Wilfrid Thibaudeau, a Quebec engineer, had outlined the nature of the terrain and conceived the genesis of a plan.

The plateau rose in a great saucer-shaped depression, catching the annual rainfall and emptying it off through hundreds of lakes and rivers at the gaps broken in its rim. The gaps, however, were comparatively few and small and the main flow entered the Hamilton by way of a narrow gorge. Five miles back from its rim the basin sloped toward the gorge and the water gathered speed. It went out over the lip, foaming in free space, for a sheer vertical plunge to a great pool below. That alone was a drop of 245 feet, a third more than the Horseshoe Falls at Niagara, but it was merely a stop en route. The pool that broke the fall was emptied again by rapids that continued the downward progress for another twenty-two miles. Between the beginning of the rapids in the saucer and the end of the rapids on the river there was a total fall of over a thousand feet. If the gaps in its rim were closed the saucer would become a reservoir about half the size of Lake

Ontario. If a tunnel replaced the gorge, bypassing the pool and rapids, there would be a direct fall for the water to the lower level of the river. That was Thibaudeau's idea and it became the essence of the plan. Some forty miles of dykes built with the glacial rubble lying ready on the plateau would seal the rim of the saucer and create a giant lake. That lake, as it was emptied down by tunnels cut through the solid rock, would provide the 'head' for turbines a thousand feet below.

In 1949, Newfoundland, the possessor of Labrador, became a province of Canada. By 1952, Joseph R. Smallwood, its first and liveliest premier, was making a deal in London, 'the biggest real estate deal of the present century'.[5] He had convinced Winston Churchill, in Churchill's own words, that 'Hamilton Falls should have a bridle'.[6] The Rothschilds had received Smallwood at Churchill's invitation and lunch at storied New Court had included Sir Eric Bowater, whose Bowater Corporation was an owner of mills in Newfoundland and one of the world's largest manufacturers of newsprint. What Joey Smallwood was offering centred on Hamilton Falls but went considerably beyond it. Pulpwood rights, mineral rights and the right to exploration were all included in a deal which drew in as it developed a highly prestigious group, including the Rothschilds, Bowater, Lord Leathers, Lord Rothermere and J. N. V. ('Val') Duncan, head of the world-wide Rio Tinto-Zinc Corporation which was soon to have a Canadian subsidiary, Rio Algom. In the meantime, by March 1953, the consortium had taken shape and established itself in St. John's. British-Newfoundland Corporation Limited, soon shortened to Brinco, was to have timbering rights, mineral and exploration rights and the right to the development of water-power over 10,000 square miles on the island of Newfoundland and over 50,000 square miles in Labrador, including Hamilton Falls.

For the next thirteen years, though there was a successful pilot development on one tributary river, Brinco's revenues from its timber and mining concessions had provided the skimpy cushion for a delayed central project. In 1954, as $3 million was budgeted for a survey of Hamilton Falls, Joey Smallwood and a series of Quebec premiers embarked on a sea of troubles. The market for power was New York, a thousand miles to the south, and the transmission lines for its delivery would cross the province of Quebec. But Quebec itself was in search of additional power; it did not relish the thought of merely serving as a pipeline, and Premier Maurice Duplessis raised a horrendous doubt. The boundary between Quebec and Labrador had been in dispute for years and Quebec's claims, if established, would include Hamilton Falls. They would do that over Smallwood's dead body but the first hints of Duplessis, echoed by two successors, were only abandoned tentatively in the time of Jean Lesage. On that point, when Daniel Johnson succeeded him in 1966, there was a rasped and sombre truce.

Meanwhile Hamilton Falls had become Churchill Falls, renamed by a grateful Smallwood in honour of the project's sponsor. Neither great names, however, nor large expenditures of money had as yet produced power. Climate, distance and geography had called for hundreds of surveys and perplexed the engineers. Innumerable major problems, technical, political and financial, had threatened the whole scheme. Smallwood had become restless in the arms of the great consortium and talked of nationalization as he waged his war with Quebec. The sister province, in 1963, had actually nationalized its then-existing resources and set up Hydro-Quebec as a public corporation. Private and public enterprise, uneasily linked together in the hopes for Churchill Falls, had met disaster in the south. Consolidated Edison of New York, the first potential customer, had backed away from the plan, mistrustful of long delays. That blow, however, had been countered by Quebec itself as the years of bickering continued and its own requirements grew. By 1965, instead of a share of the output of a plant still to be built, it was prepared to accept the whole, on due terms and conditions. By 1966, with rates and costs tentative but a date for supply set, the letter of intent was signed. Quebec would take the power to be produced at Churchill Falls, with delivery to its own transmission lines by 1972. The greatest problem was solved; there was a market now for the goods. But the Bank of Montreal was lending the company money on the security of flowing water and on work not yet begun. Gordon came to office with the letting of the first contracts, and all he needed to complete them was approximately a billion dollars.

Arnold Hart, president of the Bank of Montreal, had been prompt to renew his standing invitation. By March 1967, Gordon was one of the directors of a bank which had $10 million riding on Brinco and its subsidiary, Churchill Falls (Labrador) Limited, and was likely to have more. In the offices of Brinco itself, which had been established for the past ten years at 1980 Sherbrooke Street, there was a constant hum of planning and a coming and going of wildly assorted experts. Gordon's closest associates were Donald J. McParland, a brilliant young mining engineer in charge of technical development, and Eric G. Lambert, an imperturbable and highly congenial Scot, who was vice-president, finance. The new head of the company was often in New York, where William D. Mulholland, one of the partners in Morgan, Stanley and Company, the investment bankers, was expected to raise $500 million in long-term financing from American mortgage lenders. Val Duncan of the enormous and impregnable Rio Tinto-Zinc Corporation and the genial Edmund de Rothschild, scion of the great family, were familiar visitors to Canada and Gordon's hosts in London. At Churchill Falls itself the roads were being cleared for bulldozers and the planes and helicopters arriving with supplies, machines and workers. After fifteen years of effort at the hands of other men, the president was taking over as Brinco hit its stride. He was welcomed by Joey Smallwood and he was liked by Daniel Johnson, the premier of Quebec. He had all he could possibly wish for of the excitement of great enterprise and the prestige of large names. What he did not have, as he settled into his duties, was working money in the till.

Rio Tinto, the Rothschilds and other large shareholders had supplied some $20 million and the Bank of Montreal some $10 million for the work of preliminary development. The total cost of the project, which was to be completed in ten years but commence partial production by 1972, had been placed by early estimates in the region of $800 million. This amount, the requirement for long-term financing, was to be raised partly by the half-billion in mortgage bonds to be sold in the United States, partly by a Canadian issue and partly by long-term loans from a consortium of Canadian banks. The security for the whole was power to be supplied to the province of Quebec, and there was no doubt of the basic needs of the consumer. New York was sure that Quebec would use the power; so was Quebec itself and so were Canadian banks. Once costs were confirmed, rates would flow from that. The letter of intent that had set the project going would be transformed into a contract and the long-term loans arranged. The retiring railway president could sit at the head of Brinco, watching the great work rise.

He was to make the claim afterward that that was what he had expected from the new appointment. 'He used to call me a skunk for talking him into it,' Val Duncan recalls. Gordon, whatever he said, was hardly a financial innocent and he must have foreseen some pitfalls. Nevertheless, he was in for more than he had dreamed of. On his first northward plane-trip to the high plateau and the Falls, he left an office that could hardly meet its payrolls to be confronted with 'Heartbreak Ridge'. It was a long, hump-backed rise, somehow missed by the surveyors but lifting across the basin and decreasing the capacity of the reservoir by as much as 20 per cent. The assessed volume of water, crucial to all plans, could only be stored by building higher dykes. That work, adding at one stroke some $27 million to estimates rising everywhere, established the price for completion of the whole project at something of the order of $1,073 million.

The letter of intent between Hydro-Quebec and Churchill Falls (Labrador) had not established the rates for supplying power. These would be governed by costs, also still in the process of being established; and the deadline governed all. Quebec would have to be assured of power from Churchill Falls, at a rate it was prepared to pay, by September 1, 1972. Without that the letter of intent was worthless; there would be no basis for a contract and no long-term loans. If there was to be mortgage money from the Americans, drawing in other lenders, it would have to come on the security of assured production. And nothing could assure production but the 'bridle' placed on the falls. Somehow, and however it was going to be paid for, the work beginning at Churchill had to be pushed on.

It was devouring daily thousands that were climbing up toward millions as new contracts were let. Yet Quebec could not be pushed, for all its interest in the project and its imminent need of power. For Premier Daniel Johnson there was a huge commitment involved, there were opposed forces and alternative sources of energy, and the politics were quite as delicate as they were in Newfoundland. For Robert Boyd of Hydro the rate and cost relationships were involving months of study, and negotiations for the contract were in a state of stalled suspense. By mid-April, with the Bank of Montreal as his only source of money, Gordon's 'comfort sessions' had begun with Arnold Hart. By mid-June, as his dole of weekly advances was stretching beyond comfort, he had exhausted a range of other possibilities. Ian Sinclair of the CPR had declined an invitation to invest $50 million in Brinco bonds. Hydro-Quebec, in the absence of a completed contract, had declined to share in the financing. Nor, said Robert Boyd, in view of its own necessities, could Hydro extend the deadline. Quebec had to know by September 1967 that it would have power from Churchill Falls by September 1972. Without that certainty at a point five years ahead, it would have to turn immediately to the building of thermal plants and withdraw from the Churchill project.

In the face of these rebuffs and the prospective limit of advances from the Bank of Montreal, there was one resource remaining. If the company could not borrow it could probably sell some stock, as its first public issue. Disliked by some of the partners and muttered about by brokers, that was the plan agreed on. An equity issue of $37.5 million in Churchill Falls (Labrador) was to be set up during the summer and placed on the market in September at $15 per share.

The decision was made in June and on July 17 came the formal ceremonies of ground-breaking on the site at Churchill Falls. Brought in by the plane-load and gathered around Gordon for the launching of the great project were the high officers of the company, the multimillioned investors and a hundred and fifty dignitaries from North America and Europe. But it was Joey Smallwood's project, his dream of fifteen years, whittled down by the claims of the great consortium, by Newfoundland's financial stringencies and by the competing claims of Quebec. The premier stepped from his plane to find the assembled visitors and a rank of buses to transport them to the site of the ceremony with most of the signs in French. There were as many workers from Quebec as there were from Smallwood's province, and very few of the Newfoundlanders had high-paid technical jobs. Joey's speech of welcome became a rude political challenge to everyone there forgathered. 'This is *our* land,' he told his stiff-faced listeners. 'This is *our* province. This is *our* river. This is *our* waterfall. And we will forever make sure that it will be developed, and when developed will operate, primarily, chiefly and mainly for the benefit of the people of Newfoundland. Let there be no mistake about that.'[7] Then, turning to Gordon and presenting him with a polished lump of Labradorite, the crystalline native rock, surmounted by a gold replica of the Falls, he made it a personal injunction: 'May I ask you to accept this from the people and government of Newfoundland as a symbol of the great affection and respect they have for you—knowing, as we do, that you will protect the government and people of Newfoundland to the last drop of your blood.'[8]

Whether he was warned or warmed by these words, the president was soon chilled as the wind from the island veered. Five bills authorizing the Churchill Falls development had been pushed through the Newfoundland legislature and incorporated into an agreement which the premier had only to sign. On August 16 Joey refused to do so and emplaned for Montreal, burdened with his old resentments. Newfoundland was losing out on the returns from its great asset; Quebec and the big investors were taking the lion's share, and he did not intend to submit. That night, as a telephone call reached Gordon, he summoned his public relations men and composed a grim release: 'Smallwood Reneges—Churchill Project Closes Down'. The prose dilated on hundreds of men laid off, warned of cancelled contracts and rose to an ominous conclusion: 'Mr. Gordon reserved comment on whether legal action would be instituted, pending consultation with counsel.'[9] The work of the night, however, was not to be seen in print, or even by Joey Smallwood. At the next day's confrontation, when the giant and the bantam met, sound and fury subsided to end in a peaceful draw. Gordon would look out for Newfoundland and Joey would sign the agreement.

With that crisis surmounted, there were glints of light from Quebec. The alternatives for Daniel Johnson were privately supplied power from a plant at Churchill Falls or an expenditure by the province itself of some $400 million on thermal and other sources. Always mindful of his politics but cooperative to the last inch, Johnson instructed his Hydro-Quebec officials to pursue the first choice. Negotiations dragged, infinitely complex and difficult, but the all-important contract was becoming a nearer hope. It was hard not to be hopeful at Churchill Falls itself, where excavation for the powerhouse was begun early in September. Around the president, as the first explosives blew, were seven hundred and fifty workers, a panoply of huge machines and the neat lines of a townsite taking shape in the north. But he came back from the encouraging din of construction to the shocked gloom of finance. For Wood Gundy, the company's Canadian brokers, the Churchill Falls stock issue was 'too speculative to be sold'.[10]

With that as public knowledge, the company's chance of survival would plunge to the lower depths. It had lived for months on the Bank of Montreal, nursing the hope of that $37.5 million which now seemed to be in flight. It could market no stock without its broker's support, and through a week of bitter bickering that was unforthcoming. September 27 was the day set by the board for the formal launching of the issue, and at 9.30 in the morning Gordon called a meeting. With Wood Gundy still a determined foot-dragger, he announced immediate adjournment and resumption in the afternoon. After a stormy luncheon interval with the unpersuaded brokers he faced the board again. The underwriting of the issue, he informed the second meeting, would be delayed 'for technical reasons' and reconsidered at a third. When that meeting came, on October 2, it amounted to a polite burying; the stock issue was dead. On the 16th, however, after two weeks of sustained and desperate scrounging, the president came up with measures of resuscitation. From the Bank of Montreal there was to be another $2 million for immediate current needs, a prospective line of credit of $21 million and a loan from relenting Hydro of $16.5 million. He had actually $2 million more than he would have got from the stock issue and could breathe again for a while.

The money had come with the prospect of breaking another log-jam. Through October, November, December and on into the spring, battalions of technical experts with flanking battalions of lawyers negotiated the power contract. It came out finally in the form of a draft agreement, awaiting government approval. The 'base rate' for power was to begin at 2.7734 mills per kilowatt hour, declining after five years to 2.3787 mills, with these fractions of fractions still dependent on costs. As they rose, Hydro-Quebec within limits would assist with further financing, but the limits were sharply defined. Nor was Hydro the Quebec government; the agreement remained paper until authorized by Daniel Johnson.

By the spring of 1968 the president had got this far and on the whole seemed wearing well. Construction work at the Falls was driving forward and ever-expanding Brinco had moved to large new quarters in a tower on Westmount Square. On the top floor with his problems, musing over his project, Gordon was proclaiming confidence to all who came to listen. 'I get a certain satisfaction, a sense of power, to be associated with a thing so grand —so gigantic—in a way it's my centennial project.' Still very much himself and viewed in a better light by the French-Canadian public, he exchanged barbs with an uninhibited interviewer from *Le Magazine Maclean* who caught his fancy by informing him in advance that he intended to title his article, 'L'Abominable Monsieur Gordon'. 'Let's go,' he said with his rumbling, gravelly laugh, and proceeded to let go. He was working harder than he had at the CN. 'I have not taken the train once—I go everywhere by plane . . . at the CN I had a man for a secretary; now they think, no doubt, that I'm old enough and I have a beautiful young girl.'

Was it a legend, the writer inquired, that he worked eighteen hours a day and drank Scotch the other six? 'I ask myself if the contrary would not be more exact.' Did he play any particular sport? 'My favourite sport is to go to one or another hospital to visit my friends who have broken something in sport. It's the only physical exercise I permit myself.' He was prepared to rehash the various hangings-in-effigy, discuss the measures for bilingualism installed at the CN and even to demonstrate by attempts which his hearer found convincing that the French language was beyond him. He was proud of his wife who spoke French very well and he had a story to tell about Campbell and a broken electric train. Father's attempt to repair it had been the usual dismal failure and he had left with the usual profane words. 'Mama,' said the youngster to Norma, considering the wreck of his toy, 'is papa really the president of the CN?—you're not fooling me?' All in all, in the summing-up of the interviewer, 'he did not have the appearance of carrying Churchill Falls on his shoulders'.[11]

By the end of April, however, the buoyant mood was becoming a little forced. On the 30th, when J. L. Toole, one of the CN's vice-presidents, became director of investments, Gordon wrote to congratulate him, adding a poignant hint. 'If you have a few hundred million lying round right now, I could make at least one good suggestion.'[12] Nothing seemed to be moving except the work in the north, the roaring, churning octopus devouring its weekly millions. Through hectic weeks in the summer, with all loans exhausted, company signing officers were sent on extended field trips to postpone the payment of bills. Wood Gundy, approached again with the proposition for a stock issue, had once again refused. The comfort sessions with Hart were less and less comforting, and when Hydro came to the rescue with another $15 million it was on new and stringent terms. If, by December 15,

1968, the company had not arranged for its major long-term financing, then control of the whole project would pass to Hydro-Quebec.

Johnson had eased the condition by authorizing the signing of the contract when all other terms were met. By that very action, however, he had alerted the watchful lawyers and imposed a new delay. There was no provincial law enabling the purchase of power or enabling Hydro to do so; it would still have to be passed. That would require time; the form of the law required interminable discussion, and debate shifted to the offices of Morgan Stanley. On the wall of one of the partners, as the legal wheels ground on, was a framed quotation from Shakespeare's *Henry VI*: 'Let's kill all the lawyers!' Johnson noticed it appreciatively when he attended one of the meetings, and Gordon came back with him, bellowing the same injunction. The company, with some $77 million now sunk in the project, was still spending money at the rate of a million a week. It had to continue spending if it was to meet its power commitment and there were no more funds in hand. Worse still, it had to have full financing by the end of the current year or it would lose control to Hydro. Caught between two deadlines, at the last limit of its resources and the last months of its time, Brinco was sinking fast.

It was at the very brink of submergence when rescue finally came. Several months earlier Gordon had turned to Rio Tinto-Zinc, as one of the endangered shareholders, and suggested to Val Duncan that his company take over Brinco. It would have been a cruel abdication but it was not a possible solution. Even Rio Tinto would have been strained to find the cash and it would have been prevented by the British government from transferring sterling funds. The one answer for the North American problem was a North American investor, and a high-level safari had uncovered Bethlehem Steel. When Duncan found the Bethlehem people receptive, negotiations began, mainly in New York and London. They went on simultaneously with the crises in Montreal, urgent, complex, secret and well over Gordon's head. He was not allowed to mention them even to Arnold Hart, but the transatlantic phone calls and sheaves of coded cables could not postpone a discussion he would soon have to hold. In late July, at the fifty-ninth minute of the eleventh hour', he was supplied with a cryptic letter written by Rio Tinto and framed to be shown to Hart. It spoke vaguely enough of an interested American investor, but Gordon reinforced it. He could not name the investor but he could pledge his word, he said, that there was a sound prospect of new equity capital to repay the bank's loans. That word with Hart, and eventually with his full board, was good for the amount owing of $26 million and for a further line of credit that proved not to be required. With Bethlehem Steel as a shareholder to the tune of $42 million, Brinco was on its feet in the way of current requirements and facing the last hill. It could now go to the Americans for the half-billion in bonds.

Negotiations in New York, though they had been perplexed and stalled by the crises, were already well advanced. Mulholland at Morgan Stanley had selected his two prime targets, the Metropolitan Life Insurance Company and the Prudential Insurance Company of America. In June he had taken their executives for a view of Churchill Falls and Gordon had been there too, urgent and enthusiastic. The great wilderness and the great work had caught his imagination; he bristled with facts and statistics and the sheaf of notes he carried was written in his own hand. 'I better not sound as if I'm from Texas,' he warned himself in front of the prestigious visitors, but the results of glacial ages and millenniums of falling water were being channelled here by advanced modern technology into 'the largest single civil project under way in North America . . . a power installation, as of now, the largest in the world'. From the biggest underground powerhouse in the world more than 7,000,000 horsepower and over 34.5 billion kilowatt hours annually of electric energy would be added to Canadian resources.

> So when I look ahead and see the plans in the making, the growth of our population, the remaking of our urban areas and the pushing back of the last of our frontiers I know that energy, energy in any form, is the catalyst that is vital for results. The great housing programs, the expansion of schools and universities, the elimination of urban slums, the expansion of services industry, manufacturing and business to support them as well as to absorb a steadily growing labour force—these plans must look to energy to make them possible.[13]

Wallace McCutcheon, in a dark moment for Brinco, had recalled the lines from Browning: 'Ah but a man's reach should exceed his grasp, or what's a heaven for?' He had passed them along to Gordon and the quotation recurred often when the president talked of the possible in relation to Churchill Falls. It recurred once more that day in his talk to the American executives, and whatever they thought of Browning they were impressed by confidence and flair. And beyond that the vast basin and the bulldozers and the roar of falling water were eloquent enough to men who handled money. By late August, when Mulholland came to them with his bond offering, they were in a receptive mood.

They were, however, equipped with sharp pencils and a quarter of a percent in interest rates worked out to millions of dollars over the term of a long loan. Tough, polite and inflexible, the companies demanded 8 per cent while Mulholland backed by Gordon, with the whole issue in the balance, stood out for a quarter less. The hard bargaining in New York and the breath-holding in the offices in Montreal continued for two weeks. When it broke, it broke in a wave; Mulholland had won his point. The 'Met' came in for $150 million, Prudential followed suit, and as smaller companies came crowding in behind them the leaders were scaled down. Metropolitan and Prudential, with the issue overbid, were asked to reduce their holdings by $25 million each.

The half-billion was secure; 'the biggest straight debt issue in Wall Street history' had set Churchill Falls on the long road to completion. It remained now for St. James Street and Bay Street to clear the rest of the way. By mid-October a cooperative Wood Gundy with Morgan Stanley supporting them had placed another issue of $50 million. Quebec's confidence in the bonds brought $14.5 million from the Caisse de Depôt et Placement, the government pension fund; and of thirty-one insurance companies Sun Life, which took up 13 million of the American issue and $9 million of the Canadian, was the largest native investor.

The last of the planned requirements was a stand-by loan of $150 million from a consortium of Canadian banks. On October 29 a gustily confident Gordon and seven of the bank presidents gathered in Brinco's boardroom. 'He seemed to expect us to sign the agreement then and there,' Earle McLaughlin recalls. Nothing was to be done in that way, and the first brusque prescription from the head of the resurgent company created a slight rift.

'You send me a letter,' decreed Gordon, 'and tell me how much you're prepared to take.'

'Oh no,' said McLaughlin. 'It doesn't work that way. The Bank of Montreal is your principal banker—we'll have a syndicate meeting with the Bank of Montreal as lead bank. We'll undertake that you get what you want, but the banks themselves will arrange the distribution.'

'No.' The overbidding in New York had been a feather in Brinco's cap, and Gordon hoped for a repeat. 'I insist on your putting in bids.'

'Okay,' said McLaughlin, 'then the Royal Bank drops out.'[14]

That did not happen; Gordon grunted and yielded and the syndicate went its way. There were six more weeks of waiting but no more rifts of consequence, and on December 16 came the word from Arnold Hart. The $150 million loan was 'in place'. The last remaining millions for the last stages of the work would come from the company's earnings as it began to generate power; it was in sight of ample funds. All that remained now were the last hagglings of lawyers, the drawing-up and printing of multitudinous agreements and their distribution for signing by a watchful corps of lenders. A man could have a rest for Christmas.

He needed it. On December 11 he had taken sick at a board meeting and been put to bed by his doctor. A day later Bill Hobbs had died. It was an end to years of suffering but it darkened a sombre household where the big man could not help. Norma and her mother saw to the funeral arrangements while he stormed in bed, fighting a high temperature and just escaping pneumonia. He was over that by Christmas, relieved with the word from Hart, and insisting on a stay in Georgeville. For the subdued family, however, as the holiday came and passed, the weather was no help.

'There was a big storm,' says Norma, 'and all the power went off. We stayed up all night keeping the fires going and in the middle of the night Donnie decided the wood was burning up too fast. He went out the door in the middle of a howling blizzard to bring in wetter wood, carried loads of it upstairs and was exhausted next day.'[15] By January 3 he was sufficiently recovered from the exploit to record it for Frank Ross: 'We have just passed through a really tough two days and nights, fighting off the worst blizzard in memory. Our hydro power broke down, roads blocked with nine and ten feet drifts, absolutely impossible to get out so here we were stuck with no heat, no water and only a short supply of food. However, by keeping the fireplace roaring we managed to squeak by.' The weather, he added, was now 'wonderful' again and his own mood was improving. 'I fully expect that all formalities of Churchill Falls financing will be out of the way by the end of this month and that I will be able to have some time to myself . . . my New Year's resolution is to find more time for my friends.'[16]

January passed and there were still stubborn formalities that refused to be cleared up. Bankers, brokers and technocrats haunted the top floor office, niggling away at contracts. As always, when relief came, the president made the most of it, but he was now paying in the mornings as he had never done before. Norma noticed the change and there were no more scoldings from her. 'He'd have the most terrible hangovers—I never had the heart to say he'd behaved badly, seeing him sitting at the breakfast table white as a sheet.'[17] His eyes had bothered him since August when he had written Wallace McCutcheon that he was 'still flirting with the need for a further operation. . . . I don't really know if I can put this off beyond the next couple of months.'[18] He had put it off and now when he removed his spectacles the glare of light was painful. He went to bed at night with a black mask over his eyes; and he was no longer writing to his friend. 'He and Wally McCutcheon,' says Michael, 'had got together on one of their big benders and both came down with the flu.'[19] Half-recovered himself, Mc-Cutcheon had returned to visit his fellow-invalid and had not been welcomed by Norma. 'Well, I'm going to sit with him,' said the man not used to refusals and he had stayed on till eleven when 'she came in again'.[20] It proved to be the last visit; on January 23 McCutcheon died of a stroke.

February and March went by with no let-up for Gordon. There were still clauses of agreements to be changed and stitched together, with potential millions of dollars hinging on words and commas. He had lost two friends within six weeks of each other and he was still nagged by the flu. As April came the weekend outings at Georgeville were more welcome than ever, with their usual quota of hectic misadventures. A power boat given him by Mumford and a group of Hilton friends had come to be his pride and joy, though he risked disaster when he used it. The Land-Rover defeated him and he transferred his rage to Norma who controlled it with a sure hand. 'You're kinder to that damned Land-Rover than you are to me!' Campbell rode with his father at peril to life and limb, and on one memorable morning to Mr. Keith's store. 'Daddy—Daddy—put the brake on!' came the shrill cry of the boy as the lurching vehicle ploughed down a verandah post and ended up with its nose in the shop's doorway.[21] To old friends of the Five Lakes and some of the familiars of Luster Lake, the Gordon they saw at Georgeville was becoming a cause for worry. 'He was huffing and puffing—he didn't exercise enough and he had trouble with his legs—you wondered how his heart survived as well as it did.'[22]

On one sunny Saturday—the last Saturday in April—he sat on the verandah with Norma, looking down at the dock. He had been sick the day before with another attack of chills and had gone to bed with a fever. Still obviously tired, he was eyeing the white boat, and observed that it required a washing. That would be fine, said Norma, but it would not be done by him. 'Normally he would have just gone ahead and done it, but this time he didn't; he stayed sitting on the balcony. I thought he must be really sick and when we drove home that night he just went to sleep in the car. Then he went to work the next day and all the rest of the week. He was too busy with Brinco to see a doctor.'[23]

He hated the thought of doctors, and the job was nearing its end. The agreements had been put together, checked to the last comma and were almost ready for signature—the Bond Purchase Agreements for the fifty-two subscribers, the First Mortgage Deed of 226 pages, the General Mortgage Trust Deed of 146 pages and the copies of the power contract for every one of the lenders. It was enough even to lift those massive clusters of paper and the fine print strained the eyes, those steadily failing eyes. By late in the afternoon of May 1 there was not much left to be done. The couriers would take the documents and deliver them across the country for simultaneous signing on a day still to be set. It was mostly ceremony now; the water was married to the money and power was sure to come. Some of the men who had been close to him drifted into Gordon's office and there was a little talk and drink; not much of either for they were all of them very tired. About six o'clock Earle McLaughlin arrived. He had some tag ends of business to clear up with the president, and the two drove home together. 'He's getting old,' McLaughlin remembers thinking.[24]

The Scot from Old Meldrum was in his sixty-ninth year and, more or less to his surprise, a comparatively rich man. From his first days with the bank to his last days with the railway he had spent up to his salary and occasionally been strapped for money. He had not changed at Brinco and he had actually been paid less than he had received from the CN, but he had been dealing daily and hourly with men who dealt in millions. They had steered him quite legitimately into some of their own projects and the returns had left him gaping 'Do you know,' he said to Michael during the last and private dinner that the two would have together, 'I'm a millionaire.'[25]

That meeting, in Toronto, had been a good occasion for Michael and a suitable rounding-off—'one evening I'll always remember'. A successful graduate of law school, redeemed in his father's eyes, he was about to be called to the bar. The proud father, with his own trials surmounted, was looking ahead to relaxed years at Brinco. 'I've finished the job and now it's just a matter of serving the term of my contract.' He was content, Michael thought: 'He'd finished what he set out to do—he'd achieved, he'd become a millionaire—there were no horizons left.' Or, if there was one, it was familiar and unavoidable, common to all men. It occurred to the son afterward that they had talked a good deal of death. 'Oh yes, he was thinking of death very much that last year, and that it was just around the corner and all the rest of it . . . and he was terrified of blindness. He told me, "I just cannot let any damn doctor keep me on the hook the way they did Bill Hobbs. When my time comes I want to die in my sleep and it's done".'[26]

With Donnie there were still regrets and hardly a rounding-off, though there was a strained and painful love. The son was proud of his father and wanted the man remembered; when publishers talked of a biography he offered advice and help, though he was not prepared to write it. At the rare meetings there were subjects not to be touched on, much that was left unsaid, yet the past still rose between them. 'He came to Calgary once,' Donnie remembers, 'and it was a very pleasant visit. He was delighted to see his grandchildren—they were no responsibility. He played with them—the only time in all the years I knew him that I ever saw him play with a child. He was absolutely magical—and it broke my heart. Because all through those earlier years I'd been trying in every way to have some time with my father and it never was possible. To see him on the living room floor with my Donald—well—you know—there was an awful lot of that Celtic emotion woven through the whole thing.'27

Gordon's work at Brinco had had finance as its core but a periphery of allied problems had largely extended its reach and involved the sum of his qualities. Trained through the best years of the Canadian civil service, he remained as an individual respectful of what he had learned. He was as thrusting, hard and ambitious as private enterprise itself, but he knew where its limits lay. He was all entrepreneur, the bigger and better builder, and he was too obsessed with growth. He could rant at politicians who stood in the way of profits, but he accepted a political system and a social frame of reference that imposed legitimate bonds. Common enough himself, and a businessman himself, he could balance the claims of business with the goals of the common man.

It was a balance that often tilted with his varying moods and interests, but it usually swung back. Through his long years with the Prices Board and longer years with the railway, he had always rejected 'pussyfooting' but had met most of his antagonists in search of an honest deal. He had taken some hard blows and given them back in kind, but he had learned much that he brought along with him to Brinco and his integrity was crystal clear. He was trusted by provincial premiers, trusted by federal cabinet ministers and he was as much the master as the servant of some of the great tycoons. Churchill Falls, he had told the visiting Americans during his talk on the high plateau, was 'a most interesting example of how under our Canadian democracy private enterprise can join forces with government. This is indeed in my opinion the proper corrective for the steady drift to socialism.' Whether he was right or not, that was what he had believed in and made the partners believe in; and it had served well in his day.

As familiar in Quebec and Ottawa as he was in Montreal, he was a known figure in Europe and there were few doors closed to him in New York. Conscious of success and status, he welcomed his formal honours and was as pleased with the Order of Canada in 1968 as he had been forty years earlier with the certificate in banking from Queen's. In some ways stature did not improve him; to the last days of his life he could be the iron-fisted taskmaster and the blundering, brash buffoon. Yet for all the enemies his quirks and escapades made him, he kept most of his friends.

He found time for some of them through the hectic last months, though he had no time for a doctor. Stanley Dingle had been close to him at the CN and had retired at the same time. They had had their spots of trouble over the course of seventeen years and some of them troubled Gordon as they met for a final lunch. 'He thought he'd done some things that hurt me, but I assured him that I didn't take it that way.'[28] In the case of Lloyd Morgan he had been an unrelenting driver, and he did not forget that. 'Mr. Gordon and I never said goodbye' but the new president of Brinco invited the Morgans to Georgeville and later on to a dinner at Edgehill Road. There, awaiting the secretary who had been replaced by the beautiful girl, were half a dozen of his favourite railway executives and a prized silver tea tray with the inscription, 'Many Thanks'.[29]

J.-Louis Lévesque, the Montreal financier, had been an invaluable director of the railway and a prime target of Gordon's in his fund drives for Queen's. There was always time for Lévesque as there was for Norman MacMillan, but it was harder to see them now. 'It got to the point,' says MacMillan, 'where I don't think unless he was concentrating on the general configuration of a person he could recognize their features.'[30] To Arthur Crockett, the neighbour, Gordon himself confided. 'He told me at one time he was convinced he was going blind and he said, "That is the one thing I couldn't stand, and if that happens I'm going up on top of Place Ville-Marie and I'm jumping off".'[31] 'Donald,' said Tom Boyles, his older friend from the Bank of Nova Scotia, 'was a great man to exaggerate', but it was a thought lurking in the depths.[32]

As success neared in the long battle for Brinco he lunched with Dave Mansur and talked of the Prices Board days. They had somehow been the best; he was sure of the achievement there, but he was not so sure of the work done for the railway. Mansur himself was. 'You know, Donald,' he said, 'when you joined the company people talked of the CP and the CN— now they talk about the CN and the CP.' The big man brightened: 'You think you're right about that?' 'Of course I'm right—you made it the dominant railway.'[33]

There was that to tickle vanity and there were new offers of directorships as solid proof of regard. One from Donald Mumford, who was now president of Hilton Canada Limited, was made at another luncheon and produced a final story. Gordon was reminded somehow of a big man like himself, submitted to the ministrations of a rather small dentist. 'Little fellow had all modern equipment—swore it would be quite painless—but he practically had to climb the side of the chair to work the drill. Well, he's just ready to start when he feels a hand in his crotch, getting a grip on his knackers.

"Now, Doc," says the patient with a voice like steel filings, "*we're* not going to hurt each other, *are* we?" ' There was the usual roar at the lunch table and the big man rose with the usual rumbling chuckle. He would be glad to join the board, he said, and walked out of Mumford's life.[34]

Padre Laverty of Queen's was another with late memories. Visiting in Montreal, he had been invited to the Gordons' for dinner and later on had retired upstairs with the master. 'He sat in that big study of his with the magnificent roll-top desk. He'd got it out of CN stores as a gift for Rip Powell of Alcan, and when it was all cleaned up he looked at it and said, what am I doing, giving this to Rip Powell? Turned out Rip couldn't accept it—it wouldn't fit in his office, so here it is. "I hope I concealed my pleasure". ' They had a laugh over that and it was time for the padre to go; he was driving back to Kingston. Gordon came down while he made his farewell to Norma and waited to see him off. 'He stood there filling the whole doorway and waved as I got in the car. "Now you take it easy, Padre," the big bellow came. "I'll be down that way in three or four days—give you a call." Three days later I was out driving near Kingston and the word came over the radio. Donald Gordon was dead.'[35]

If he had been strained and tired when he drove home with McLaughlin on the evening of May 1, he seemed relaxed to Norma. They had a quiet drink and dinner and he went on up to his study. During the last few weeks he had been talking about his will and he wanted to work on his papers. He could not have had much to do. 'To my surprise,' said Howard Ross whom he had appointed one of his executors, 'his affairs were in perfect order.'[36] He went to bed around eleven and when Norma woke in the morning he seemed to be still asleep, with his spectacles on the table beside him and the mask over his face. She went out to look after Campbell and came back à little later to suggest that he get up; they could have their breakfast together. But the big form did not move; there was no breath stirring the black cloth of the mask.[37]

It was a Saturday holiday for Campbell and he was playing in Westmount Park with half a dozen of his friends. A week short of his thirteenth birthday now, he had become enamoured of war games, acquired some of the accoutrements and devised means for their use.

It was the usual crazy thing—I put up a Russian flag in the middle of the lawn and we all collected. Then we trooped to Westmount Park and did a lot of running around and had a picnic. About two o'clock Mrs. Creighton from across the street came by and called Danny, her eldest son, who was my best friend. 'Have any of you got a radio?' she asked and we said no, so she said, 'All right—carry on.' So we played a lot more and finally we got very tired and about five o'clock we came back to my house. We were collected in the driveway when another friend, Mrs. Patterson, arrived and said to her son, 'We're going home' and she piled him into the car, much against everyone's will. Then Mrs. Creighton came and took the Creighton children home and I went into the house. There were hundreds of people there and the neighbours looking upset and unpleasant. I wandered around among them with my First World War helmet and green camouflage suit and guns and knives and finally came into the living room where ten or twenty people were sitting around looking very glum, and father wasn't there but I didn't think anything of it. Then somebody took me into the library and I was told to stay there. So I picked up the phone and called Danny across the street and told him to come over. He said, 'Are you sure?' and I said yes. So Danny came over and then somebody told me Mom wanted to see me and I went to Mom's room. She told me to sit down and said, 'Campbell, your father— '—and right there, at something in her face or voice, I panicked. I said, 'Is it a stroke—or a heart attack?'—and she said, 'No. He is dead.' I collapsed and wept for about five minutes and then recovered very quickly—went back to the library, turned on the television and just watched television for a long time . . . it didn't really sink in.[38]

As it sank in on the friends of the man and the business community that had known him there was the sense of a passing era. The Seventies would not be the Sixties and the entrepreneurs of the future would differ from Donald Gordon. Even in his own late years the burly individualist with the stamp of Old Meldrum had been a little behind his times, a little lost in the age of social planning. His roots went back to the Canada of khaki puttees and the war for King and Country that had come, embittered by carnage, to weather the great depression. He had been one of the green improvisers who had worked by guess and by God through the strains of the second war. If the country had held together, if it had made its way in peace, if it was bigger, richer, better, he could claim some credit for that. There were still innumerable shortfalls and he shared in them too, for a man is tied to his roots, limited by his own time. There would be new dimensions and definitions of progress, there might well be taller figures, but at least in the haunts of business and even the halls of government there would probably be less fun.

It was that thought, perhaps, that hovered over the funeral as the cabinet ministers and business leaders, the small fry and the great, sat in the pews together. Later at Edgehill Road, where the closest of the friends gathered for talk and a parting drink, there were stories of the old times in the mood of the old times. Dave Mansur, listening, conceived a startling thought which he was to deliver years later. 'When I think of Donald,' he said, 'I think of that song—"Embraceable You". He just embraced everybody—he gathered you in with that personal magnetism of his, that beautifully developed sense of the ridiculous.'[39] It applied, perhaps, to the chosen who were gathered in that day, each with his own recital from the long list of adventures and the wide reach of the career. Bill Zeckendorf was there and given a royal welcome though he was an adventurer now in eclipse; Webb and Knapp was bankrupt. Jimmy Gardiner of Saskatchewan, the old foe of the Prices Board, had motored from his own province though he was a man dying of cancer. Walter Gordon was there, the inconvenient namesake, sometimes friendly enemy and disapproving friend. He looked round, he remembers, and said to someone near him: 'This is the part that Donald would like to be in on.'[40]

List of interviews

Transcription

TR 55 Douglas Abbott
TR 56 Walter Gordon
TR 57 Mrs. Donald Gordon

TR 58 Mrs. Donald Gordon
TR 59 Fred V. Stone
TR 60 Pierre Taschereau
*recorded by W. R. Wright

Notes

Transcribed interviews are indicated by the letters TR, followed by the number of the interview as listed on pages 271–72 and the relevant page number(s) of the transcription.

Chapter 1

1. *Weekly Scotsman*, Edinburgh, Nov. 17, 1960, Donald Gordon Papers, Queen's University Archives (hereafter cited as Gordon Papers).
2. Willie Gordon to Gordon, Dec. 12, 1960, ibid.
3. *Scottish Daily Mail*, Oct. 14, 1949, ibid.
4. Campbell Gordon, TR 7:5.
5. John Macnaughton, *Lord Strathcona*, Makers of Canada series (Toronto: Oxford University Press, 1927), pp. 1–14.
6. Donald R. Gordon, TR 10:46.
7. John Gordon to Gordon, July 11, 1926, Gordon Papers.
8. 'The Cowgate' by John Gordon, ibid.
9. Mrs. Margaret Garbig, TR 19:2.
10. Ainslie Kerr, TR 3:22–23.
11. Note on letter from Toronto *Telegram*, Gordon Papers.
12. 'Soakers' by 'Watchie' Gordon, Toronto *Telegram*, Apr. 24, 1915, ibid.
13. Gordon Papers.
14. Ibid.

Chapter 2

1. Report quoted in telegram, William Nicks to Gordon, Bank of Nova Scotia personnel file.
2. Bank of Nova Scotia personnel file.
3. Ibid.
4. Ibid.
5. Ainslie Kerr, TR 3:22.
6. Gordon Papers.
7. Article on Gordon, Bank of Nova Scotia personnel file.
8. Mrs. Margaret Garbig, TR 19:2, 3, 19.
9. Thomas A. Boyles, TR 25:5.
10. *Journal of the Canadian Bankers Association* XXXIII (October 1925): 529ff.
11. Donald R. Gordon, TR 10:44.
12. John Gordon to Gordon, July 11, 1926, Gordon Papers.

Chapter 3

1. Mrs. Wallace McCutcheon, TR 13:13.
2. R. L. Dales, TR 23:2.
3. Ibid., pp. 3–4.

4. Thomas A. Boyles, TR 25:21.
5. Gordon Papers.
6. Dales, TR 23:3.
7. Boyles, TR 25:17.
8. Dales, TR 23:7.
9. Gordon Papers.
10. Dales, TR 23:10.
11. Boyles, TR 25:4.
12. Article quoting staff report, Bank of Nova Scotia personnel file.
13. Note of letter, ibid.
14. J. Ross Tolmie, J. R. Beattie, TR 20:8.
15. Boyles, TR 25:2.
16. Donald R. Gordon, TR 10:2.

Chapter 4

1. George Watts, TR 43:3.
2. Thomas A. Boyles, TR 25:3.
3. Five Lakes, TR 20:2.
4. Notes, p. 2, Bank of Canada Archives.
5. Ibid.
6. J. R. Beattie, TR 20:14.
7. R. M. Fowler, TR 27:1-2.
8. Joseph Barter, TR 21:8, 9, 14.
9. Watts, TR 43:2.
10. Barter, TR 21:16.
11. W. Earle McLaughlin, TR 41:5.
12. Louis Rasminsky, TR 33:4.
13. Five Lakes, TR 20:78.
14. Sidney Turk, 'The Foreign Exchange Control Board: Its Genesis and Exodus', *The Canadian Banker* 63, no. 2 (1956).
15. Rasminsky, TR 33:2.
16. Turk, 'The Foreign Exchange Control Board'.
17. Ibid.
18. Maxwell W. Mackenzie, TR 32:1-2.
19. Fraser Bruce, TR 20:2-3.
20. Gordon Papers.
21. The following account of the *Emile Bertin* episode draws upon Donald Gordon's résumé in the Gordon

Papers and naval signals.
22. J. W. Pickersgill, TR 20:45.

Chapter 5

1. Quoted by Louis Rasminsky, 'Foreign Exchange Control: Purposes and Methods', in *Canadian War Economics*, ed. J. F. Parkinson (Toronto: University of Toronto Press, 1941), p. 126.
2. J. Douglas Gibson, TR 15:4.
3. Donald Gordon, *Journal of the Canadian Bankers Association* XLVII (July 1940):426.
4. *Report of the Wartime Prices and Trade Board, Sept. 3, 1939 to March 31, 1943*, p. 3.
5. Mitchell Sharp, TR 31:6.
6. J. W. Pickersgill, TR 20:43-44.
7. Pauline Jewett, 'The Wartime Prices and Trade Board: A Case Study in Canadian Public Administration' (Ph.D. thesis, Harvard University, 1950), p. 23.
8. Pickersgill, TR 20:45.
9. J. Ross Tolmie, TR 20:85.
10. David Sim, TR 20:30.
11. Address to administrators, Nov. 20, 1941, Gordon Papers.
12. Radio address, Nov. 21, 1941, ibid.
13. Address to publishers and press, Nov. 27, 1941, ibid.
14. Radio address, Nov. 28, 1941, ibid.
15. Frederick Griffin, Toronto *Star*, Nov. 30, 1941.

Chapter 6

1. Remarks to administrators, Dec. 7, 1941, Gordon Papers.
2. WPTB Release No. 2, ibid.
3. Grattan O'Leary, *Maclean's Magazine*, n.d., ibid.
4. 'Chairman's Remarks to Econ-

omists', Jan. 2, 1942, ibid.

5. Address to Canadian Club, Montreal, Mar. 20, 1942, ibid.

6. Grattan O'Leary, *Maclean's Magazine*, n.d., ibid.

7. Mitchell Sharp, TR 31:4.

8. Frederick Griffin, Toronto *Star*, n.d., Gordon Papers.

9. R. M. Fowler, TR 27:13.

10. J. Douglas Gibson, TR 15:12.

11. Mrs. F. Mackenzie Ross, TR 39:2.

12. Byrne Hope Sanders, TR 14:3, 8.

13. Gordon to Ilsley, June 4, 1942, Gordon Papers.

14. B. H. Sanders, TR 14:10.

15. Ibid., pp. 12–13.

16. Ibid., p. 27.

17. R. M. Fowler, TR 27:20.

18. M. W. Mackenzie, TR 32:5.

19. Gordon to Ilsley, Sept. 19, 1942, Gordon Papers

20. Five Lakes, TR 20:39.

21. Gibson, TR 15:8.

22. Gordon to Ilsley, Sept. 19, 1942, Gordon Papers.

23. Gibson, TR 15:17.

24. Fowler, TR 27:19–20.

25. Ibid., p. 18.

26. Five Lakes, TR 20:27.

27. Ibid., p. 97.

28. *Maclean's Magazine*, May 1, 1942.

29. Ibid.

30. From 'Donald Gordon' by Ruth C. Smith, MS draft in Mrs. Donald Gordon's private papers.

31. Mary Jukes, TR 12:12.

Chapter 7

1. Gordon Papers.

2. Toronto *Star Weekly*, n.d., ibid.

3. July 29, 1942, M. W. Mackenzie files.

4. Correspondence résumé, Oct. 19, 1943, ibid.

5. Fred V. Stone, TR 59:2

6. Ibid., pp. 5–6.

7. Gordon to W. C. Ronson, Feb. 26, 1943, Gordon Papers.

8. Correspondence, Feb. 27, July 28, Nov. 26, 1943, ibid.

9. J. Douglas Gibson, TR 15:12–14.

10. Byrne Hope Sanders, TR 14:15.

11. Chicago Better Business Bureau to Gordon, Feb. 9, 1943, Gordon Papers.

12. Gordon to Ilsley, Aug. 12, 1943, ibid.

13. Paul Martin, TR 5:10.

14. Toronto *Star*, Aug. 14, 1943.

15. Summary of press reaction to speech of Aug. 14, 1943, Gordon Papers.

16. Gordon Papers.

17. *Financial Post*, Sept. [?], 1943.

18. *House of Commons Debates*, Mar. 19, 1943.

19. *WPTB Report*, 1943, p. 5.

20. Gordon to Ilsley, Dec. 10, 1943, Gordon Papers.

21. Donald R. Gordon, TR 10:12.

22. Ibid., pp. 4, 14.

23. Ibid., p. 14.

24. Ibid., p. 32.

25. Michael Gordon, TR 11:15.

26. Ibid., pp. 17, 18.

27. Donald R. Gordon, TR 10:5

28. Gordon to Ilsley, Aug. 12, 1943, Gordon Papers.

29. Donald R. Gordon, TR 10:12.

Chapter 8

1. *Wavell: The Viceroy's Journal*, ed. Penderel Moon (Oxford University Press, 1973), p. 49. See also *International Journal*, Canadian Institute of International Affairs (Autumn 1976): 727.

2. Gordon to Dewar, Apr. 20, 1944, Gordon Papers.

3. Michael Gordon, TR 11:16.

4. Ibid., p. 14.

5. Gordon to Dewar, Apr. 20, 1944, Gordon Papers.

6. Donald R. Gordon, TR 10:25–26.

7. *Fortune Magazine*, quoted in Ottawa *Journal*, Sept. 11, 1944.

8. Gordon to Ilsley, Feb. 29, 1944, Gordon Papers.

9. Memorandum, Towers to Gordon, Sept. 19, 1944, ibid.

10. Gordon to Dewar, Nov. 6, Nov. 23, 1944, ibid.

11. Report of speech to Trades and Labour Congress, *Financial Times*, Oct. 27, 1944.

12. C. C. Whittaker, *Saturday Night*, Sept. 23, 1944.

13. Gordon to Dewar, Nov. 23, 1944, Gordon Papers.

14. Mary Jukes, TR 12:; Louis Rasminsky, TR 33:7.

15. Michael Gordon, TR 11:18.

16. Donald R. Gordon, TR 10:47.

17. Ibid., p. 20.

18. Michael Gordon, TR 11:18.

19. R. M. Fowler, TR 27:6.

20. Ibid., pp. 12–13.

21. Michael Gordon, TR 11:12.

22. Kitchener *Record*, Oct. 26, 1945.

23. David Sim, TR 20:4.

24. Mrs. Wallace McCutcheon, TR 13:2.

25. Speech to Board of Trade, Winnipeg *Free Press*, Oct. 5, 1945.

26. Edmonton *Journal*, Oct. 3, 1945; Sydney *Post Record*, Oct. 12, 1945.

27. Vancouver *News Herald*, Sept. 28, 1945.

28. Sydney *Post Record*, Oct. 13, 1945.

29. Gordon to Ilsley, Nov. 17, Gordon Papers.

30. Michael Gordon, TR 11:35.

31. Donald R. Gordon, TR 10:16.

32. Ibid., p. 7.

Chapter 9

1. Gordon to Ilsley, Jan. 4, 1946, Gordon Papers.

2. Ibid.

3. Ibid.

4. Gordon to W. L. Murray, president, Murphy Gamble, Ottawa, Jan. 29, 1946, ibid.

5. Douglas Gibson, TR 15:10.

6. Ottawa *Journal*, July 26, 1946.

7. Ibid.

8. Montreal *Gazette*, Aug. 21, 1946.

9. Gordon to Ilsley, Oct. 4, 1946, Gordon Papers.

10. Montreal *Gazette*, Nov. 9, 1946.

11. Montreal *Herald*, Nov. 15, 1946.

12. Toronto *Globe and Mail*, Nov. 22, 1946.

13. Ottawa *Journal*, Nov. 13, 1946.

14. Montreal *Gazette*, Nov. 26, 1946.

15. Winnipeg *Free Press*, Dec. 25, 1946.

16. Dec. 12, 1946, Gordon Papers.

17. Sudbury *Star*, Jan. 30, 1947.

18. *WPTB Report, Jan. 1–Dec. 31, 1946*, p. 5.

19. Ibid.

20. Ottawa *Journal*, Feb. 3, 1947.

21. *Le Canada*, Mar. 20, 1947.

22. *La Presse*, Mar. 20, 1947.

23. Ottawa *Journal*, Mar. 25, 1947.

24. Henderson to Gordon, Mar. 16, 1947, Gordon Papers.

25. *Le Canada*, Mar. 21, 1947.

26. *La Presse*, Mar. 20, 1947.

27. Gordon Papers.

28. Ibid.

29. Michael Gordon, TR 11:10–11.

30. Gordon Papers.

31. Text of speech by J. L. Ilsley, ibid.

32. Mitchell Sharp, TR 31:2.

Chapter 10

1. Louis Rasminsky, TR 33:8.

2. Ibid., p. 7.

3. Paul Martin, TR 5:10.

4. *Journal of Commerce*, New York, Nov. 2, 1949.

5. J. Douglas Gibson, TR 15:30.

6. *Western Producer*, May 19, 1949.
7. R. M. Fowler, TR 27:22.
8. Five Lakes, TR 20:49; Ottawa *Journal*, n.d., Gordon Papers.
9. Stuart Garson to McGregor, Nov. 4, 1949, Gordon Papers.
10. Martin, TR 5:5.
11. Five Lakes, TR 20:28–29.
12. Ibid., p. 93.
13. J. Ross Tolmie, TR 20:118.
14. Bill of sale, Gordon Papers.
15. Donald R. Gordon, TR 10:17, 18.
16. Joseph Barter, TR 21:6, 16.
17. Gordon Papers.
18. Sir Alexander Ross, TR 4:1.
19. Ibid., p. 5.
20. Barter, TR 21:9.
21. Memorandum of conversation with L. B. Pearson, June 7, 1963, Gordon Papers.
22. Michael Gordon, TR 11:31–35.
23. Byrne Hope Sanders, TR 14:93.
24. Donald R. Gordon, TR 10:46.
25. Ibid., pp. 18–19.
26. Michael Gordon, TR 11:23.
27. Donald R. Gordon, TR 10:19, 44–46.
28. J. W. Pickersgill, TR 20:59.
29. Memorandum, June 7, 1963, Gordon Papers.
30. Norman J. MacMillan, TR 38:5.
31. Memorandum, June 7, 1963, Gordon Papers.
32. MacMillan, TR 38.6.
33. Michael Gordon, TR 11:23, 25.
34. MacMillan, TR 38.7.

Chapter 11

1. David Mansur, TR 47:5.
2. E. A. Bromley, TR 37:1.
3. Norman J. MacMillan, TR 38:2.
4. Ibid.
5. Montreal *Star*, Feb. 10, 1950.
6. Blair Fraser, 'Big Donald at the Throttle', *Maclean's Magazine*, August 1952.
7. MacMillan, TR 38.8.
8. S. F. Dingle, TR 16:1.
9. Ibid.
10. J. A. McDonald, TR 26:3.
11. Maynard Metcalf, TR 35:12, 13.
12. Michael Gordon, TR 11:24.
13. Dingle, TR 16:4.
14. Donald R. Gordon, TR 10:48.
15. Montreal *Gazette*, Mar. 4, 1950.
16. Dingle, TR 16:17, 18.
17. Bromley, TR 37:1.
18. MacMillan, TR 38:20–21.
19. *Proceedings of the Sessional Committee on Railways and Shipping* (hereafter cited as *Sessional Committee*), March 1950, pp. 27, 33.
20. Ibid., p. 267.
21. MacMillan, TR 38:20–21.
22. McDonald, TR 26:7, 8.
23. Paul Martin, TR 5:6, 12.
24. McDonald, TR 26:7, 8.
25. Donald R. Gordon, TR 10:29, 30.
26. Dingle, TR 16:3, 14.
27. Vancouver *Sun*, May 15, 1950.
28. Donald R. Gordon, TR 10:29–30.
29. Ibid., p. 30.
30. McDonald, TR 26:7, 8.
31. Ibid., p. 31.
32. MacMillan, TR 38:8.
33. Mansur, TR 47:14.
34. MacMillan, TR 38:8–9.
35. Fraser, 'Big Donald at the Throttle'.
36. *Labour Gazette* L (1950):1640.
37. Donald R. Gordon, TR 10:31–32.
38. MacMillan, TR 38:9.
39. Radio address, Aug. 15, 1950, Gordon Papers.
40. *Labour Gazette* L (1950):1643.
41. William Dodge, TR 29:3.
42. Ibid.
43. William J. Smith, TR 30:2–3.
44. MacMillan, TR 38:10.
45. Metcalf, TR 35:6.
46. *Report of the Royal Commission on Transportation, 1961*, I, 8.
47. Fraser, 'Big Donald at the

Throttle'.
48. Donald R. Gordon, TR 10:27.

Chapter 12

---

1. E. A. Bromley, TR 37:1.
2. *CNR Annual Report*, 1950, pp. 4–5.
3. Quoted in Peter Newman, *Flame of Power* (Toronto: Longmans, Green, 1959), p. 208.
4. *CNR Annual Report*, 1950, pp. 4, 21.
5. Norman J. MacMillan, TR 38:2.
6. Blair Fraser, 'Big Donald at the Throttle', *Maclean's Magazine*, August 1952.
7. S. F. Dingle, TR 16:6.
8. Bromley, TR 37:5.
9. Ibid., pp. 3, 4.
10. Ibid., pp. 4–5, 7–8.
11. W. J. Smith, TR 30:2.
12. R. H. Tarr, TR 45:7.
13 Ibid., pp 1–2.
14. David Mansur, TR 47:6.
15. MacMillan, TR 38:17–19.
16. *Sessional Committee*, 1951, pp. 122–23.
17. George Lach, TR 9:9.
18. *CNR Annual Report*, 1952, letter of transmittal, p. 5.
19. MacMillan, TR 38:14.
20. Lloyd Morgan, TR 44:1–2.
21. Grattan O'Leary to Gordon, Dec. 11, 1951, Gordon Papers.
22. C. A. Harris, TR 28:6.
23. William Dodge, TR 29:4ff; also Five Lakes, TR 20:40ff.
24. Donald R. Gordon, TR 10:24.
25. Michael Gordon, TR 11:43.
26. Donald R. Gordon, TR 10:24.

Chapter 13

---

1. J. W. Pickersgill, *My Years With Louis St. Laurent* (Toronto: University of Toronto Press, 1975), pp. 177–78.

2. Ibid.
3. *Sessional Committee*, 1953, p. 105.
4. Ottawa *Journal*, Mar. 24, 1953.
5. Ibid., Mar. 25, 1953.
6. Ibid.
7. Ibid.
8. Mrs. Donald Gordon, TR 1:1.
9. Mrs. W. H. Hobbs, TR 8:3.
10. Ibid.
11. Ibid.
12. Donald R. Gordon, TR 10:36.
13. Ibid., p. 26.
14. Ibid., p. 36.
15. Ibid., p. 39.
16. Ibid., p. 38.
17. Michael Gordon, TR 11:25.
18. Ibid.
19. Mrs. Donald Gordon, TR 58:1.
20. Ibid., p. 2.
21. Mrs. W. H. Hobbs, TR 8:1, 5.
22. Walter Gordon, TR 56:2.
23. Leonard L. Knott, *La Place* (Montreal: Rolph, Clark, Stone, Benallack, 1962), p. 54.
24. Grattan O'Leary, TR 51:2.
25. Norman J. MacMillan, TR 38:16.
26. Montreal *Star*, Oct. 29, 1953.
27. Ibid.
28. MacMillan, TR 38:16–17.

Chapter 14

---

1. *CNR Annual Report*, 1956.
2. Maynard Metcalf, TR 39:23.
3. Ainslie Kerr, TR 3:21.
4. Norman J. MacMillan, TR 38:14, 15.
5. Ibid.
6. Toronto *Telegram*, Nov. 4, 1954.
7. Ottawa *Journal*, Mar. 30, 1955.
8. *Canadian Transportation* (May 1955), p. 60.
9. *Sessional Committee*, Mar. 22, 1956, p. 243.
10. MacMillan, TR 38:17.
11. Lionel Chevrier, *The St. Lawrence Seaway* (New York: St.

Martin's Press, 1959), p. 67.
12. Ibid.
13. Ibid.
14. Ibid.
15. MacMillan, TR 38:16.
16. Chevrier, *St. Lawrence Seaway*, p. 70.
17. MacMillan, TR 38:17.
18. Vancouver *Province*, Aug. 19, 1954.
19. Ibid.
20. W. J. Smith, TR 30:5.
21. *CNR Annual Report*, 1955.
22. MacMillan, TR 38:22.
23. Kitchener *Record*, Jan. 13, 1955.
24. Ottawa *Journal*, Jan. 13, 1955.
25. *Sessional Committee*, 1955, p. 134.
26. Charlottetown *Guardian*, Nov. 3, 1954.
27. Ibid.
28. MacMillan, TR 38:16.
29. Toronto *Telegram*, Feb. 21, 1955.
30. Lloyd Morgan, TR 44:3.
31. Zeckendorf, with Edward Mc-Creary, *Autobiography* (New York: Holt, Rinehart and Winston, 1974), p. 168.
32. Ibid., pp. 166–67.
33. David Mansur, TR 47:2.
34. Leonard L. Knott, *La Place* (Montreal: Rolph, Clark, Stone, Benallack, 1962), pp. 72–76.
35. Ibid., p. 74.
36. Ibid.
37. Mrs. Donald Gordon, TR 57:1.
38. Dr. J. A. Corry, TR 6:14.
39. Donald Mumford, TR 48:4.
40. Mrs. Donald Gordon, TR 57:3.
41. Mumford, TR 48:3.
42. *Le Devoir*, Montreal, Apr. 10, 1956.
43. Mansur, TR 47:7.
44. Mrs. W. H. Hobbs, TR 8:4.
45. Mrs. Donald Gordon, TR 57:5.
46. Gordon to Symington, Mar. 7, 1955, Gordon Papers.
47. Rev. C. C. Cochrane, TR 2:2, 3, 6.
48. Ibid.
49. Michael Gordon, TR 11:38.

Chapter 15

1. *Sessional Committee*, Mar. 19, 1957, pp. 145–46.
2. Montreal *Star*, Mar. 28, 1957.
3. Ainslie Kerr, TR 3:11.
4. *Sessional Committee*, May 5, 1959, p. 176.
5. Ibid.
6. Sudbury *Star*, May 15, 1959.
7. *Sessional Committee*, Mar. 30, 1960, p. 210.
8. Douglas Fisher, TR 54:5.
9. Toronto *Star*, Nov. [?], 1960.
10. Walter Gordon, TR 56:1.
11. R. H. Tarr, TR 45:3.
12. Walter Gordon, TR 56:1.
13. Tarr, TR 45:3.
14. Walter Gordon, TR 56:1.
15. *CNR Annual Report*, 1960, pp. 4, 5.
16. S. F. Dingle, TR 16:9.
17. Norman MacMillan, TR 38:13.
18. R. A. Bandeen, TR 52:3.
19. Tarr, TR 45:7.
20. C. A. Harris, TR 28:1.
21. Ibid., p. 2.
22. Ibid.
23 *CNR Annual Report*, 1960, p. 6.
24. *Sessional Committee*, 1961, p. 166.
25. Zeckendorf, *Autobiography* (New York: Holt, Rinehart and Wilson, 1974), p. 176.
26. Wilfrid Gagnon, remarks at Board of Trade luncheon, Apr. 16, 1958, CN-QE press kit.
27. Lloyd Morgan, TR 44:4.
28. Zeckendorf, *Autobiography*, pp. 16–17.
29. Ibid., pp. 175–76.
30. W. Earle McLaughlin, TR 41:2.

31. Ibid.

32. MacMillan, TR 38:25–26.

33. Zeckendorf, *Autobiography*, p. 193.

34. McLaughlin, TR 41:3.

35. Dr. J. B. Stirling, TR 17:10.

36. Dr. J. A. Corry, TR 6:1.

37. Rev. A. Marshall Laverty, TR 34:1.

38. Mrs. Margaret Garbig, TR 19:3.

39. Gordon to Mrs. J. D. Strachan, Jan. 15, 1959.

40. Mrs. J. D. Strachan to Gordon, n.d., Gordon Papers.

41. Michael Gordon, TR 11:9.

42. James A. Gordon, TR 18:11.

43. Michael Gordon, TR 11:9.

44. Mrs. J. D. Strachan to Gordon, n.d., Gordon Papers.

45. Excerpt from address, n.d., Gordon Papers

46. Aberdeen *Journal*, Aug. 29, 1959.

47. Aberdeen *Evening Express*, Aug. 20, 1959.

48. Campbell Gordon, TR 7:1.

49. Michael Gordon, TR 11:38–39.

50. Winnipeg *Free Press*, Nov. 15, 1957.

51. Donald R. Gordon, TR 10:22.

Chapter 16

1. R. A. Bandeen, TR 52:1, 6, 7.

2. *Report of the Royal Commission on Transportation*, 1961, I, 7–8.

3. Bandeen, TR 52:7.

4. Dr. J. B. Stirling, TR 17:4–5.

5. *Royal Commission on Transportation*, I, 74.

6. *House of Commons Debates*, Feb. 27, 1961, p. 2478.

7. J. A. McDonald, TR 26:16.

8. *House of Commons Debates*, Feb. 27, 1961, p. 2477.

9. Ottawa dispatch to New York *Herald Tribune*, June 11, 1961.

10. Douglas Fisher, TR 54:7.

11. McDonald, TR 26:15.

12. Mrs. Donald Gordon, TR 1:5.

13. *Sessional Committee on Railways, Airlines and Canals*, June 19, 1961, pp. 291–93.

14. Fisher, TR 54:8.

15. *Sessional Committee*, 1961, pp. 317–18.

16. Jeannine Locke, 'Rebel on Rails', Toronto *Star Weekly*, Feb. 12, 1962.

17. Saskatoon *Star-Phoenix*, July 2, 1961.

18. Louis Rasminsky to Gordon, July 26, 1961, Gordon Papers.

19. John Diefenbaker, TR 22:5.

20. W. R. Wright, interviewing Grattan O'Leary, TR 51:1.

21. McDonald, TR 26:9.

22. Confidential memorandum, Sept. 25–29, 1961, Gordon Papers.

23. Ibid.

24. Ibid.

25. Montreal *Gazette*, Sept. 14, 1962.

26. Toronto *Star*, Nov. 25, 1962.

27. Ottawa *Citizen*, Sept. 1, 1962.

28. *Sessional Committee*, 1961, pp. 326–27.

29. McDonald, TR 26:10.

30. Fisher, TR 54:4.

31. *Sessional Committee*, Nov. 19, 1962, p. 59.

32. C. A. Harris, TR 28:4.

33. Norman J. MacMillan, TR 38:16, 17.

34. *La Presse*, Montreal, Nov. 20, 1962.

35. Montreal *Star*, quoting Pelletier, Nov. 26, 1962.

36. Montreal *Gazette*, Nov. 30, 1962.

37. Mrs. Donald Gordon, TR 58:5.

38. Jean de Guise, Montreal *Star*, Dec. 12, 1962.

39. Donald Foley, ibid.

40. Ibid.

41. William Dodge, TR 29:5.

42. *La Presse*, Dec. 1962 (English translation, Gordon Papers).

43. Montreal *Star*, Dec. 18, 1962.

44. J. V. Clyne to author, Dec. 12, 1977.

45. Mrs. Donald Gordon, TR 58:5, 6.

46. Donald R. Gordon, TR 10:23–24.

47. Michael Gordon, TR 11:41–42.

48. Mrs. W. H. Hobbs, TR 8:10.

49. Mrs. Donald Gordon, TR 58:4.

Chapter 17

1. J. A. McDonald, TR 26:10.

2. Dr. J. B. Stirling, TR 17:9, 10.

3. Grégoire to Gordon, June 5, 1963, Gordon Papers.

4. Gordon to Pearson, Sept. 14, 1963, ibid.

5. *Sessional Committee*, Dec. 12, 1963, p. 369.

6. Ibid.

7. Richard J. Gwyn, *The Shape of Scandal* (Toronto: Clarke, Irwin, 1965), p. 142.

8. *Sessional Committee*, Dec. 12, 13, 1963, pp. 338–44.

9. Ibid., p. 352.

10. Ibid., p. 366.

11. Ibid., p. 354.

12. Ibid., p. 367.

13. Ibid.

14. Henri Poulin, *Journal de Montréal*, Nov. 6, 1964.

15. Douglas Fisher, TR 54:1.

16. Ibid.

17. Ibid., p. 2.

18. Winnipeg *Tribune*, Oct. 2, 1964.

19. J. W. Pickersgill, TR 20:89ff.

20. *Report of the Industrial Commission on Canadian National Railways 'Run-Throughs'*, Nov. 17, 1965, p. 1.

21. Ibid., p. 125.

22. Ibid., p. 134.

23. Ibid., p. 136.

24. Ibid., p. 135.

25. Ibid., pp. 130–31.

26. Fisher, TR 54:7.

27. O'Leary to Gordon, June 14, 1963, Gordon Papers.

28. *Report on 'Run-Throughs'*, p. 80.

29. Gordon Papers.

30. Montreal *Star*, May 27, 1964.

31. Confidential memorandum, Feb. 3, 1965, Gordon Papers.

32. *CNR Annual Report*, 1964, p. 15.

33. *Reader's Digest*, November 1966, p. 174.

34. Ibid., p. 178.

35. *Montreal '66*, May 1966.

36. Ibid.

37. *Reader's Digest*, November 1966, p. 172.

38. Norman J. MacMillan, TR 38:11–12.

39. Notes, Oct. 7, 1965, Gordon Papers.

40. McDonald, TR 26:16–17.

41. Five Lakes, TR 20:96.

42. Gordon to Frank Ross, May 12, 1966, Gordon Papers.

43. MacMillan, TR 38:14.

44. Gordon to Gordon Robertson, June 13, Gordon Papers.

45. Montreal *Gazette*, July 6, 1966.

46. Mrs. Donald Gordon, TR 57:3.

47. J. W. Pickersgill, TR 20:25–26, 89.

48. Jeannine Locke, 'Rebel on Rails', Toronto *Star Weekly*, Feb. 24, 1962.

49. Office memorandum, n.d., Gordon Papers.

50. Mrs. Donald Gordon, TR 58:4.

51. Donald R. Gordon, TR 10:17.

52. Bill of sale, Sept. 29, 1966, Gordon Papers.

53. Speech at Queen's, Apr. 7, 1958, ibid.

54. Gordon to MacMillan, Dec. 30, 1966, ibid.

55. List in Mrs. Donald Gordon's papers.

56. Arthur Crockett, TR 24:3–4.

57. 'Hello Donald' booklet, CNR PR files.

58. Notes, Gordon Papers.
59. Gordon to MacMillan, Dec. 21, 1966, ibid.
60. Montreal *Star*, Jan. 13, 1967.

Chapter 18

---

1. Mrs. Donald Gordon, TR 57:8.
2. Gordon Papers.
3. Quoted in Philip Smith, *Brinco, The Story of Churchill Falls* (Toronto: McClelland and Stewart, 1975), p. 39.
4. Ibid., p. 43.
5. Richard J. Gwyn, *Smallwood* (Toronto: McClelland and Stewart, 1968), pp. 256–57.
6. Smith, *Brinco*, p. 16.
7. Ibid., p. 276.
8. Ibid., p. 278.
9. Ibid., pp. 290–91.
10. Ibid., p. 283.
11. Alain Stanké in *Le Magazine Maclean*, April 1968.
12. Gordon to J. L. Toole, Apr. 30, 1968, Gordon Papers.
13. 'Welcome US Visitors', notes, ibid.
14. W. Earle McLaughlin, TR 41:2.
15. Mrs. Donald Gordon, TR 57:4.
16. Gordon to Frank Ross, Jan. 3, 1969, Gordon Papers.
17. Mrs. Donald Gordon, TR 58:3.
18. Gordon to McCutcheon, Aug. 29, 1968, Gordon Papers.
19. Michael Gordon, TR 11:47.
20. Mrs. Wallace McCutcheon, TR 13:9.
21. Mrs. Donald Gordon, TR 58:2.
22. Five Lakes, TR 20:93.
23. Mrs. Donald Gordon, TR 57:4.
24. McLaughlin, TR 41:5.
25. Michael Gordon, TR 11:33.
26. Ibid., pp. 47–48.
27. Donald R. Gordon, TR 10:41.
28. S. F. Dingle, TR 16:7.
29. Lloyd Morgan, TR 44:3.
30. Norman J. MacMillan, TR 38:28.
31. Arthur Crockett, TR 24:4.
32. Thomas A. Boyles, TR 25:19.
33. David Mansur, TR 47:5.
34. Donald Mumford, TR 48:3.
35. Rev. A. Marshall Laverty, TR 34:3.
36. Grattan O'Leary, TR 51:2.
37. Mrs. Donald Gordon, TR 1:3.
38. Campbell Gordon, TR 7:7–8.
39. Mansur, TR 47:6.
40. Walter Gordon, TR 56:3.

Index